MULTIMEDIA IN EDUCATION AND SPECIAL EDUCATION

EDUCATION IN A COMPETITIVE AND GLOBALIZING WORLD SERIES

Motivation in Education
Desmond H. Elsworth (Editor)
2009. ISBN: 978-1-60692-234-7

The Reading Literacy of U.S. Fourth-Grade Students in an International Context
Justin Baer, Stéphane Baldi, Kaylin Ayotte, Patricia J. Gree and Daniel McGrath
2009 ISBN: 978-1-60692-138-3

Teacher Qualifications and Kindergartners Achievements
Cassandra M. Guarino, Laura S. Hamilton, J.R. Lockwood, Amy H. Rathbun and Elvira Germino Hausken
2009 ISBN: 978-1-60741-180-2

Effects of Family Literacy Interventions on Children's Acquisition of Reading
Ana Carolina Pena (Editor)
2009 ISBN: 978-1-60741-236-6

Nutrition Education and Change
Beatra F. Realine (Editor)
2009. ISBN: 978-1-60692-983-4

Reading at Risk: A Survey of Literary Reading in America
Rainer D. Ivanov
2009. ISBN: 978-1-60692-582-9

Evaluating Online Learning: Challenges and Strategies for Success
Arthur T. Weston (Editor)
2009. ISBN: 978-1-60741-107-9

Learning in the Network Society and the Digitized School
Rune Krumsvik (Editor)
2009. ISBN: 978-1-60741-172-7

Rural Education in the 21st Century
Christine M.E. Frisiras (Editor)
2009 ISBN: 978-1-60692-966-7

IT- Based Project Change Management System
Faisal Manzoor Arain
2009. ISBN: 978-1-60741-148-2

Reading: Assessment, Comprehension and Teaching
Nancy H. Salas and Donna D. Peyton
2009 ISBN: 978-1-60692-615-4

Mentoring: Program Development, Relationships and Outcomes
Michael I. Keel (Editor)
2009. ISBN: 978-1-60692-287-3

Enhancing Prospects of Longer-Term Sustainability of Cross-Cultural INSET Initiatives in China
Chunmei Yan
2009. ISBN: 978-1-60741-615-9

Multimedia in Education and Special Education
Onan Demir and Cari Celik
2009. ISBN 978-1-

EDUCATION IN A COMPETITIVE AND GLOBALIZING WORLD SERIES

MULTIMEDIA IN EDUCATION AND SPECIAL EDUCATION

ONAN DEMIR
AND
CARI CELIK
EDITORS

Nova Science Publishers, Inc.
New York

LIBRARY OF CONGRESS CATALOGING-IN-PUBLICATION DATA

Multimedia in education and special education / [edited by] Onan Demir and Cari Celik.
    p. cm. -- (Education in a competitive and globalizing world)
  Includes bibliographical references and index.
  ISBN 978-1-60741-073-7 (hardcover : alk. paper)
  1. Audio-visual education. 2. Special education--Audio-visual aids. 3. Media programs (Education) I. Demir, Onan. II. Celik, Cari.
  LB1043.M843   2009
  371.9'04335--dc22   2009009101

Published by Nova Science Publishers, Inc. ✦ New York

CONTENTS

PREFACE

Advances in media, technology and psychology have had an enormous effect on how students learn and how teachers teach. This book presents new media applications for teaching as well as new methodologies to help students with special needs. An investigation of the effectiveness of multimedia computer assisted instruction is presented. The needs of the autistic are addressed in this book as well, with attention given to the use of Virtual Reality applications that may improve the learning, training and quality of life of people with autism as well as other learning difficulties. Musculoskeletal diseases such as rheumatoid and osteoarthritis are some of the major causes of chronic disability. Education is considered to be an integral part of their treatment, equipping patients to cope with the different stages of these progressive diseases. Continued development and innovative use of new media will most likely broaden its appeal and enhance their educational efficacy.

Chapter 1 - This chapter investigates the effectiveness of multimedia computer assisted instruction. Sixty-three first-year university students were randomly assigned to 3 experimental groups receiving the same sequence of lessons, but with different presentation media: (i) 'Text'; (ii) Text and 'Stills'; and (iii) Text, Stills and 'Audio'. Wickens' (1992) model, an elaboration of dual code theory (Paivio, 1971), was used to investigate the *why* of multimedia effectiveness. Knowledge type (declarative/procedural) and cognitive learning style (Verbal/Visual) were used to explore *when* and *to whom* multimedia is beneficial. Learning was assessed through a 20-item multiple-choice test, immediately following instruction, and 1 week later. Half the recall questions featured a graphic cue, so that the role of visual images in long-term recall could be examined. The mono-medium group (i.e., 'Text') demonstrated superior gains in learning over the other groups, with a trend for the 'Text' participants to have the highest recall test scores emerged, and was maintained across all hypotheses. The results were not in accordance with dual code theory, and challenged the widely accepted view that multimedia, especially graphic media, leads to increased learning.

Chapter 2 - The paper addresses the question whether the illustrations which are associated to texts in instructional books match the multimedia principles supported by empirical research. A sample of textbooks devised for primary school was analysed by classifying the quantity, type, and use of pictures. The choices which led to devise picture-text combinations failed to parallel completely the principles of multimedia learning, even though they seemed to reflect criteria consistent with the cognitive development of the children for whom books were designed. Findings allowed us to draw conclusions about multimedia learning tools which are not as negative as previously reported in literature, even if a more substantial awareness concerning cognitive processes might help book illustrators to structure text-pictures relationships more effectively and teachers to select and employ illustrated books according to multimedia principles.

Keywords: Multimedia; Learning; Multimedia learning; Illustrated textbook; Cognitive psychology

Chapter 3 - Musculoskeletal diseases such as rheumatoid and osteo- arthritis are some of the major causes of chronic disability. Their incidence is predicted to increase as the proportion of elderly people in the population increases. These conditions can result in long-term and variable effects on the sufferer. Education is considered to be an integral part of their treatment equipping patients to cope with the different stages of these progressive diseases.

The range and complexity of information needed has seen the medical discipline of rheumatology embrace technology in support of a wide variety of educational interventions. Early pioneers demonstrated how computer assisted learning could benefit both patients and medical students by increasing their knowledge about these conditions. The establishment of the Internet has provided a new medium for wide spread dissemination of information. As this digital evolution continues there is increasing interest in how video games might be used to stimulate learning in younger generations who have grown up with this type of media.

These educational initiatives have proven to be measurably successful. Patients have access to a broad knowledge base from which they are able to increase their understanding of their illness, resulting in beneficial changes in behaviour. Medical students and qualified doctors have ready access to current research and best practise. The flexibility of the delivery medium supports more adaptable and distance modes of study whilst encouraging students to be more self-sufficient learners.

Computer assisted education has established itself as an invaluable resource in support of medical teaching and learning. But it will not appeal to everyone. Given the challenges facing each individual in education, these resources can only be commended, with learners now having access to a range of resources from which they can meet their educational needs. Continued development and innovative use of new media is likely to broaden their appeal and enhance their educational efficacy.

Chapter 4 - The past ten to fifteen years have seen a rapid resurgence of behavioral approaches in the teaching of language and social skills to young children with developmental delays. Particularly in the area of autism, this has been most evident with the advent of Early Intensive Behavioral Intervention (EIBI) programs in both home and Special Education settings. These "traditional" EIBI programs are often criticized, however, for fostering a rather rigid use of language. Learners who have participated in EIBI are often seen to demonstrate highly formal or "robotic" conversational skills. While these children respond very well to the contrived stimulus conditions that characterize many EIBI programs and clearly benefit from their ability to master rote skills such as verbal imitation, labeling, and receptive language, they often fall short in generating novel language responses. Moreover, the current evidence-based methods found in EIBI programs (discrete trial instruction and incidental teaching), are often found lacking in their ability to consistently produce the kind of flexibility in language and social skill repertoires that is necessary for these children to be successfully integrated with their peers in the classroom and on the playground.

Alternatively, relational frame theory and its formulation of derived relational responding may provide a conceptual framework on which to build a line of applied research to develop and test interventions that will bolster existing EIBI programs in these areas of generality and flexibility of language skills. Derived relational responding refers to an individual's ability to discriminate and respond psychologically to the relationships between stimuli without having those relationships directly taught. The following study, representing some of the early work being done in this new area of applied research, investigated the possibility of children with autism acquiring and demonstrating novel mands without direct teaching. The results indicated success on several levels. The study replicated previous findings that the establishment of an equivalence class through conditional discrimination training is a viable means to facilitate the derived transfer of mand function. Secondly, by addressing the conversational use of complex mands, the present study extended previous findings beyond basic manding for tangible reinforcers to more advanced applications, such as manding for information. Finally, this work can be seen as a positive step toward improving the current teaching technology so that it may eventually foster more natural, flexible language repertoires for young children with autism and other developmental delays.

Chapter 5 - The history and development of racetrack procedures in special education were outlined. The outcomes of employing a game like procedure called racetracks were reviewed and discussed. The basic tenants of racetrack procedures were presented. The various formats of racetracks were provided. Data for various action research projects completed at Gonzaga University were presented. The use of these procedures has been effective in both resource and self-contained classroom settings. In addition, racetracks were found to be effective with a wide range of student populations ranging from those at-risk for school failure to students with autism. Racetracks have been effective in reading (reading racetracks), math (math racetracks, and spelling (spelling racetracks). Directions for future research and possible uses of racetrack procedures were made.

Educators as well as policy makers have become very concerned about teaching students with and without disabilities academic skills (Heward, 2005; National Institute of Child Health and Human Development, 2000; National Reading Panel, 2002; Osborne, 1994). Students who have low academic skills are more likely to drop out of school (Chambers, Dunn, & Rabren, 2004; Lloyd, 1978, have difficulty with the law (Gersten & Keating, 1987; Howard, McLaughlin & Vacha, 1996), and experience chronic unemployment or underemployment (Livingstone, 1998; Rivera-Batiz, 1992).

With the recent advent to evidence-based procedures, a wide range of teacher implemented interventions are now available to those who work with children with and without disabilities (Alberto & Troutman, 2008; Heward, 2005). Several research studies (Greenwood, 1998; Marchand-Martella, Slocum, & Martella, 2004; Slavin et al., 1994) have found that providing students with excellent instruction in the basic skills has social as well as economic benefits. A common set of characteristics employed in many of these studies include (a) teaching appropriate pre skills (Greenwood, 1996; Marchand et al., 2004; Johnson, Luiten, Derby, McLaughlin, Weber, & Johnson, 2002) (b) frequent evaluation of student performance (Marchand-Martella et al., 2004; Rinaldi, Sells & McLaughlin 1996; Slavin, 1996; Slavin, Karweit, & Wasik, 1994); (c) error correction procedures (Greenwood et al., 1998; Marchand-Martella et al., 2004; (d) use of students or other school personnel to provide additional instruction or review (Greenwood, 1996, 1996, Greenwood, Delquadri, & Carta, 1988; Slavin, 1996; Slavin, Madden, Dolan, & Wasik, 1996; Wasik & Slavin, 1993); (e) additional time in instruction (Greenwood et al., 1998; Kameenui, 1993; 1998; Slavin, 1996; Slavin, R. E., et al., 1996).); (f) use of well planned lessons or clear concise teaching procedures (Marchand-Martella et al., 2004; Greenwood et al., 1998; Slavin, Madden, Dolan, Wasik, Ross, S. & Smith, 1994; Slavin et al., 1996); and (g) increased the opportunity for students to respond in the curricula (Heward, 1994; Greenwood, 1996; Greenwood, Hart, Walker & Risley, 1994; Kameenui, 1998; Rinaldi et al., 1996; McLaughlin & Skinner, 1996; Skinner, McLaughlin, & Logan, 1997; Slavin, 1996; Slavin et al., 1994, 1996). Racetrack procedures contain many of these evidence-based instructional components.

Chapter 6 - Literature on Social Stories refers to the method as a "popular trend" in the instruction of students with ASD and describes potential benefits but also cautions that there is little empirical evidence to demonstrate their effectiveness. A recent review of the literature reports highly variable effects, primarily due to inconsistencies in Social Story structure, research design, and variation across participants and behaviors. Because of a conflict between recommendations for story construction and actual results with conformist or non-conformist stories, researchers have called for further investigations to determine the components of Social Stories that contribute to their efficacy. The present study included two phases. In Phase 1, a review of the literature was conducted to identify the core characteristics of documented procedures. This resulted in a 10-step approach to constructing and evaluating Social Stories for students with ASD. In Phase 2, the 10-step model, as a new method to guide and monitor a controlled implementation of Social Stories, was implemented with six students with ASD. Procedural fidelity could be established, and the implementation resulted in behavioral goals being attained by all participants.

A Social Story is a short story defined by specific characteristics that describes a situation, concept, or social skill using a format that is meaningful for people with autism spectrum disorders (ASD) (Reynhout & Carter, 2006). Originally, Social Stories™ were developed by Gray to teach children with autism how to play games while increasing their ability to interact socially with others (Gray, 1995). Social Stories have been used to teach children with varying degrees of severity of autism or Asperger syndrome the cues and behaviors they need to know to interact with others in a socially appropriate manner. Behavioral targets included aims to decrease disruptive or challenging behaviors, and to increase social interaction, communicative behaviors, or on-task behavior (Barry & Burlew, 2004; Reynhout & Carter, 2006).

Literature indicates that Social Stories often are used in the instruction of students with ASD (Barry & Burlew, 2004). Potential benefits have been reported but authors also caution that there is little empirical evidence demonstrated about their effectiveness (Yarnall, 2000; Elder, 2002; Reynhout & Carter, 2006). A recent review of the literature (Reynhout & Carter, 2006) reported highly variable effects, mainly due to inconsistencies in Social Story structure, research design, and a broad variation across participants and behaviors. Because of a conflict between recommendations for story construction and actual results with conformist or non-conformist stories, Reynhout and Carter (2006) have called for further research to determine the exact components of Social Stories that are central to their efficacy.

Typically, Social Stories are constructed with six basic sentence types (Reynhout & Carter, 2006). Gray (2003) recommended a ratio of two to five descriptive, perspective, and/or affirmative sentences for every directive and/or control sentence in a Social Story™. However, as Reynhout and Carter (2006) point out, these recommendations for story construction are not based on empirical evidence; and in some cases, their own review of the literature yielded higher percentages of non-overlapping data (PND) for "inappropriately modified" stories (p. 462) that violated Gray's ratio by using less descriptive and more directive sentences, or using a higher proportion of consequence sentences.

Besides the ratio of basic sentence types, practitioner-oriented literature (e.g., Scott et al., 2000; Gray, 2003) also describes, and suggests the use of, additional research-based instructional strategies to make Social Stories more effective for students with ASD. According to these authors, the perspective of the child for whom the story is written should always be adopted and maintained. Adherently, stories are typically written in the first (or sometimes in the third) person singular. Further, behavioral responses should be stated in positive terms (e.g., 'I am going to use my low voice' vs. 'I am not going to yell out'). Words and/or images may be used to supply the student with a permanent product to which he or she can refer back when practicing the target social skill. The student's comprehension of the story should be checked before proceeding to skill practice with the story. This is typically done either in a written or spoken questions-and-answers format, with a comprehension checklist, or by letting the student fill in a version of the story that has blanks. Gray (2003) suggested that the Social Story first be read in close proximity to a situation where the student is likely to need to use the target skill, which can then be practiced in relevant real-life contexts and situations. Depending on progress made, the reading of the story can become less frequent, parts of it may be faded out, leaving the student with an increasingly simpler procedural facilitator until the target behavior becomes a routine part of the student's repertoire.

Chapter 7 - In the last 10 years, the research in the area of Technology and Computer Science applied to specific treatment and training has increased. In the recent literature it is possible to find research in a wide variety of areas, from applications developed to treat phobias to systems for learning, training and improving the skills of people with special needs. Virtual Reality (VR) has been claimed as one of the most powerful environments to help in the learning and training process of people with special needs. This kind of application offers the possibilities of teaching in a controlled and structured environment, with opportunities for repetition and generalization to the real world, and facilitates the social participation and the representation of abstract concepts. These characteristics are suitable for helping people with autism and learning difficulties.

In this paper authors focus our attention on the use of VR applications for improving the learning, training and quality of life of people with autism and learning difficulties. After revising the most recent developments in the area of computer graphics applied to people with learning difficulties, authors will try to highlight the most relevant issues of this kind of application to better fit the necessities of the final user. As an example, authors describe our two main applications developed for helping people with autism and learning difficulties in their learning process: a virtual supermarket and a virtual school. On one hand, the virtual supermarket was developed with the main objective of training people with autism in concept development and imagination. VR makes it possible to explicitly show imaginary/magic transformations in how an object can act as if it were a different one, which is useful for training both abstract concepts and imagination understanding. Additionally, this virtual environment allows the interaction with different virtual objects, making possible to learn more about their correct usage or how to play with them, both skills where people with autism has problems.

On the other hand, the virtual school is an application under development with the main purpose of training people with autism in social understanding and interaction, another problematic skill for this group. The integration of virtual characters who can interact with the user allows simulation of social situations in which users can participate and be involved, obtain affective engagement, and try to develop their social skills and communication. Also, it is possible to train them in emotion recognition and understanding and associate each emotion with specific situations.

This chapter concludes with a revision of the methodology used to test this type of application with people with autism, and with more relevant research outcomes obtained in this field.

Chapter 8 - The overrepresentation of minority students in special education programs has been cause for concern since the original enactment of legislation requiring special education for children with disabilities. Current data suggest that the trend persists.

Given the increasing number of ethnically diverse students in our nation's schools, coupled with the potentially negative outcomes associated with misidentification, it is imperative that educational professionals understand the disproportionality phenomenon as a prerequisite for creating equitable learning environments.

This chapter explores disproportionality in special education. First, it provides an introduction and literature review to acquaint readers with disproportionality and its effects. This includes an overview of definitions, measurement issues, historical and current estimates of disproportionality at the state and national level, factors hypothesized to contribute to disproportionality, and unanswered questions. Next, the methods and results of a study analyzing data from all public school districts in the state of Ohio during the 2006-2007 academic school year are presented to illustrate disproportionality incidence. Ohio has been chosen as the illustration since data are available from every public school district. The state is populous and racially representative of the USA, according to US Census reports, and for many factors it is viewed as a bellwether state reflecting national trends. This study displays the degree to which disproportional identification of African American students continues to exists across disability categories, and displays the association between school district type (e.g., rural, urban, suburban) and disproportionality rates. Finally, the chapter provides discussion of the implications and resulting recommendations for addressing disproportionality at the school, district, and state level.

Chapter 9 - Although individuals with mental retardation, learning disability, autism and the Gifted are considered to be and treated as separate populations, they share many common characteristics due to the heavy reliance on IQ for diagnosis within the special educational system. By reviewing evidence found in educational, psychological, and legal research over the past century, this chapter demonstrates how a child's special educational diagnosis is based, in part, on his or her race, socio-economic background, year of evaluation, and geographic location rather than his or her educational needs and cognitive ability. The authors also reveal how minor changes in diagnostic policies across the country can have a significant impact on the lives of millions of school children, parents, educators, and school administrators each year. Implications regarding the use of IQ in special education diagnoses as well as variability in diagnostic criteria across the country are discussed. Furthermore, recommendations for future researchers and policy-makers are provided.

Keywords: Diagnosis, IQ, autism, Gifted, Learning Disability, Mental Retardation

Chapter 10 - The common instruction format for students with special educational needs in mathematics education is individually based instruction. We challenge this approach by guided, interactive instruction. The starting point is the student's own informal way of thinking, or in the words of Freudenthal (1991), their 'common sense'. This is the basis for construction, and student interaction in the classroom. The confrontation with each other's ways of thinking can stimulate students' reflection, leading to a higher level of semantization and formalization. We translate this theory into school practice by presenting an instruction format in which students are confronted with rich math problems that are embedded in a context. Working in pairs the students discuss, inquire and construct solutions. Through writing down solutions and conjectures, they have a means to communicate their ideas to their classmates and their teacher. The arising interaction, authors think, is an essential element for the emergence of reflective thinking in learning mathematics.

Keywords: Realistic mathematics education, special needs education, guided instruction, learning by interaction

Chapter 11 - Consultation has become common among special education teachers since the 1997 and 2004 reauthorizations of the Individuals with Disabilities Education Act (IDEA), which require teachers to use positive behavior support interventions in addressing the behavioral needs of children who exhibit challenging behavior. At present, many school teachers and school systems lack the capacity to effectively utilize these research validated practices and oftentimes they rely on consultation in order to meet these legal requirements. The purpose of this chapter is to describe a university based consultation model for implementing evidence based practices in positive behavior support interventions in classroom settings. A case illustration is presented to demonstrate how such a model can be utilized effectively to maximize positive outcomes.

Chapter 12 - Patient education is crucial in preventive medicine to achieve and maintain a healthy and appropriate lifestyle and hereby minimize the burden of morbidity due to chronic disease. The framework concept of shared decision making encourage health care professionals to apply a participatory approach in patient education. Feasability and effects of such an approach has already been described in ambulatory settings but little is known about implementation in acute care. Also participatory approaches are often referred as less appropriate in the elderly. To examine the feasability and medium-time effects of a participatory educational session offered in an acute care setting a pilot-study was done in elderly patients with diabetes and hypertension.

Patients were recruited from general internal medicine and geriatric wards. They were eligible if acute illness was controlled or partially recovered. Exclusion criteria were dementia, delirium, instable clinical condition and remaining prognosis below 1 year. Patients were randomized to an intervention group consisting of a short (30 minutes) participatory education session focussing on self-management of hypertension. Reassessment of participants by telephone took place 3 months thereafter.

44 patients (29 women and 15 men, age 57-88) took part in the study. After three months in the intervention group (N=20) significantly more participants showed reduced blood pressure values, both systolic (120-160mmHg) and diastolic (70-90mmHg), body weight (50-121kg) and HbA1c (5.8-11.3%). However, only 4 patients in the intervention group achieved blood pressure values of 130/80mmHG or below. Also median weight reduction was limited (2kg).

Participatory patient education when applied in an acute care setting is feasible and provides beneficial effects on blood pressure control, weight reduction and metabolic control in elderly but well-functioning patients with diabetes. Therefore this approach may effectively supplement usual ambulatory patient education.

Keywords: Hypertension, HbA1c, diabetes, patient education, participatory decision making

Chapter 13 - Business and government have embraced data logging applications to provide for a more comprehensive web-based user experience. The vast majority of web-based educational applications have yet to incorporate even the most rudimentary forms of data-logging. The incorporation of data-logging and tracking applications can aid in the enhancement of a individual's learning experience by aiding in the creation and maintenance of community, logistical planning and instructional individualization. Educational researchers and application developers can apply lessons learned in the commercial and government marketplace when using data collection tools to advance an online learners educational experience.

In: Multimedia in Education and Special Education
Editors: O. Demir and C. Celik
ISBN 978-1-60741-073-7
© 2009 Nova Science Publishers, Inc.

Chapter 1

THE EFFECTS OF TEXT, GRAPHIC IMAGES AND AUDIO ON LEARNING

Janice Langan-Fox[1],, Kim Albert[2], James Canty[1], and Michael Sankey[1]*

[1]Swinburne University of Technology, Australia
[2]TNS Global

ABSTRACT

This chapter investigates the effectiveness of multimedia computer assisted instruction. Sixty-three first-year university students were randomly assigned to 3 experimental groups receiving the same sequence of lessons, but with different presentation media: (i) 'Text'; (ii) Text and 'Stills'; and (iii) Text, Stills and 'Audio'. Wickens' (1992) model, an elaboration of dual code theory (Paivio, 1971), was used to investigate the *why* of multimedia effectiveness. Knowledge type (declarative/procedural) and cognitive learning style (Verbal/Visual) were used to explore *when* and *to whom* multimedia is beneficial. Learning was assessed through a 20-item multiple-choice test, immediately following instruction, and 1 week later. Half the recall questions featured a graphic cue, so that the role of visual images in long-term recall could be examined. The mono-medium group (i.e., 'Text') demonstrated superior gains in learning over the other groups, with a trend for the 'Text' participants to have the highest recall test scores emerged, and was maintained across all hypotheses. The results were not in accordance with dual code theory, and challenged the widely accepted view that multimedia, especially graphic media, leads to increased learning.

---

* Correspondence should be addressed to Professor Janice Langan-Fox, Faculty of Business and Enterprise, Swinburne University of Technology, P.O. Box 218, Hawthorn, 3122, Victoria, Australia. Telephone: +61392144619; Fascimile: +61392145336. Email: jalanganfox@swin.edu.au

INTRODUCTION

Multimedia and Instruction

Recently, there has been an explosion in the production and utilization of multimedia computer assisted instruction (CAI) packages, which present information by way of text, still graphics, animation, audio and/or video. Three reasons for the dramatic increase have been proposed by Najjar (1996a): (i) the rapidly declining cost of computers with sophisticated multimedia capabilities; (ii) the finding that learners prefer multimedia instruction; and (iii) the belief that multimedia helps people learn. In educational and training environments, multimedia CAI has been uncritically accepted, based mainly on the latter assumption, that multimedia of increasing technological complexity helps people learn more effectively (Langan-Fox & Griffin, 1999). Thus, the general research question for the current investigation was: "Does increasing the complexity of media in CAI foster increased learning outcomes?"

History of Instructional Media Research

The efficacy of CAI has been the subject of ongoing debate for over a decade (Chen, Ghinea, & Macredie, 2006; Kalyuga, Chandler, & Sweller, 2000; Langan-Fox, Anglim & Wilson, 2004; Langan-Fox, Grant, & Anglim, 2007; Langan-Fox, Platania-Phung, & Waycott, 2006; Leahy, Chandler, & Sweller, 2003; Mayer & Johnson, 2008; Mousavi, Low, & Sweller, 1995). Meta-analyses have been used to examine over 200 studies comparing multimedia CAI to traditional classroom lectures (see Najjar, 1996b; Bhowmick et al., 2007). Participants in these studies were derived from various milieus (e.g., schools, tertiary institutions, industry, and the military), and the instructional content areas ranged from foreign languages to electronic equipment operation. Typically, learning outcomes have been measured using achievement or performance tests. The results of the meta-analyses showed that learning was higher when the instruction was presented via the computer-based multimedia system than traditional lectures (Najjar, 1996b; Bhowmick et al., 2007), supporting the belief that multimedia increases learning. In concordance with these findings, recent studies using both self-report and objective outcome testing have found that compared to classes with a traditional teacher-leading approach, those using multimedia-based instruction are better liked by students and yield improvements in student learning (Dimitrov, McGee & Howard, 2002; Feeg, Bashatah & Langley, 2005; Mayer, 1997; McKethan & Everhart, 2001; Moreno & Valdez, 2005; Sneddon, Settle & Triggs, 2001).

However, alternative explanations have been offered. Clark (1985) pointed out the terms "media" and "method" are often confused with each other, prompting misleading statements regarding the attribution effectiveness in CAI. Method refers to characteristics such as text organization and pace of learning. Najjar (1996b) noted that improved organization of material in CAI, compared to lectures, may be responsible for learning advantages. Other confounding variables include the effects of teacher, delivery system and content. Clark (1983) has stated that media are simply vehicles for instruction and concludes that "media do not influence learning under any conditions" (p. 445). This view is supported by a large body of studies which provide no strong evidence to warrant the use of multimedia as an effective tool for learning (see Hede, 2002). Clark and Craig (1992) have also claimed that most studies showing positive results for CAI have serious methodological problems and ignore the effects of novelty. Clark's (1983, 1985) assertions have since instigated many counteractions (Kozma, 1991; Bagui, 1998; Hede, 2002; Nathan & Robinson, 2001; Rieber, 2000), with Kozma (1991) arguing that medium and method have an inseparable relationship and therefore, both are key components for the design of instruction.

Ultimately, the comparative research paradigm, used for many years to evaluate the effectiveness of computer versus traditional instruction (a teacher), failed to control "the myriad variables bearing upon teaching and learning" (Williams & Brown, 1990, p.102). However, this does not deny that closely controlled studies can be designed, with media as an independent experimental variable. One way to achieve this is to compare learning when the "method" (organization, content and delivery system) is the same. This can be achieved by replacing the traditional lecture with a second version of CAI, and systematically varying the independent variable of interest. In 1987, Gillingham and Guthrie reviewed all CAI research since 1980. Only 13 studies reported data that could be used in a meta-analysis. Of these, only six compared two versions of CAI (mean effect size = 1.05; range = 3.29). Williams and Brown (1990) emphasized that the mean effect size resulting from comparing two versions of CAI reveals that elements of the instructional package can indeed be varied to provide optimal learning conditions. This finding is exciting, but in isolation, not meaningful. If CAI research is to be truly worthwhile, it needs to be anchored to theoretical models that yield information about these optimal learning conditions. In 1992, Mayes stated "there has been little work on the...fundamental issues of why and when multimedia techniques would be of benefit" (p. 3). Research has since been devoted towards addressing these questions (Mayer, 2001; Mayer & Moreno, 1998, 1999; Moreno & Valdez, 2005), although results warranting for the use of multimedia as an effective alternative to learning have been inconsistent (Hede, 2002). Williams and Brown (1990) advocate an information-processing model as a suitable theoretical framework as it provides fertile ground for the development of hypotheses about instructional technology. In recent times, another question has emerged: *"To whom* is multimedia CAI of benefit?" Researchers (e.g., Grimley, 2007; Lusk et al., 2008; Samaras, 2006) have signaled the importance and need for additional research in the area of individual differences in multimedia learning.

The present chapter aims to: (a) utilize an extension of dual code theory (Paivio, 1971) proposed by Wickens (1992) to account for *why* learning outcomes may vary across different media conditions; (b) investigate *when* specific media attributes may be of benefit by examining the relationship between media and lesson content (declarative or procedural knowledge); and (c) explore individual differences (Verbal/Visual cognitive learning style) that may indicate *to whom* multimedia instruction is of value. What follows is a review of the relevant literature in relation to these aims, before presenting the research hypotheses.

Table 1. Review of literature combining CAI and Cognitive Learning Styles

Author	Year	Cognitive Learning Style	Measure of CLS	Instructional Design	Content	Outcome
Hagen	2001	FI/FD	Group Embedded Figures Test (Witkin et al., 1971)	2 computer groups and a traditional classroom group	Piano sight play	No effects of CLS and no interaction with instructional design
Hart	1995	Assimilator, accomodator, diverger, converger (AM, AC, DV, CN)	Kolb Learning Style Inventory (1984)	Hypertext –tracked navigation strategies	Statistics	No effects for CLS and instructional design
Whyte et al.	1995	Field-independent or field dependent (FI/FD)	Group Embedded Figures Test (Witkin, Oltman, Raskin & Karp, 1971)	Different types of feedback (Knowledge of Response; Knowledge of Correct Response)	Learning a new concept	Partial support that CLS interacts with instructional design for improved learning
Weller et al.	1995	FI/FD	Group Embedded Figures Test (Witkin et al., 1971)	4 hypermedia conditions differing by: organizer, titles and map	Computer ethics	Learning varied by CLS. FD student outcomes varied according to instructional treatment. FI did not vary much.
Korthauer & Koubek	1994	FI/FD	Hidden Figures Test (Ekstrom et al., 1976)	Structured and unstructured hypertext navigation	Industrial ergonomics	CLS, structure and level of prior knowledge lead to differences in navigation & learning outcomes
Riding & Douglas	1993	Verbal/Imager & Wholist/ Analyst	Cognitive Styles Analysis (Riding, 1991)	Text-plus-text versus text-plus-picture	Car braking systems	CLS interacted with media condition
Riding & Sadler-Smith	1992	Verbal/Imager & Wholist/ Analyst	Cognitive Styles Analysis (Riding, 1991)	3 conditions differing by: structure, advance organizer, verbal emphasis, diagram type	Home hot-water systems	CLS interacted with instructional condition

Author	Year	Learning style dimension	Instrument	Treatment	Content domain	Findings
Allinson	1992	Reproducing versus meaningful orientation	Approaches to Studying Inventory (Entwistle, 1983)	Hypertext –tracked navigation strategies	Physiological feedback	No learning differences, but distinct navigation strategies used by two groups
Sein & Robey	1991	AM, AC, DV, CN	Kolb Learning Style Inventory (1976)	Analogical versus abstract model of task	Electronic mail filing system	Learning style with a matched design was a predictor of performance
Cordell	1991	AM, AC, DV, CN	4MAT Learning Styles Inventory (Kolb, 1975)	Linear versus branching sequencing of lessons	Weight management	No main effects for learning style and no interaction for CLS and instructional design
Carlson	1991	Deductive or inductive	See Carlson & Falk (1986)	Altered sequencing of CAI: examples then concepts; concepts then examples	Observation skills training	Skills were significantly higher when the student's learning style was matched
Rowland & Stuessy	1988	Holist or serialist	Study Preference Questionnaire (Ford, 1985)	Tutorial versus simulation	Home energy conservation	Matched condition (holist-simulation & serialist-tutorial) produced higher scores
Canino & Cicchelli	1988	FI/FD	Embedded Figures Test (Witkin et al., 1971)	Algorithmic (structured) versus discovery (unstructured)	Algebra	No interaction between CLS and instructional treatment
Smith	1984	FI/FD	Closure Flexibility Test (Thurston & Jeffrey, 1980)	Mildly adaptive – students can skip a sub-lesson if pass a pre-test	Comma usage	Learning style differentiated student achievement using CAI (FI scored higher than FD)

The Information Processing System

Current cognitive theory views learning as a set of three interrelated processes (encoding, storage and retrieval) that intervene between the input of information via the senses and the output of human behavior (Kyllonen & Alluisi, 1987). Encoding refers to the process of transforming an external stimulus into a format that can then be stored in memory; storage refers to the process of retaining the encoded information in memory; and retrieval is the process of recovering encoded information stored in memory (Quealy & Langan-Fox, 1998). Williams and Brown (1990) nominated two aspects of memory as relevant to comparative instructional technology research, working memory (WM) and long-term memory (LTM). The optimal assignment of media to the dual codes of WM is proposed as a means of overcoming the limited capacity of the system

Visual Images and LTM

Many studies have suggested that visual images facilitate retrieval of information from LTM (Tulving, 1985). The principle of encoding specificity (Tulving, 1985) states that retrieval cues, such as visual images, provide access to information in LTM if, and only if, the cues are stored as part of the original memory. It has also been found that congruent cues, those that best fit the context of encoding, resulted in improved retrieval (Tulving, 1985). Thus, image-linked knowledge should be more effectively recalled to a degree mediated by the meaningfulness of the presentation (Gagné & Glaser, 1987). Table 1 gives an overview of the literature and demonstrates the benefit of image-linked knowledge and suggests an interaction between memory subsystems and visual images in learning and recall. In accordance with this view, multiple-channel theories have the underlying assumption that when more than one medium is used to transmit information, additional processing channels are utilized. This leads to increased efficiency at the WM stage, hence enhancing learning (Barron & Kysilka, 1992). The most widely recognized multiple-channel theory in the current literature proposes two processing channels allowing the dual coding of information (Paivio, 1971).

Multiple-Channel Theory: Dual Coding of Information

Paivio (1971) proposed that information is processed through two independent channels, the verbal and the nonverbal. Thus, information retained in WM can be represented by either of two codes: (i) a phonetic/linguistic verbal form; or (ii) an analogue spatial form, such as a visual image (Baddeley, 1990; Estes, 1989; Wickens, 1992). These two kinds of WM appear to operate in a largely independent way (Najjar, 1996b; Wickens, 1992). Dual code theory suggests that related information presented in both verbal and non-verbal codes will result in learning gains beyond those from presentation through either the verbal or non-verbal channel alone (Moreno & Valdez, 2005). Information processed through two channels is called 'referential processing' and has been shown to have an additive effect on recall (Mayer & Anderson, 1991; Paivio, 1991; Shih & Alessi, 1996). Referential processing may produce an additive effect on recall due to the creation of additional cognitive paths that can be followed to assist in retrieval (Najjar, 1996b). The presentation of concurrent verbal and nonverbal instructional material should therefore produce better learning outcomes. Empirical studies on both computer and non-computer based multimedia tend to support dual code theory

(Atkinson, 2002; Baek & Layne, 1988; Mayer & Moreno, 1998; Moreno & Mayer, 1999; Mousavi, Low, & Sweller, 1995; Sadoski, Getz & Rodriguez, 2000). For example, Baek and Layne (1988) found that for high school students asked to complete a computer-based tutorial, participants assigned to a 'text with still graphics' condition out-performed a 'text' only group. Moreover, a body of research by Mayer and colleagues (Mayer & Anderson 1991; 1992; Mayer & Gallini 1990; Mayer 1989) compared retention and transfer test scores for students learning from 'text and illustrations' and 'text' alone. Participants in the multimedia group (text and illustrations) showed a 23% median improvement over text-only groups (Mayer 1997; 2001). These results are consistent with what Mayer (2001) calls the multimedia effect: people learn better from words and pictures than from words alone.

A criticism of dual code theory is that with multiple formats for the presentation of information available on a computer (e.g., speech, print, pictures, etc.) the question still remains: "Which types of media optimize dual coding in working memory?" Thus, dual code theory is only one step towards an understanding of learning from multimedia instruction. A model developed by Wickens (1992) supports and elaborates on dual code theory, by drawing attention to the attributes of input information, and identifying the optimum assignment of display format for compatibility with the codes in WM.

Display Modality and Working Memory Code

Wickens (1992) described four possible formats of information display (speech, sound localization & pitch, print, analog pictures) that are defined by the auditory and visual input modalities (Figure 1). These four formats can potentially be associated with either of the two different codes in WM (spatial or verbal). Nonetheless, experimental data suggest that the allocation of formats to memory codes should not be arbitrary (Wickens, Sandry & Vidulich, 1983). In general, Wickens prescribed speech as the most appropriate display for processing in verbal WM, and analog pictures as the ideal display for spatial WM. Wickens' (1992) model has a broad human-machine orientation. For example, the model has been used to investigate physical displays such as nuclear power control consoles, and is not confined to the human-computer interface. Past research into CAI, especially media at the interface level has not been approached from a theoretical perspective. This presented a challenge to the present investigation - to see whether current knowledge about cognitive processes, in particular coding of media in WM as described by Wickens, could be used to explain and predict learning outcomes.

While some studies have supported optimal assignment of display format to WM, overall results have been inconclusive (for a review, see Wickens, 1992). Wickens (1992) proposed two explanations for these inconsistencies: (i) the different properties of the tasks under investigation; and (ii) individual differences in preferred modes of cognition. The relation of task and individual differences to Wickens' model are shown in Figure 1, taken from Quealy & Langan-Fox (1998).

Knowledge Type and Multimedia Instruction

Subject matter for CAI lessons in previous studies has covered wide content domains and tasks, and this has made generalizations difficult. As discussed earlier, Wickens (1992) noted task differences as one reason why support for the optimum assignment of display format to

WM code has been inconclusive. An alternative, that may aid comparisons across studies, is to analyze disparate content areas in terms of general types of knowledge, for example, declarative knowledge ("knowing that") and procedural knowledge ("knowing how"). The distinction between declarative and procedural knowledge is somewhat artificial, and subject to a great deal of overlap in real-life situations. Yet, Williams and Brown (1990) noted that the cognitive requirements of procedural and declarative learning are so different that researchers must categorize the type of learning being examined. Hence, another reason for investigating the declarative and procedural knowledge types is that they may shed light on LTM subsystems.

Declarative and Procedural Knowledge

Anderson (1980) viewed declarative knowledge as being typically verbal in nature, while Wickens (1992) proposed that the auditory format is the most appropriate for verbal WM processing in the short term - indicating that for optimum learning, declarative knowledge should be presented in the auditory mode. Quealy and Langan-Fox (1998) found a non-significant trend indicating that learning of declarative knowledge was most effective from auditory presentations. Following an immediate recall test, ranking of media conditions from highest to lowest scores were as follows: (i) text, stills and audio; (ii) text, audio and video; followed by (iii) text and stills. This ordering was maintained at a re-test approximately two weeks later. Wickens (1992) did not suggest that retention of information presented by auditory displays would be better than retention of information presented by text displays. The pattern found by Quealy and Langan-Fox could be explained by increased efficiency in WM leading to an overall improvement in performance, both on immediate and delayed memory tests. This pattern also suggests that the complexity of video as a medium is not particularly advantageous for conveying declarative knowledge.

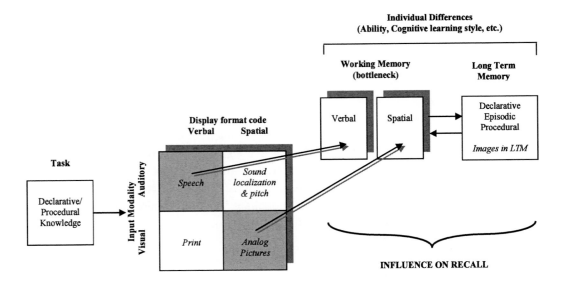

Figure 1. Integrating the optimum assignment of display format to working memory code model (from Quealy & Langan-Fox, 1998), and the influence of task and individual differences, on learning outcomes.

Anderson (1980) distinguished declarative knowledge from procedural knowledge on the basis of difficulties in communicating procedural knowledge verbally. If procedural knowledge is mainly processed by spatial WM, then the optimum display format would most likely be pictures/images (Wickens, 1992). In line with this logical deduction, a review by Park and Hopkins (1993) found that video and animation were effective for demonstrating sequential actions in a procedure. Similarly, Palmiter and Elkerton (1993) found that recall of procedural information was better when presented via animation than text. However seven days later, recall was equivalent. The immediate test did not emphasize differences in long-term encoding. Nor could retention be enhanced by initially presenting animation with accompanying spoken procedural text. This led Palmiter and Elkerton to conclude that animated procedural demonstrations may encourage superficial processing and a disregard for procedural text. This pattern was also evident in Quealy and Langan-Fox (1998) who found that recall scores clustered on an immediate test of procedural knowledge, but converged after a two week delay. Quealy and Langan-Fox noted this may have been a result of confounding of declarative and procedural knowledge that may have occurred because the categorizations of knowledge were based on the predominant type of knowledge contained in entire lessons. Alternatively, the result could be accounted for by the superficial processing described by Palmiter and Elkerton.

Thus, differences in processing of declarative and procedural knowledge extend from WM to LTM. Gagné and Glaser (1987) recognized that image-linked knowledge should aid recall from LTM, to a degree mediated by the meaningfulness of the presentation. In other words, images may be more effective in enhancing recall of one knowledge type over the other, from LTM. For instance, Quealy and Langan-Fox (1998) found a highly significant complexity interaction between knowledge type and recall when cued by a graphic.

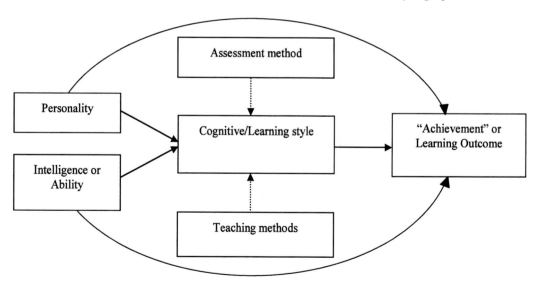

Figure 2. The role of cognitive learning styles (after Furnham, 1995).

Individual Differences and Multimedia Instruction

After reviewing experimental data, Wickens (1992) was unable to conclude that one display mode was superior to another and attributed this ambivalence in part, to individual differences in preferred modes of cognition, corresponding with cognitive styles research.

Cognitive (Learning) Styles, Strategies and Instruction

Cognitive style refers to an individual's typical or habitual manner, mode, or form of perceiving, processing and using information (Riding & Rayner, 1998). While this definition sounds unequivocal, cognitive styles are often elusive for two reasons. First, confusion exists between terms such as cognitive styles and learning styles, and styles versus strategies (Hodgkinson, Langan-Fox, & Sadler-Smith, 2008). Second, a proliferation of style constructs has emerged, without regard for other research in the same field (Hayes & Allinson, 1993). Cognitive style has been defined as "an individual's characteristic and consistent approach to organizing and processing information" (Tennant, 1988, p.4) whereas *learning style* has been referred to as "a student's consistent way of responding to and using stimuli in the context of learning" (Claxton & Ralston, 1978, p.7).

Although cognitive learning styles are regarded as habitual modes of information processing, they are not simple habits, in the technical sense of learning theory. Unlike habits, cognitive learning styles are not directly responsive to principles of acquisition and extinction (Messick, 1976) and cannot be modified easily by training (Ausburn & Ausburn, 1978; Kogan, 1971). Cognitive learning styles then, are stable over time and across a wide variety of tasks (Jonassen & Grabowski, 1993), indicating a physiological basis (Riding, 1997). More recently however, the fixed nature of cognitive style has been challenged by a number of researchers (Skehan, 1998; Adey et al., 1999; Driver, 2000; Sitko-Lutek et al., 2000; Armstrong, 2002; Thies, 2003). This literature has raised questions over the degree of style malleability (Armstrong, 2002) and also whether some individuals are more amenable to a change in style than others (Evans, 2004).

Cognitive strategies are regularities in information processing that are at least partly a function of particular situations (Messick, 1976). In comparison to styles, strategies may be learned and developed and are more likely to be responsive to change through training. Since cognitive learning styles are not as likely to change with intervention, Whyte, Karolick, Nielsen, Elder and Hawley, (1995) suggested that instruction should be adapted to the learner rather than the learner to instruction. Furnham (1995) developed a model to illustrate some more established ideas relating cognitive learning style to instructional methods and achievement, as well as methods of assessment, intelligence, and personality.

Furnham's model (1995) (Figure 2) suggests that the variation in *style* of cognition implies more than ability (Ausburn & Ausburn, 1978). Messick (1976) summarized the main distinctions between cognitive style and ability. In particular, abilities are *value directional* (having more is better than having less), whereas styles are *value differentiated* (neither pole is necessarily better); and abilities *enable* learners to perform tasks, whereas styles organize and *control* the ways in which the tasks are performed. In this sense, style is distinct from ability in that it does not measure how well we do something but, rather, how we approach something (Grimley & Banner, 2008). According to Allinson and Hayes (1990), it is now "generally accepted that educational attainment depends not simply upon…the ability of the student, but also upon the individual's learning style" (p. 859). Riding (1997) viewed style as not impacting critically on learning outcomes when the task was simple, and more importantly, when a task was difficult.

The Matching Hypothesis: Learning Style and Instructional Methods

The dashed arrows in Furnham's (1995) model indicate that there may or may not be a match between a persons cognitive learning style and the teaching (instructional) methods used. The essence of this relationship was described by Snow (1978) as an Aptitude-Treatment Interaction (ATI). Snow recognized that individual differences, such as cognitive learning style, not only predict individual differences in learning outcome, but they also interact with alternative instructional treatments. Cronbach and Snow's (1977) further assertion that different instructional methods are necessary to accommodate these individual differences was supported by Ford and Chen (2001), who found that matching a user's cognitive style with content presentation enhanced performance and improved perception. The matching of students to instruction can become a reality by virtue of technological advances in individualized and interactive CAI. Studies of cognitive learning styles and CAI showed support for the proposition that instructional methods are differentially effective for students with different cognitive learning styles (Carlson, 1991; Chen & Macredie, 2002, 2004; Ford & Chen, 2000, 2001; Ghinea & Chen, 2003; Kim, 2001; Korthauer & Koubek, 1994; Riding & Douglas, 1993; Riding & Sadler-Smith, 1992; Rowland & Stuessy, 1988; Sein & Robey, 1991; Smith, 1985; Weller, Repman, Lan & Rooze, 1995; Whyte, Koralick, Nielsen, Elder & Hawley, 1995).

Multimedia CAI and the Verbal/Visual Cognitive Learning Style

There has been a paucity of research examining relationships between cognitive learning style, multimedia CAI and learning. For example, Riding and Douglas (1993) used their Verbal/Imagery (hereafter referred to as Verbal/Visual) model to examine the effect of cognitive learning style and mode of presentation on learning performance. Results indicated that Visualizers' performance on recall tasks was a great deal better when the presentation mode was text-plus-picture, rather than the entirely verbal mode. Intermediates, as expected, performed similarly in both instructional conditions. However, there was an unexpected lack of effect of presentation mode for Verbalizers' performance. One factor that may have contributed to this effect was knowledge type. Riding and Douglas acknowledged that some types of information may be easier to visualize and suggested that recall may be affected by an interaction between information type, cognitive learning style, and mode of presentation. A recent study conducted by Massa & Mayer (2006) found no evidence to support the hypothesis that visual and verbal learners learn better from different modes of multimedia instruction. Two replication experiments and the examination of 51 interactions across all three experiments yielded no significant results to support differentiated multimedia for verbalizers and visualizers.

Validity of the Verbal/Visual Cognitive Learning Style

Work by Riding and Douglas (1993) indicated that the Verbal/Visual cognitive learning style may be an appropriate variable for comparative media investigations. However, other styles have been identified. Messick (1976) identified 19 cognitive styles, and Riding and

Cheema (1991) found over 30 style labels in a literature search. A notable problem with past research is that researchers often fail to mention the existence of other types of cognitive learning styles (Riding & Cheema, 1991). Lewis (1976) recognized this problem and suggested that "the right thing to do is to focus…on the search for individual differences that are basic, in the sense that they underlie (and to that extent, *explain*) a whole range of more readily observable differences" (p.304). Evidence for the existence of the Verbal/Visual style has been mounting since the early work of Francis Galton in 1883 on imagery types, and the observation by Bartlett in 1932 that participants tended to fall into two imagery categories: visualizers, who claimed that their recall was based on visual imagery, and verbalizers, who claimed to rely on words rather than images (e.g., Laing, 2001). [For a review of experimental, physiological and behavioural research into the Verbal/Visual dimension refer to Richardson (1977)]. The Verbal/Visual style has been suggested as one of two underlying individual differences in cognition (Rayner & Riding, 1997; Riding, 1997; Riding & Cheema, 1991). Thus, Lewis' demand for a focus on fundamentals, so as to avoid trivialities, has been met, and the appropriateness of this cognitive learning style for the current study has been established.

In sum, a review of the literature suggests that by reducing demands on the limited capacity of WM by optimum assignment of media to WM, learning and retention will be improved, and that this effect will vary with task and individual differences.

The Present Investigation

The design of the present study was determined by three aims: to investigate the *why*, *when* and *to whom* of multimedia CAI efficacy. A controlled comparison was made between three computer assisted instruction conditions that varied only in media complexity: (i) 'Text'; (ii) text with 'Still' graphic; and (iii) text with still graphic and an 'Audio' track. The audio track was read by a female. Mirenda, Eicher and Beukelman (1989) found no gender interaction for preference of male/female voice output when learning from a computer. To account for *why* learning outcomes, as assessed by a multiple-choice recall test, may vary across different media conditions, two aspects of memory were considered, WM and LTM. WM will be examined with reference to Wickens' (1992) optimum assignment of display format to WM codes by comparing the learning outcomes of individuals in the three media conditions: (i) a mono-media control group ('Text'); (ii) a dual-coding multimedia group ('Stills'); and (iii) an optimum coding multimedia group ('Audio'). Learning outcome was measured by a recall test, which was administered twice, immediately after the instruction and one-week later. Half the recall questions featured a graphic cue and the remainder had no cue, so that the role of visual images in LTM recall could be examined. To explore *when* specific media attributes may be of benefit, the instructional content was categorized as either declarative or procedural knowledge. While learning of declarative knowledge can be tested via simple recall, the validity assessing procedural knowledge with text-based recall questions, rather than application of the skill, is questionable. This problem is not unique to the current study. To investigate *to whom* multimedia instruction is of value, the Verbal/Visual cognitive learning style was assessed. Other individual difference variables such as verbal and spatial ability, prior knowledge, interest in lesson, and time taken to complete the lesson were also measured. While no hypotheses were drawn with respect to these latter variables, they were examined in preliminary analyses to check for group differences and influence on the dependent variable, learning outcome. Participants were randomly allocated to experimental conditions to control for potentially intrusive variables.

Hypotheses

H1: *Impact of media condition and WM codes on learning.* In accordance with Wickens (1992) it was expected that the optimum assignment of display format to WM code (Wickens, 1992) will reduce short-term memory demands on learners thereby improving overall performance and retention. Wickens specified audio and analog pictures as the most appropriate media for dual coding in WM. Therefore, it was hypothesized that: (i) Participants in the 'Audio' condition would achieve significantly higher scores than participants in the 'Stills' condition who would in turn achieve significantly higher scores than participants in the 'Text' condition, on an immediate recall test. (ii) Initial presentation group rankings will be maintained on a delayed test of recall.

H2: *Effect of cue graphics on information retrieval from LTM across media conditions.* In accordance with the principles of encoding specificity (Tulving, 1985) and multimedia design (Mayer, 2001), it was expected that participants assigned to conditions with still graphics in the lessons ('Stills' and 'Audio') would obtain significantly higher scores on cued-questions than subjects assigned to the condition without still graphics in the lessons ('Text') on a delayed recall test.

H3: *Effects of knowledge type and media condition on learning and retention.* Anderson (1980) stated that declarative knowledge is verbal in nature, and Wickens' (1992) model indicates that audio is most appropriate media for processing in verbal WM. In contrast, procedural knowledge has spatial properties, and Wickens' model indicates that analog pictures are the most appropriate media for spatial processing. Therefore, it was expected that: (i) Participants in the 'Audio' condition would score higher than participants in the 'Stills' condition, who would in turn score higher than participants in the 'Text' condition for declarative knowledge on both the immediate and delayed recall tests; (ii) Participants assigned to conditions with still graphics in the lessons ('Stills' and 'Audio') would obtain significantly higher scores than participants assigned to the condition without still graphics in the lessons ('Text') on an immediate test of procedural knowledge; but this difference would not be evident on a delayed recall test of procedural knowledge.

H4: *Effects of knowledge type, cue graphics and media condition on long term learning.* Gagné and Glaser (1987) suggested that cued-recall of declarative and procedural knowledge from LTM will result in differential learning outcomes. It was expected that: (i) Participants assigned to conditions with still graphics in the lessons ('Stills' and 'Audio') would obtain significantly higher scores for cued-recall of procedural knowledge than cued-recall of declarative knowledge, on a delayed test; (ii) For participants assigned to the 'Text' condition, there would be no significant differences in recall scores for cued procedural knowledge and cued declarative knowledge, on a delayed test; (iii) There would be no significant difference in recall scores of non-cued declarative and procedural knowledge across media conditions.

H5: *Effect of matching cognitive learning style with media condition on learning simple and complex tasks.* The matching hypothesis posits that learning outcomes depend (in part) on the match or mismatch of an individual's cognitive learning style and the instructional methods used to present information (Furnham, 1995). Riding (1997) further asserted that cognitive learning styles are critical only for complex tasks. Therefore, it was expected that: (i) on a simple task, learning of Visualizers in the 'Stills' condition and Verbalizers in the 'Text' condition (matched) would not be significantly different from learning of Visualizers in the 'Text ' condition and Verbalizers in the 'Stills' condition (mismatched), as assessed by a recall test; (ii) On a complex task, learning of Visualizers in the 'Stills' condition and Verbalizers in the 'Text' condition (matched) would be significantly higher than learning of Visualizers in the 'Text' condition and Verbalizers in the 'Stills' condition (mismatched), as assessed by a recall test.

H6: *Effect of cue graphics on information retrieval from LTM for students with differing cognitive learning styles across media conditions.* In accordance with the empirical finding that Visualizers in media conditions with graphics were more inclined to utilize diagrams in information recall than Verbalizers (Riding & Douglas, 1993), it was expected that: (i) On a complex task, Visualizers assigned to media conditions with still graphics ('Stills' and 'Audio') would score significantly higher on the cued-recall test questions than Verbalizers in the same conditions ('Stills' and 'Audio'); (ii) On a complex task, there would be no significant difference in cued-recall test scores between Visualizers and Verbalizers assigned to the 'Text' media condition.

H7: *The effect of media conditions, knowledge type, and cognitive learning styles, on learning outcomes.* Riding and Douglas (1993) suggested that some types of information may be easier to visualize for certain learners. Thus, an exploratory investigation into the interaction of mode of presentation, knowledge type and cognitive learning style was undertaken. It was expected that: Learning outcomes on a complex task would be affected by the interaction of media condition ('Text', 'Stills', and 'Audio'), knowledge type (declarative/ procedural) and cognitive learning style (Verbalizers/Visualizers).

METHOD

Participants

Participants were 63 first year psychology students at a major university in the state of Victoria, Australia. Participants were recruited from the first year subject pool, and received two hours credit for their participation. The sample comprised 23 males and 40 females with 84% of the participants aged between 17 and 19 years. Participants were randomly allocated to one of the three experimental groups corresponding to the three different presentation media conditions. The 'Text' group comprised of 22 participants (10 males, 12 females); the 'Stills' group comprised of 21 participants (seven males, 14 females); and the 'Audio' group comprised of 20 participants (six males, 14 females).

**Table 2. Between- and Within-Subjects Groups for the Dependent Variable
(Recall Score)**

Knowledge Type	Graphic Cues	Presentation Media Conditions		
		Text	Stills	Audio
		Session A (Time=1)		
Declarative (D)				
	Yes (Y)	TextDY1	StillsDY1	AudioDY1
	No (N)	TextDN1	StillsDN1	AudioDN1
Procedural (P)				
	Yes (Y)	TextPY1	StillsPY1	AudioPY1
	No (N)	TextPN1	StillsPN1	AudioPN1
		Session B (Time=2)		
Declarative (D)				
	Yes (Y)	TextDY2	StillsDY2	AudioDY2
	No (N)	TextDN2	StillsDN2	AudioDN2
Procedural (P)				
	Yes (Y)	TextPY2	StillsPY2	AudioPY2
	No (N)	TextPN2	StillsPN2	AudioPN2

Note: The individual difference classification factors are not illustrated.

Experimental Design

The experiment utilized a repeated-measures design consisting of one between-groups factor with three levels (delivery media) and two within-subjects factors: (i) type of learning task, which has two levels, declarative or procedural; (ii) the presence or absence of a picture cue presented with the recall questions (two levels). Classification factors relating to individual differences in cognitive learning style and verbal/spatial ability were also assessed. The dependent variable was the learning outcome: knowledge of mobile telecommunications as measured by immediate and a delayed recall tests. Table 2 gives an overview of the design.

Measures

Background Questionnaire

Demographic information included age and sex, and variables believed to have an influence on the learning outcome measure. These were: (a) past experience with computers; (b) familiarity with mobile telecommunications; (c) degree of eyestrain from looking at a computer screen; (d) visual impairments; (e) auditory impairments; (f) attitude to computers; and (g) general attitude to computer assisted instruction and mobile telecommunications.

Ability Tests

Verbal ability was measured by the Higher Test, Form ML (ACER, 1981). Among an Australian college and TAFE sample, the Higher Test was found to have a Kuder-Richardson (KD-20) reliability of .85. This pencil-and-paper test is a broad measure including items assessing vocabulary, verbal similarities, verbal reasoning, and verbal analogy problems.

The Surface Development Test (VZ-3) from the Kit of Factor-Referenced Cognitive Tests (Ekstrom, French, Harman, & Dermen, 1976) was selected as a measure of spatial visualization. Spatial visualization is "one of the factors most frequently found in factorial investigations" of spatial ability (Carroll, 1993, p.316). Spatial visualization emphasizes power, rather than speed, when solving increasingly difficult problems involving spatial forms (Lohman, 1979) and has been said to be relevant to learning from the visual mode (Kirby, Moore, & Schofield, 1988). The VZ-3 is a pencil-and-paper test that requires subject's to judge the results of mentally folding a complex shape. Using a college sample, the VZ-3 has a reliability coefficient of .90.

Cognitive Learning Style Questionnaire

The 20-item self-report Verbal and Visual Learning Styles Questionnaire designed by Kirby, Moore and Schofield (1988) was utilized as a measure of the Verbal/Visual cognitive learning style. To date, the measure has only been used in a handful of other empirical investigations (e.g. Plass et al., 1998; Schofield & Kirby, 1994). The questionnaire contains two scales, verbal and visual, each consisting of 10 items. Kirby et al. analyzed the items by a principal components analysis, and found that the items for both dimensions of this cognitive learning style possess good construct validity. The verbal and the visual scales were tested for reliability and found to have adequate alpha coefficients of .70 and .59 respectively. In the current study, a test-retest reliability analysis revealed a Cronbach's alpha of .92 for the verbal scale, and .90 for the visual scale. For the purpose of the present study, this measure was computerized. The response format involved answering statements such as: "I find illustrations or diagrams help me when I'm reading."

Attitude to Lesson

Apart from extraneous effects of attitudes to computers, participants responded to a series of 10 questions following each of the two short CAI lessons: interest in the topic of mobile telecommunications; affective response to the method of presentation and the content of the lesson; confidence that they had learned the material presented; and an indication of how well the lesson had kept their attention. Questions were presented on the computer, and were identical across all three media presentation conditions. Participants responded on a 5-point rating scale from strongly agree to strongly disagree.

Recall Test

The recall test was used to assess learning outcomes and was administered on two occasions, immediately after the lessons were completed, and after a delay of approximately one week ($M = 7.00$ days, $SD = 3.02$). There were 10 questions relating to declarative knowledge, and 10 questions relating to procedural knowledge (half the questions each from Lesson 1 and Lesson 2). The 20 questions were multiple choice and presented in random order. Overall, the recall test was found to have a Cronbach's reliability alpha of .66. Half the recall questions were supplemented by a visual cue, being the image seen during instruction, and half the questions had no cues. The cued question screens had the question positioned to the left of the screen, and the cue graphic – taken from the corresponding screen of the instructional task – positioned to the right. The no-cue type did not have any graphics, rather it merely featured the question. The computer automatically recorded the responses to the questions. If an incorrect answer was chosen, the correct answer was displayed on the left of the screen, prior to the next question being presented.

Apparatus

Computer Hardware

The hardware used in the experiment included five IBM compatible computers each equipped with a standard keyboard, a mouse, a 16-inch color monitor, and high quality audio capabilities. For Session A, two computers were permanently set up for the 'Audio' condition. Audio output was received via headphones. Two computers were set up for the 'Text' group and one computer for the 'Stills' group, and vice versa for every alternate session.

Computer Software

The computer assisted instruction task was developed specifically for the current investigation using Microcraft's authoring software. Lessons were delivered and results recorded using Microcraft's Lesson Management System.

Computer Assisted Instruction Task

The three experimental groups received the same lessons, with only the presentation media being manipulated, and were as follows: (1) The 'Text' presentation had lessons where the information was presented with written text centered on the screen. The lessons were self-paced. (2) The 'Stills' presentation had the same lesson content. The written text appeared on the left side of the screen and an illustrative graphic was added on the right side of each screen. The lessons were self-paced. (3) The 'Audio' presentation again involved identical lesson content to the other two groups. In addition to the written text on the left and still graphic on the right of the screen ('Stills'), as soon as new text appeared on the screen, a digitally recorded audio track of the text being read verbatim by a female voice came through on the participants' headphones. Once the audio track was finished, participants could decide when to move onto the next screen.

Lesson Design

The lessons were based on a simplified version of commonly used commercial CAI. For example, to control the order of delivery of the material, navigational options were minimized. There were no page-up options, and participants were only able to attempt each lesson once. In addition, the tutorial was linear, requiring all users to follow the same designated sequence. The first screen of each lesson contained the following information: the lesson number and title; the main topics covered in the lesson; how to proceed to the next screen; and a note reminding participants to take their time to understand the concepts presented as the lesson could not be repeated. So as to avoid the confounding of declarative and procedural knowledge, the categorization of knowledge type was based on each screen in each lesson, rather than the knowledge type predominantly represented in entire lessons. Each lesson featured eight screens describing facts (declarative knowledge) and eight screens explaining how to correctly perform sequential procedures (procedural knowledge). With the exception of the differing presentation media, the lessons were identical for every participant. At the end of each lesson, participants were presented with a summary screen repeating the main points of the lesson. The time taken to complete the CAI tutorial was automatically recorded by the computer.

Screen Layout

There was a maximum of 50 words per screen. The screen layout consisted of three main areas:(i) the text in the centre or on the left side of the screen; (ii) the graphic on the right of the screen; and (iii) an arrow button that could be clicked on, using the mouse, to continue moving through the lesson on the bottom right of the screen (Figure 3). By dividing each screen into these areas, a standard interface was provided for the user. For all screens: the background was a neutral pale grey; the text was black, with a large and standard font; and the graphics were 256 color.

Lesson Content

The content domain of mobile telecommunications was selected as it supported both declarative and procedural knowledge. The source of the lesson content was literature provided by a corporation in the telecommunications industry.

Lesson 1: Introducing Mobile Telecommunications

The declarative topics covered: analogue versus digital networks; analogue versus digital mobile telephones; SIM (Smart) cards; and security mechanisms. The procedural topics covered: making a call; receiving a call; storing and recalling frequently used numbers.

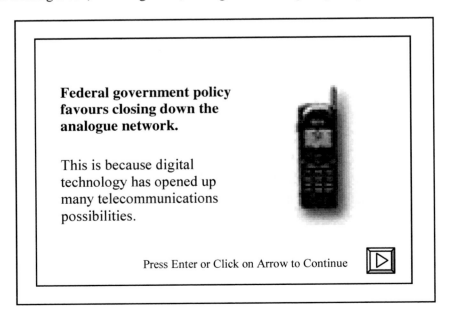

Figure 3. Basic design of a CAI information screen containing declarative knowledge.

Lesson 2: Using Messaging Services

The declarative topics covered: what various answering and messaging services are available and what they provide (voicemail, on-screen messaging, call forwarding, etc.). The procedural topics covered the steps involved in using these answering and messaging options.

Procedure

Research Context

A pilot study was conducted to test and refine the CAI task.

Small groups were tested over two experimental sessions (A & B), with a maximum of five participants per session. Both sessions were conducted in a computer laboratory setting. Participants were seated across five separate rows, with ample desk space for the pencil-and-paper tests and the computer, which presented the CAI task and the cognitive learning style questionnaire.

Experimental Overview

Before experimentation began, participants listened to an introductory briefing. Participants were only recruited if a consent form was signed. Upon entering the experiment at Session A, participants were allocated a number, and this was retained for Session B, so individuals remained anonymous, but their data from both sessions could be matched. Figure 4 gives an overview.

Session A

During the first session, which was 1 hour and 40 minutes duration, the background questionnaire and the two ability tests were administered using a standard pencil-and-paper format. Participants were then randomly assigned to one of the three media conditions ('Text', 'Stills', or 'Audio'). The experimenter specified to the participants that they would be asked to answer 20 quiz questions on the material presented in the CAI tutorial. While past research has failed to find a difference in intentional and incidental learning outcomes (Craik & Tulving, 1975), the informed method ensured that participants approached the lesson in the same way as any other piece of formal instruction. Participants were then guided through the log-on procedure on the computer. The participants assigned to the 'Audio' condition were then asked to put on their headphones. From this point onwards participants followed identical computerized instructions, and responded using a keyboard and/or mouse. However, participants could raise their hands if they had questions concerning the use of the program. No help about the learning content was provided. The two CAI lessons about mobile telecommunications were then presented. Each of the experimental groups received the same lessons, but using different presentation media. After each of the two lessons, participants responded to the questions entitled "Attitude to Lesson". Participants then completed the computerized multiple-choice recall test and the cognitive learning style questionnaire.

Session B

In the second session, one week later, participants were redirected as to the log-on procedure. They then repeated the on-screen recall test and the computerized cognitive learning styles questionnaire (to establish test-retest reliability). This was followed by individual subject debriefing, explaining the purpose and design of the experiment, and giving participants an opportunity to ask questions and make comments.

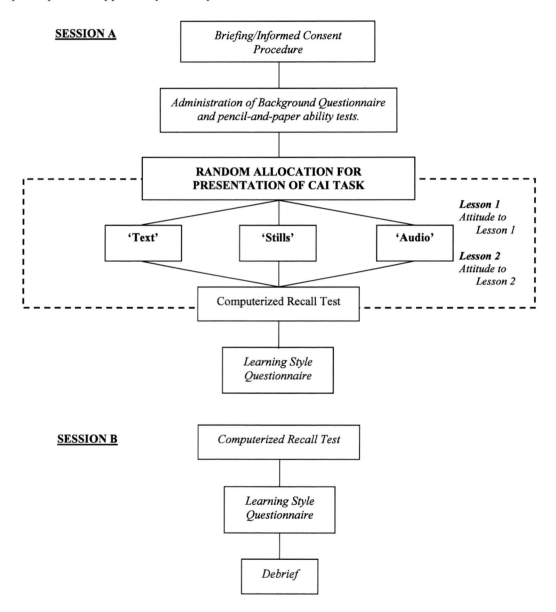

Figure 4. Overview of experimental procedure.

Table 3. Intercorrelations of Verbal Ability, Spatial Ability, and Recall Test Scores for Sessions A and B

Test	1.	2.	3.	4.
1. Session A Recall	—	.63**	.38**	.48**
2. Session B Recall		—	.38**	.46**
3. Verbal Ability			—	.31*
4. Spatial Ability				

Note: $N = 63$
* $p < .05$. ** $p < .01$.

RESULTS

Preliminary Analyses

Background Questionnaire

To ensure that performance on the CAI task was not influenced by extraneous background variables a multiple regression analysis was conducted, using a standard simultaneous regression model. The responses to the background questionnaire, regarding age, prior experience with mobile telecommunications, visual impairments, and so on, were used to predict score on the recall test at Session A. Overall, the regression was close to reaching formal significance ($R^2 = .26$, $F(9, 53) = 2.06$, $p = .051$), but an examination of the independent variables in the equation revealed that no background variable made a unique contribution to predicting learning outcomes. A multivariate analysis of variance (MANOVA) was then conducted to determine whether the 'Text', 'Stills' and 'Audio' groups were equivalent on all the background variables. As would be expected with random allocation, the three media conditions showed no significant between-group differences for background questionnaire responses, Pillai's trace statistics: $F(22,102) = 1.187$, $p = .276$.

Ability Tests

Intercorrelations of the ability tests and learning outcomes are presented in Table 3. Not surprisingly, both verbal and spatial ability were highly correlated with the dependent variable, learning outcome. A multivariate analysis of variance was conducted, with verbal and spatial ability as dependent variables, and one between-subjects factor defining cases as 'Text', 'Stills', or 'Audio'. With the use of Pillai's trace, the combined DVs were not significant, $F(4,120) = .96$, $p = .434$. Thus, both verbal and spatial ability were controlled for by the random allocation of participants to media conditions.

Learning Styles Questionnaire

The learning styles questionnaire was measured along two dimensions, the Verbal and the Visual, each scored out of a maximum of ten. To check the convergent and discriminant validity of the Verbal and Visual Learning Styles Questionnaire, the two dimensions were correlated with measures of spatial and verbal ability (Table 3). The Visual dimension was mildly and positively correlated with spatial ability but not verbal ability. The Verbal dimension was mildly and positively correlated with verbal ability but not spatial ability.

These results indicate that Verbal style is not the same as verbal ability, but the constructs are related; and that Visual style is not the same as spatial ability, but again the constructs are related.

A discrete difference score was calculated by subtracting Visual scores from Verbal scores, and participants were then classified as Visualizers ($n = 23$), Intermediates ($n = 16$), or Verbalizers ($n = 24$) based on a three-way split (after Riding & Douglas, 1993). Due to the sample size ($N = 63$), and since the main thrust of the hypotheses was to investigate the effects of habitual Visualizers and Verbalizers, the Intermediates were excluded from further analyses.

Attitude to Lessons

To ensure that learning on the instructional lessons was not influenced by extraneous variables two multiple regression analyses were conducted, using the standard simultaneous regression model. All 10 attitude-to-lesson variables were specified as predictors including: affective response to the method of presentation, participants' interest in the mobile telecommunications, how well the lesson had kept their attention, etc. The first analysis revealed that participants' attitudes to Lesson 1 were significant predictors of recall score at Lesson 1, $R^2 = .33$, $F(10, 52) = 2.550$, $p = .014$. One attitude variable uniquely predicted learning outcome (*I thought the material was well presented*). The relationship was negative ($sr_i^2 = -.248$), suggesting that participants who thought the material was not well presented obtained higher recall scores for Lesson 1. In the second regression analysis, recall score for Lesson 2 was not significantly predicted by participants' attitudes to Lesson 2, $R^2 = .13$, $F(10, 52) = .804$, $p = .626$. Two multivariate analyses of variance (MANOVAs) were then conducted to determine whether the 'Text', 'Stills' and 'Audio' groups were equivalent in their attitudes to CAI Lesson 1 and Lesson 2. With the use of Pillai's statistic, the combined DVs were not significant for either CAI Lesson 1 or CAI Lesson 2: $F(20,104) = 1.025$, $p = .441$, and $F(20,104) = .925$, $p = .557$, respectively.

Recall Test

Examination of recall test scores at Session A ($M = 12.302$; $SD = 3.206$) revealed no univariate outliers, and a normal distribution. Similarly, when recall scores at Session A were examined by media condition, the distribution appeared normal and no univariate outliers were found. A multivariate analysis of variance was conducted with time taken to complete the CAI lessons, time taken to complete the recall test at Sessions A and B, and the number of days elapsed between Session A and Session B as dependent variables, and one between-subjects factor defining cases as 'Text', 'Stills', or 'Audio'. With the use of Pillai's trace, the combined DVs showed no significant between-group differences, $F(6,118) = 1.578$, $p = .160$.

Hypothesis Testing

H1: The impact of media condition and working memory codes on learning. A repeated-measures analysis of variance was conducted on one between-subjects factor, media, and one-within subjects factor, time of measurement, with two levels, recall score at Session A and recall score at Session B. The assumption of homogeneity of variance-covariance matrices was not violated (Box's M = 1.438, $F(6,86028)$ = .228, p = .968). There was no need to test sphericity as the within-subjects factor had only two levels.

There were no significant main effects for either media or time measurement, $F(2,60)$ = 2.00, p = .144 and $F(1,60)$ = .08, p = .780 respectively, and no significant media by time interaction, $F(2,60)$ = .92, p = .404. The media by time differences, while not significant are illustrated in Figure 5. The ranking of participants according to media condition for Session A was expected to be 'Audio' > 'Stills' > 'Text'. Figure 6 shows that the pattern of results for Session A was not as expected, with 'Text' > 'Audio' > 'Stills'.

Nor were the initial group rankings maintained on the test of long-term retention at Session B. The 'Audio' scores dropped to the lowest ranked group. Interestingly, 'Stills' and 'Text' participants showed a slight, but non-significant, increase in mean recall scores from Session A to Session B.

H2: The effect of cue graphics on learning across media conditions. It was expected that participants assigned to the 'Stills' and 'Audio' conditions would score significantly higher on cued-recall questions than participants in the 'Text' condition, on a delayed recall test. An analysis of variance was conducted, with cued-recall score at Session B as the dependent variable and one between-subjects factor defining cases as 'Text', 'Stills' or Audio'. There were no significant media differences for cued-recall scores at Session B, $F(2,60)$ = 1.794, p = .175, and the pattern of cued-recall scores for the groups was in the opposite direction than predicted (Figure 7).

H3: The effects of knowledge type and media condition on learning and retention. A three-factor, analysis of variance was performed with one between-subjects factor, media condition, and two within-subjects factors, type of knowledge (declarative/procedural), and time of measurement (Session A/Session B). In Table 4, no significant main effects for media or time of measurement were found.

The only significant main effect was for type of knowledge, $F(1,60)$ = 31.43, p < .001, reflecting overall better learning of participants on declarative knowledge than procedural knowledge, as assessed by scores on recall test. This effect can be seen by comparing Figure 8 (i) and (ii).

(i) Effect of declarative knowledge and media condition on learning/retention. For declarative knowledge, the ranking of participants according to media condition for Session A was expected to be 'Audio' > 'Stills' > 'Text'. Mean scores indicated that the pattern of results was not as expected. 'Text' and 'Stills' were approximately equal, with participants in the 'Audio' condition having the lowest mean recall score. At Session B, the rankings were in the opposite direction to predicted, due to increase in mean recall of 'Text' participants.

Table 4. Intercorrelations of the Verbal Dimension, the Visual Dimension, Verbal Ability, and Spatial Ability

Source	1.	2.	3.	4.
1. Verbal Dimension	—	-.07	.29*	-.07
2. Visual Dimension		—	.10	.32*
3. Verbal Ability			—	.31*
4. Spatial Ability				—

Note: N = 63.
* p < .05. ** p < .01.

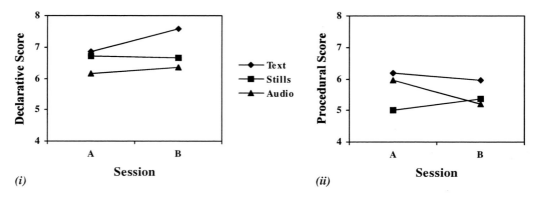

Figure 5. Mean recall scores (maximum score = 10) of (i) declarative knowledge and (ii) procedural knowledge by media condition and time of measurement.

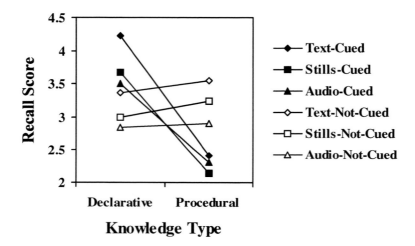

Figure 6. Mean Cued and Non-cued Recall Scores (maximum score = 5) for knowledge type (declarative/procedural) by media condition at Session B.

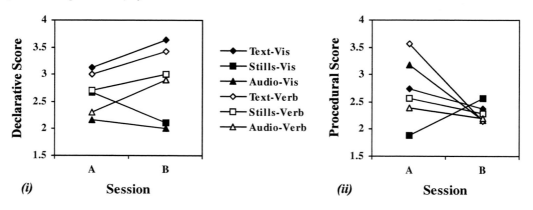

Figure 7. Mean recall scores (maximum score = 5) of (i) declarative knowledge and (ii) procedural knowledge, by media condition and time of measurement.

(ii) Effect of procedural knowledge and media condition on learning/retention. For procedural knowledge the 'Audio' and 'Stills' conditions were expected to rank higher than the 'Text' condition at Session A. As mentioned, no significant interaction between knowledge type and media was found. However, close examination of mean scores indicated that the pattern of results was not as expected. 'Text' and 'Audio' were approximately equal, with participants in the 'Stills' condition having the lowest mean recall score. For Session B, the rankings were expected to converge, by virtue of a hypothesized decline in 'Audio' and 'Stills' scores over time. The 'Audio' condition showed such a decline, but the 'Stills' condition showed a slight increase in mean recall.

H4: The effects of knowledge type, cue graphics and media condition on long-term learning. It was expected that cued recall and non-cued recall of declarative and procedural knowledge from LTM would result in differential learning outcomes. A multivariate analysis of variance was conducted with one between-subjects factor defining cases as 'Text', 'Stills' for Audio', and four dependent variables relating to the breakdown of recall scores at Session B: cued declarative; cued procedural; non-cued declarative; and non-cued procedural.

Cued-recall of declarative and procedural knowledge. There were no significant media differences for either declarative or procedural cued-recall scores at Session B, $F(2,60) = 2.275, p = .112$, and $F(2,60) = .319, p = .728$, respectively. The pattern of results is described below. (i) 'Stills' and 'Audio'. It was expected that participants in the 'Stills' and 'Audio' conditions, would obtain higher recall scores for cued procedural knowledge than cued declarative knowledge, on a delayed test. The reverse trend was apparent, with cued procedural scores being lower than cued declarative scores. It is worth noting that cued-recall scores for procedural knowledge were lower than non-cued scores for procedural knowledge. (ii) 'Text'. As expected cued-recall scores of 'Text' paraticipants did not significantly differ for declarative and procedural knowledge.

Non-cued recall of declarative and procedural knowledge. As expected, no difference in recall scores of non-cued declarative and procedural knowledge across media conditions at Session B was found, $F(2,60) = 1.145, p = .325$, and $F(2,60) = 2.144, p = .126$, respectively.

H5: The effect of matching cognitive learning style and media condition on learning simple and complex tasks. Before testing this hypothesis, it was necessary to establish that a subset of the recall test was simple and another subset was complex. The design of the CAI task consisted of two lessons, "Lesson 1. Introducing mobile telecommunications" and "Lesson 2. Using messaging services". Based on recall scores for each lesson at Session A, the former lesson was viewed as simple ($M = 6.79, SD = 1.69$) and the latter lesson complex ($M = 5.51, SD = 2.06$), and this was confirmed by a repeated-measures t-test, $t(62) = 5.20, p < .001$.

Effect of matching cognitive learning style and media condition on a simple task. An analysis of variance was conducted, with two between-subjects factors defining subjects according to their cognitive learning style (Verbal/Visual) and media condition ('Text', 'Stills', or 'Audio'), and one dependent variable, recall score for Lesson 1 (Session A). There were no significant main effects for media or cognitive learning style, $F(2,41) = .216, p = .807$ and $F(1,41) = .406, p = .528$ respectively. As expected, on a simple task (Lesson 1), there was no significant interaction of media condition and cognitive learning style on recall score, $F(2,41) = 1.326, p = .277$. In other words, matched Visualizers and Verbalizers obtained the same mean recall scores as mismatched Visualizers and Verbalizers, on a simple task (Lesson 1) (see Table 5).

Table 5. Recall Scores for Visualizers and Verbalizers by Media Condition

Cognitive Learning Style	'Text'		'Stills'		'Audio'	
	M	SD	M	SD	M	SD
Lesson 1						
Visualizer	6.75	1.04	6.22	2.11	7.50	2.07
Verbalizer	7.43	1.72	7.29	1.60	6.70	1.34
Lesson 2						
Visualizer	5.88	1.81	4.56	2.40	5.33	2.34
Verbalizer	6.57	1.99	5.29	2.14	4.70	1.64

Note: Maximum score = 10.

(ii) Effect of matching cognitive learning style and media condition on a complex task. An analysis of variance was conducted, with two between-subjects factors defining subjects according to their cognitive learning style (Verbal/Visual) and media condition ('Text', 'Stills', 'Audio'), and one dependent variable, recall score for Lesson 2 (Session A). On a complex task (Lesson 2), there were no significant main effects for media or cognitive learning style, $F(2,41) = 1.901$, $p = .162$ and $F(1,41) = .191$, $p = .665$, respectively. Contrary to predictions, there was no significant interaction of media condition and cognitive learning style on recall score, $F(2,41) = .546$, $p = .583$. However, the pattern of results indicated a trend in the expected direction, with Verbalizers in the 'Text' condition (matched) performing better than Visualizers in the 'Text' condition (mismatched). In contrast to predictions, Visualizers in the 'Stills' condition (matched) did not perform as well as Verbalizers in the 'Stills' condition (mismatched). Only in the 'Audio' condition did Visualizers show a trend towards outperforming Verbalizers (Table 5), but no "matching" hypotheses for the 'Audio' condition were specified a priori.

H6: The effect of cue graphics on learning for students with differing cognitive learning styles across media conditions. It was expected that on a complex task, Visualizers and Verbalizers would obtain different cued-recall scores across the media conditions. An analysis of variance was performed with one dependent variable, cued-recall score for Lesson 2 at Session B, and two between-subjects factors, defining subjects according to their cognitive learning style (Verbal/Visual) and media condition ('Text', 'Stills', or 'Audio'). There were no significant main effects for media or cognitive learning style, $F(2,41) = .028$, $p = .972$ and $F(1,41) = .847$, $p = .363$ respectively. Contrary to predictions, there was no significant interaction of media condition and cognitive learning style on cued-recall score, $F(2,41) = 1.614$, $p = .212$.

(i) Stills and audio. It was expected that Visualizers assigned to the 'Stills' and 'Audio' conditions would score significantly higher on the cued-recall test questions than Verbalizers in the 'Stills' and 'Audio' conditions.

(ii) Text. As expected, there were no significant differences in cued-recall test scores between Visualizers and Verbalizers assigned to the 'Text' media condition.

H7: The effect of media condition, knowledge type, and cognitive learning styles, on learning outcomes. A repeated-measures analysis of variance was performed with two between-subjects factors defining cases according to their cognitive learning style (Verbal/Visual) and media condition ('Text', 'Stills', or 'Audio'), and two within-subjects factors assessing recall scores on a complex task: type of knowledge (declarative/procedural), and time of measurement (Session A/Session B).

No significant main effects for media, cognitive learning style, knowledge type or time of measurement were found. The time of measurement by knowledge type interaction was significant. Declarative scores diverged over time and procedural scores converged over time. Since this interaction did not focus on differences between media conditions it was not pursued post hoc.

Media, knowledge type and time of measurement also interacted significantly. A series of One-way ANOVAs, using Tukey's HSD to control for Type I errors associated with multiple post hoc comparisons, were conducted to investigate this interaction. It was found that participants in the 'Text' condition scored significantly higher for procedural recall at Session A than participants in the 'Stills' condition, $F(2,62) = 3.321$, $p < .05$; and participants in the 'Text' condition scored significantly higher declarative recall at Session B than participants in the 'Stills' condition, $F(2,62) = 3.847$, $p < .05$.

Two interactions were particularly relevant to the current hypothesis: (i) media, cognitive learning styles and type of knowledge; and (ii) media, cognitive learning styles, type of knowledge, and time of measurement. Neither of these interactions were statistically significant. However, several trends were apparent from the mean recall scores. Verbalizers in the 'Text' condition (matched) evinced a trend for higher scores than Visualizers in the 'Text' condition (mismatched) for procedural knowledge at Session A. In contrast, Visualizers in the 'Stills' condition (matched) showed a trend for lower scores than Verbalizers in the 'Stills' condition (mismatched) for declarative knowledge at Session B and procedural knowledge at Session A. Although no hypotheses were specified, a pattern showed Verbalizers in the 'Audio' condition obtained higher scores than Visualizers in the 'Audio' condition for declarative knowledge at Session B, and that Visualizers in the 'Audio' condition obtained higher scores than Verbalizers in the 'Audio' for procedural knowledge at Session A.

CONCLUSION

The general research question for the investigation was: "Does increasing the complexity of delivery media in computer assisted instruction enhance learning outcomes?" The research design required participants to complete a computer assisted instruction task in one of three media conditions: (i) 'Text'; (ii) Text and 'Stills'; or (iii) Text, Stills and 'Audio'. In the past, comparative media studies have failed to adopt a theoretical approach when addressing the research question. Consequently, the current study set out to explore this question in light of a major theoretical model proposed by Wickens (1992). Wickens' model elaborates on dual code theory (Paivio, 1971) by specifying the display media required for optimal processing in WM, thereby facilitating learning outcomes. From this model, it was anticipated that the combination of audio and images would result in maximum learning performance. Previous results concerning the optimum assignment model have been ambiguous, and Wickens' stated that this may have been due to task differences and individual differences, hence both these variables were investigated. The study also examined the role of visual images in retrieving knowledge from LTM.

Broadly, the study results indicated that the data were not congruent with Wickens' (1992) model, demonstrating no significant differences in learning outcomes across the three media conditions. Furthermore, a trend pointed to the highest ranked recall scores being obtained by participants in the single medium 'Text' condition. The results for knowledge type were predominantly non-significant and the rank orderings of the media conditions were not as predicted. Nonetheless, several notable trends emerged. Scores for procedural knowledge converged over time, replicating a pattern found in previous studies (Palmiter & Elkerton, 1993; Quealy & Langan-Fox, 1998), whereas declarative scores diverged over time. This may have been a reflection of the finding that procedural knowledge was more difficult to learn than declarative knowledge. Contrary to predictions, it appeared that the graphic cues interfered with the recall of procedural knowledge; while not significant, cued procedural scores were poorer than non-cued procedural scores.

Likewise, it appeared that the graphic cues interfered with Visualizers' retrieval of knowledge from LTM. While non-significant, a trend pointed to Visualizers obtaining lower cued recall scores than Verbalizers in the 'Stills' and 'Audio' conditions; whereas in the 'Text' only condition, where no graphics were initially presented, Visualizers showed a trend towards higher cued recall scores than Verbalizers. This is contrary to Riding and Douglas (1993), who found that in a text-plus-picture condition, Visualizers, but not Verbalizers, utilized images in retrieving information. There were no significant differences in learning outcomes for Visualizers and Verbalizers across the three media conditions. As expected, Verbalizers in the 'Text' condition (matched) showed a trend for higher scores than Visualizers in the 'Text' condition (mismatched). However, this was complicated by the finding that Verbalizers in the 'Stills' condition (mismatched) showed a trend for higher scores than Visualizers in the 'Stills' condition (matched). On the whole, therefore, these results did not support the matching hypothesis (Furnham, 1995). Nevertheless, preliminary findings reinforced the validity and reliability of the Verbal and Visual Learning Style Questionnaire (Kirby, Moore, & Schofield, 1988).

Surprisingly, this study also failed to support the assumption that learners prefer multimedia CAI, as results revealed no group differences in attitude to the two CAI Lessons. A positive attitude to multimedia has been linked with novelty effects (Quealy & Langan-Fox, 1998) which have been proposed to account for any media differences seen in comparative studies (Clark & Craig, 1992). Thus, the absence of media differences could be attributed to the lack of novelty of the multimedia CAI task.

In considering the lack of effect of presentation mode upon learning outcomes, there appear to be several contributing factors. These included the sample size and problems inherent in the task. While the participants were all unfamiliar with mobile telecommunications, as first year university students they may have been well-practiced in concentrated study, especially from text-based materials (see Langan-Fox, Platania-Phung & Waycott, 2006 for more on this perspective). A wider range of learners/trainees, particularly those from working environments, may expose more varied learning outcomes across media conditions. A problem with the design of the CAI task concerned feedback for incorrect answers on the recall tests. The motivation behind the inclusion of feedback was to emulate current practice in education and training. 'Stills' and 'Text' participants showed a slight, but non-significant, increase in mean correct recall scores from Session A to Session B, which suggested that these participants attended to the feedback for incorrect answers given in Session A. However, the 'Audio' scores decreased (but not significantly) over time. An explanation for this decrease, in accordance with Palmiter and Elkerton's (1993) findings for dynamic visual media, is that the audio medium encouraged superficial processing and neglect of informative text and textually presented feedback. This highlights the objection raised by Clark (1985), that media and method (e.g., feedback) become inextricable when attributing causality to learning from multimedia CAI.

The results also pointed to the inadequacy of the still images used in the 'Stills' and 'Audio' conditions of the CAI task. The finding that still images did not appear to have an additive effect on learning outcomes is inconsistent with dual code theory (Paivio, 1971). Furthermore, in contrast to the principal of encoding specificity (Tulving, 1985), retrieval of information from LTM was not aided by image-based cues, and the aforementioned results for procedural knowledge and cognitive learning styles suggested that the cues may actually have interfered with recall. These findings indicate that a method of accurately defining the important characteristics of still images to be used in CAI must go beyond a simple elimination of ambiguous and/or unhelpful images based on a small pilot study. For example, various scaling operations have been developed to describe interrelations among words and images, such as, concretenesss-abstractness, familiarity, and recognizability (Paivio, 1971).

An issue that was recognized at the outset of the chapter relates to the presentation and evaluation of procedural knowledge, which is different from declarative serial recall, and must certainly go beyond a tutorial followed by a pen and paper test, or even a mouse and keyboard test. A drill-and-practice format for computerized instruction and a performance/transfer test may be a more appropriate operationalizing of procedural knowledge. Media differences may be more pronounced under these circumstances.

Another interpretation of the results is that the CAI task and subsequent recall test were not sensitive enough. There was some support for this proposition was based on the interaction of media, knowledge type and time. This interaction was examined twice, first in Hypothesis 3 where total recall score (Lesson 1 and Lesson 2) was the dependent variable, and again in Hypothesis 7 where the recall score for the complex task (Lesson 2) was the dependent variable. The former result was not significant, while the latter result was significant, suggesting the influence of media on learning outcomes may only be apparent when the task is complex. Similarly, Riding (1997) claimed that cognitive learning styles are only crucial when tasks are complex. Although Lesson 2 was deemed more complex than Lesson 1, the results regarding the matching of cognitive learning styles to media condition at Lesson 2 were non-significant. This is suggestive that the task was not complex enough.

Contributions to the Literature

Given these caveats, there are still a number of ways in which the current research has contributed to the information processing approach to multimedia CAI. Firstly, the design illustrated that a controlled comparative methodology can be utilized in multimedia CAI research. Secondly, the investigation situated the *why* of multimedia efficacy in a theoretical model, and placed the theoretical model in a larger more practical framework which incorporates *when* and *to whom* multimedia CAI is of value. Finally, the study challenged the widely held assumption that multimedia helps people to learn more effectively. A discussion of each of these contributions to the literature follows.

Reconsidering the Comparative Research Design

A controlled comparative design was utilized that countered many of the criticisms of previous comparative research (Clark, 1985; Najjar, 1996b; Williams & Brown. 1990). In particular, the investigation demonstrated that it is possible to manipulate the mode of presentation, while controlling the method of presentation. In future studies, the controlled comparative design could be used to help distinguish whether multimedia has other differencial effects, for example levels of arousal or mental workload.

Theoretical Considerations

Paivio's (1971) dual code theory was not supported in the current study. Under these circumstances, the data were therefore also incompatible with Wickens' (1992) model, which was founded on dual code theory. Nonetheless, Wickens highlighted the need to move beyond a simplistic dual code approach, in order to identify media that optimize dual coding in WM. Wickens' model also provided focus and direction at the level of information processing, in an area of research that has been theoretically weak in the past.

Reconciling Single- and Multiple-Channel Theories

Overall, the results were consistent with Barron and Kysilka's (1992) single-channel filter theory of information processing. In accordance with the single channel theory, based on Braodbent's (1958) filter theory, only one medium is attended; any additional media are ignored and therefore do not lead to increased learning outcomes. However, multiple-channel theory cannot be dismissed, given that the additive nature of dual coding on learning has been well established in the empirical literature (Baek & Lane, 1988; Clark & Paivio, 1991; Levie & Lentz, 1982; Mayer, 1997, 2001; Mayer & Anderson, 1991; Mayer & Moreno, 2003; Moreno & Valdez, 2005; Paivio, 1986; van Merrienboer & Ayres, 2005). Therefore, a gap between the single- and multiple-channel theories of information processing could be said to exist. This gap needs to be bridged, and one possible way to achieve this would be by proposing a "switching mechanism" between both the single and multiple channel theories. The trigger for the switch may be physiological (e.g., arousal), psychological (e.g., selective attention, and/or individual differences), or based on the features of the multimedia CAI task. Researchers have only recently begun to examine the effect of individual differences such as prior knowledge (Kalyuga, Chandler, & Sweller, 1998, 2000; Kozma, 2003; Lowe, 2003; Stern, Aprea & Ebner, 2003), gender (Riding & Grimley, 1999; Grimley, 2007), motivation (Najjar, 1998) and working memory capacity (Lusk et al., 2008) on multimedia learning. Additional research in this area may prove fruitful in providing additional insight into ways of enhancing the design, structure and delivery of multimedia environments to accommodate diverse learner requirements.

Implications of the Developed Framework

Wickens' (1992) model was also used to construct a framework for studying the relationships between media, task and individual differences. Generalizations about multimedia effectiveness have been difficult in the past due to task differences. Thus, the current study categorized the content of the CAI task as declarative knowledge and procedural knowledge. The main effect for knowledge type, the interaction of media, knowledge type and time on a complex task, the dissimilar trends for procedural and declarative knowledge over time, and the distinct patterns of results for cued and non-cued procedural and declarative knowledge, all suggest that this type of task categorization is indeed useful. Furthermore, these results support the theoretical distinction of declarative and procedural sub-systems in LTM (Estes, 1989; Tulving, 1983). This illustrates the potential of CAI as a test-bed for study into memory, learning, and other cognitive phenomena, as discussed by Quealy and Langan-Fox (1998).

Turning to individual differences, this study did not hypothesize, a priori, any interaction among the Verbal/Visual cognitive learning style and the 'Audio' condition. Exploratory analyses, although non-significant, indicated that the addition of a redundant verbal medium has differential effects on learning of Visualizers and Verbalizers. Research is needed to clarify this relationship, as the integration of the individual difference approach with comparative media studies has substantial practical utility. With the introduction and strengthening of intelligent/adaptive systems, relevant individual differences of each student can be automatically compensated.

Challenging the Role of Multimedia

From the present research, it was found that no media condition demonstrated superior gains in learning over the other groups. In so far as there was a trend, it indicated that participants in the 'Text' only condition obtained the most accomplished learning outcomes. Therefore, in the frenzied rush to adopt new technologies, it may be time to reflect on the notion that conventional wisdom may be wrong, and that multimedia may not help people learn more effectively. Only further research on media and instruction may provide prudent guidelines regarding multimedia effectiveness to prevent the production and application of expensive programs that may have little effect on learning outcomes.

REFERENCES

Abouserie, R., Moss, D., & Barasi, S. (1992). Cognitive style, gender, attitude toward computer assisted learning and academic achievement. *Educational Studies, 18*(2), 151-160.

Adey, P., Fairbrother, R., Wiliam, D., Johnson, B., Jones, C. (1999). *Learning Styles and Strategies: A Review of Research*. King's College London: London.

Allinson, C. W., & Hayes, J. (1990). Validity of learning styles questionnaire. *Psychological Reports, 67*, 859-866.

Allinson, L. (1992). Learning styles and computer-based learning environments. In I Tomek (Ed.), *Computer Assisted Learning: ICCAL 1992* (pp.4-28). Berlin: Springer-Verlag.

Anderson, J. R. (1980). *Cognitive Psychology and its Implications*. San Fransisco: Freeman.

Armstrong, S.J. (2002), "Effects of cognitive style on the quality of research supervision", in Francis, A., Armstrong, S., Graff, M., Hill, J., Rayner, S., Sadler-Smith, E., Spicer, D.

(Eds). *Proceedings of the 7th Annual Conference of the European Learning Styles Information Network*, Ghent University, Belgium, 26-28 June 2002, 13-24.

Atkinson, R. (2002). Optimizing learning from examples using animated pedagogical agents. *Journal of Educational Psychology, 94*, 416–427.

Atkinson, R. C., & Shiffrin, R. M. (1971). The control of short-term memory. *Scientific American, 225*, 82-90.

Ausburn, L. J., & Ausburn, F. B. (1978). Cognitive styles: Some information and implications for instructional design. *Educational Communications Technology Journal, 26*, 337-354.

Australian Council for Eductaional Research [ACER]. (1981). *Higher Test, Form ML*. Hawthorn, Australia: ACER.

Baddeley, A. (1990). *Human Memory: Theory and Practice*. Hillsdale: Lawrence Erlbaum.

Baek, Y., & Lane, B. (1988). Color, graphics and animations in a computer assisted learning tutorial lesson. *Journal of Computer Based Instruction, 15*, 131-135.

Bagui, S. (1998). Reasons for increased learning using multimedia. *Journal of Educational Mutlimedia and Hypermedia, 7*(1), 3-18.

Barron, A. E., & Kysilka, M. L. (1992). The effectiveness of digital audio in computer-based training. *Journal of Research on Computing in Education, 25*(2), 277-289.

Bhowmick, A., Khasawneh, M. T., Bowling, S. R., Gramopadhye, A. K., & Melloy. B. J. (2007). Evaluation of alternate multimedia for web-based asynchronous learning. *International Journal of Industrial Ergonomics, 37*, 615-629.

Broadbent, D. E. (1958). *Perception and Communication*. New York: Pergamon Press.

Burger, K. (1985). Computer assisted instruction: Learning style and academic achievement. *Journal of Computer-Based Instruction, 12*(1), 21-22.

Canino, C., & Cicchelli, T. (1988). Cognitive styles, computerized treatments on mathematics achievement and reaction to treatments. *Journal of Educational Computing Research, 4*(3), 253-254.

Carroll, J. B. (1993). *Human Cognitive Abilities: A Survey of Factor-Analytic Studies*. Cambridge: Cambridge University Press.

Carlson, H. L. (1991). Learning style and program design in interactive multimedia. *Educational Technology Research and Development, 39*(3), 41-48.

Chen, S. Y., & Macredie, R. D. (2002). Cognitive styles and hypermedia navigation: Development of a learning model. *Journal of the American Society for Information Science and Technology, 53*, 3–15.

Chen, S. Y., & Macredie, R. D. (2004). Cognitive modelling of student learning in web-based instructional programmes. *International Journal of Human–Computer Interaction, 17*(3), 375–402.

Chen, S. Y., Ghinea, G., & Macredie, R. (2006). A cognitive approach to user perception of multimedia quality: An empirical investigation. *International Journal of Human-Computer Studies, 64*, 1200–1213.

Clark, J. M., & Paivio, A. (1991). Dual coding theory and education. *Educational Psychology Review, 3(*3), 149-208.

Clark, R. E. (1983). Reconsidering research on learning from media. *Review of Educational Research, 53*(4), 445–459.

Clark, R. E. (1985). Evidence for confounding in computer-based instruction studies: Analyzing the meta-analyses. *Educational Communication and Technology Journal, 33*, 249-263.

Clark, R. E., & Craig, T. G. (1992). Research and theory on multi-media learning effects. In G. M. Giardina (Ed.), *Interactive Multimedia Learning Environments: Human Factors and Technical Considerations on Design Issues* (pp.19-30). New York: Springer-Verlag.

Claxton, C., & Ralston, Y. (1978). *Learning styles: Their impact on teaching and administration*. Washington DC: American Association for Higher Education.

Cordell, B. (1991). A study of learning styles and CAI. *Computers and Education, 16*(2), 175-183.

Craik, F. I. M., & Tulving, E. (1975). Depth of processing and the retention of words in episodic memory. *Journal of Experimental Psychology: General, 104*(3), 268-294.

Cronbach, L. J., & Snow, R. E. (1977). *Aptitudes and Instructional Methods: A Handbook for Research on Interactions*. New York: Irvington.

Das, J. P. (1988). Implications for school learning. In R. R. Schmeck (Ed.), *Learning Strategies and Learning Styles*. New York: Plenum Press.

Dimitrov, D. M., McGee, S., & Howard, B. C. (2002). Changes in students' science ability produced by multimedia learning environments: Application of the linear logistic model for change. *School Science and Mathematics, 102*(1), 15-24.

Driver, M. J. (2000). "Decision style: past, present and future research", in Riding, R., Rayner, S. (Eds). *International Perspectives on Individual Differences*, Ablex, Stamford, CT, Vol. Volume 1, Cognitive Styles.

Ekstrom, R. B., French, J. W., Harman, H., & Dermen, D. (1976). *Kit of Factor Referenced Cognitive Tests*. Princeton: Educational Testing Service.

Enochs, J. R., Handley, M. M., & Wollenberg, J. P. (1986). Relating learning style, reading vocabulary, reading comprehension, and aptitude for learning to achievement in the self-paced and computer-assisted instruction modes. *Journal of Experimental Education, 54*(3), 135-139.

Entwistle, N. (1981). *Styles of Learning and Teaching*. Chichester: Wiley.

Ester, D. P. (1994-95). CAI, lecture, and student learning style: The differential effects of instructional method. *Journal of Research on Computing in Education, 27*(2), 129-140.

Estes, W. K. (1989). Learning theory. In A. Lesgold & R. Glaser (Eds.), *Foundations for a Psychology of Education*. Hillsdale, NJ: Lawrence Erlbaum.

Evans, C. (2004). Exploring the relationship between cognitive style and teaching style. *Educational Psychology, 24*(4), 509-30.

Feeg, V. D., Bashatah, A., & Langley, C. (2005). Development and testing of a CD-ROM based tutorial for nursing students: Getting ready for HIPAA. *Journal of Nursing Education, 44*(8), 381-386.

Fletcher-Flinn, C. M., & Gravatt, B. (1995). The efficacy of computer-assisted instruction (CAI): A meta-analysis. *Journal of Educational Computing Research, 12*(3), 219-242.

Ford, N., & Chen, S. Y. (2000). Individual differences, hypermedia navigation, and learning: An empirical study. *Journal of Educational Multimedia and Hypermedia, 9*, 281–311.

Ford, N., & Chen, S. Y. (2001). Matching/mismatching revisited: an empirical study of learning and teaching styles. *British Journal of Educational Technology, 32*(1), 5–22.

Furnham, A. (1995). The relationship of personality and intelligence to cognitive learning style and achievement. In D. H. Saklofske & M. Zeidner (Eds.), *International Handbook of Personality and Intelligence* (pp. 397-413). New York: Plenum Press.

Gagné, R. M., & Glaser, R. (1987). Foundations in learning research. In R. M. Gagné (Ed.), *Instructional Technology Foundations* (pp.49-83). Hillsdale, NJ: Lawrence Erlbaum.

Ghinea, G., & Chen, S. Y. (2003). The impact of cognitive styles on perceptual distributed media quality. *British Journal of Educational Technology, 34,* 393–406.

Gillingham, M. G., & Guthrie, J. T. (1987). Relationships between CBI and research on teaching. *Contemporary Educational Psychology, 12,* 189-199.

Grimley, M. (2007). Learning from multimedia materials: The relative impact of individual differences. *Educational Psychology, 27*(4), 465-485.

Hart, G. (1995). Learning styles and hypertext: Exploring user attitudes. *ASCILITE 1995: Learning with Technology,* 238-245.

Hayes, J., & Allinson, C. W. (1993). Matching Learning style and instructional strategy: An application of the person-environment interaction paradigm. *Perceptual and Motor Skills, 76,* 63-79.

Hede, A. (2002). An integrated model of multimedia effects on learning. *Journal of Educational Multimedia and Hypermedia, 11*(2), 177-191.

Hodgkinson, G. P., Langan-Fox, J., & Sadler-Smith, E. (2008). Intuition: A fundamental bridging construct in the behavioural sciences. *British Journal of Psychology, 99,* 1–27

Jonassen, D. H., & Grabowski, B. L. (1993). *Handbook of Individual Differences, Learning and Instruction.* Hillsdale: Lawrence Erlbaum.

Kalyuga, S., Chandler, P., & Sweller, J. (1998). Levels of expertise and instructional design. *Human Factors, 40,* 1–17.

Kalyuga, S., Chandler, P., & Sweller, P. (2000). Incorporating learner experience into the design of multimedia instruction. *Journal of Educational Psychology, 92,* 126–136.

Kim, K. S. (2001). Implications of user characteristics in information seeking on the World Wide Web. *International Journal of Human–Computer Interaction, 13,* 323–340.

Kirby, J., Moore, P., & Schofield, N. (1988). Verbal and visual learning styles. *Contemporary Educational Psychology, 13,* 169-184.

Kogan, N. (1971). Educational implications of cognitive style. In G. S. Lesser (Ed.), *Psychology and educational practice.* Glenview, Ill.: Scott Foresman.

Korthauer, R. D., & Koubek, R. J. (1994). An empirical evaluation of knowledge, cognitive style, and structure upon the performance of a hypertext task. *International Journal of Human-Computer Interaction, 6*(4), 373-390.

Kozma, R. (1991). Learning with media. *Review of Educational Research, 61*(2), 179-211.

Kozma, R. (2003). The material features of multiple representations and their cognitive and social affordances for science understanding. *Learning and Instruction, 13,* 205-226

Kyllonen, P. C., & Alluisi, E. A. (1987). Learning and forgetting facts and skills. In G. Salvendy (Ed.), *The Handbook of Human Factors* (pp.124-150). New York: Wiley.

Laing, M. (2001). Teaching learning and learning teaching: an introduction to learning styles. *New Frontiers in Education, 31*(4), 463–475.

Langan-Fox, J., Anglim, J., & Wilson, J. R. (2004). Mental models, team mental models and performance: Process, development and future directions. *Human Factors and Ergonomics in Manufacturing.* 14(4), 331-352.

Langan-Fox, J., Armstrong, K., Balvin, N., & Anglim, J. (2002). Process in skill acquisition: Motivation, interruptions, memory, affective states and metacognition. *Australian Psychologist.* 37(2), 104-117

Langan-Fox, J., Grant, S., & Anglim, J. (2007). Modelling skill acquisition in acquired brain injury. *Australian Psychologist, 42*(1), 39-48.

Langan-Fox, J. & Griffin, M. (Eds.). (1999a). *Human Performance and the Workplace Vol. 1: Training and Performance*. Brisbane: Imprint Books.

Langan-Fox, J. & Griffin, M. (Eds.). (1999b). *Human Performance and the Workplace Vol. 2: Motivation at Work*. Brisbane: Imprint Books

Langan-Fox, J., Platania-Phung, C., & Waycott, J. (2006). Effects of advance organizers, mental models and abilities on task and recall performance using a mobile phone network. *Applied Cognitive Psychology, 20*(9), 1143-1165.

Langan-Fox, J., & Shirley, D. (2003). The nature and measurement of intuition: Cognitive and behavioral interests, personality and experiences. *Creativity Research Journal, 15*(2,3), 207-222

Langan-Fox, J., Waycott, J., & Albert, K. (2000). Linear and graphic advance organizers: Properties and processing. *International Journal of Cognitive Ergonomics,4*(1),19-34.

Leahy, W., Chandler, P., & Sweller, P. (2003). When auditory presentation should and should not be a component of multimedia instruction. *Applied Cognitive Psychology, 17*, 401–418.

Levie, W. H., & Lentz, R. (1982). Effects of text illustrations: A review of research. *Educational Communication and Technology Journal, 30*, 195-232.

Lewis, B. N. (1976). Avoidance of aptitude-treatment trivialities. In S. Messick & Associates (Eds.), *Individuality in Learning* (pp.301-308). San Fransisco: Jossey-Bass.

Lohman, D. F. (1979). *Spatial Ability: A Review and Reanalysis of the Correlational Literature*. (Tech. Rep. No. 8). Stanford, CA: Aptitude Research Project, School of Education.

Lowe, R.K. (2003). Animation and learning: Selective processing of information in dynamic graphics. *Learning and Instruction, 13*(2), 157-176

MacGregor, S., Shapiro, J., & Niemiec, R. (1988). Effects of computer augmented learning environment on math achievement for students with different cognitive styles. *Journal of Educational Computing Research, 4*, 453-465.

Mayer, R. E. (1997). Multimedia learning: Are we asking the right questions? *Educational Psychologist, 32*, 1–19.

Mayer, R. E. (2001). *Multimedia learning*. New York: Cambridge University Press.

Mayer, R. E., & Anderson, R. B. (1991). Animations need narrations: An experimental test of a dual-coding hypothesis. *Journal of Educational Psychology, 83*, 484-490.

Mayer, R. E., & Johnson, C. I. (2008). Revising the redundancy principle in multimedia learning. *Journal of Educational Psychology, 100*(2), 380-386.

Mayer, R. E., & Moreno, R. (1998). A split-attention effect in multimedia learning: Evidence for dual processing systems in working memory. *Journal of Educational Psychology, 90*, 312–320.

Mayes, J. T. (1992). The 'M-word': Multimedia interfaces and their role in interactive learning systems. In A. D. Edwards & S. Holland (Eds.), *Multi-media Interfaces and Learning* (pp.2-26). Heidelberg: Springer-Verlag.

McKethan, R., & Everhart, B. (2001). The effects of multimedia software instruction and lecture-based instruction on learning and teaching cues of manipulative skills on preservice physical education teachers. *Physical Educators, 58*(1), 2-13.

Melton, A. W. (1963). Implications of short-term memory for a general theory of memory. *Journal of Verbal Learning and Verbal Behaviour, 2*, 1-21.

Messick, S. (1976). Personality consistencies in cognition and creativity. In S. Messick & Associates (Eds.), *Individuality in Learning* (pp.4-37). San Fransisco: Jossey-Bass.

Miller, G. A. (1956). The magical number seven, plus or minus two: Some limits on our capacity for processing information. *Psychological Review, 63*(2), 81-97.

Mirenda, P., Eicher, D., & Beukelman, D. R. (1989). Synthetic and natural speech preferences of male and female listeners in four age groups. *Journal of Speech and Hearing, 32*(1), 175-183.

Moreno, R., & Mayer, R. E. (1999). Cognitive principles of multimedia learning: The role of modality and contiguity. *Journal of Educational Psychology, 91*, 358–368.

Moreno, R., & Valdez, A. (2005). Cognitive load and learning effects of having students organize pictures and words in multimedia environments: the role of student interactivity and feedback. *Educational Technology Research & Development, 53*(3), 35-45.

Mousavi, S. Y., Low, R., & Sweller, J. (1995). Reducing cognitive load by mixing auditory and visual presentation modes. *Journal of Educational Psychology, 87*, 319–334.

Najjar, L. J. (1996a). *The Effects of Multimedia and Elaborative Encoding on Learning* [On-line]. Available FTP://ftp.gvu.gatech.edu:/pub/gvu/tech-reports/96-05.ps.Z

Najjar, L. J. (1996b). Multimedia information and learning. *Journal of Educational Multimedia and Hypermedia, 5*(2), 129-150.

Najjar, L.J. (1998). Principles of educational multimedia user interface design. *Human Factors, 40*(2), 311-323.

Nathan, M., & Robinson, C. (2001). Considerations of learning and learning research: Revisiting the "media effects" debate. *Journal of Interactive Learning Research, 12*, 69-88

Paivio, A. (1971). *Imagery and Verbal Processes*. New York: Holt, Reinhart & Winston.

Paivio, A. (1986). *Mental Representations: A Dual Coding Approach*. New York: Oxford University Press.

Paivio, A. (1991). Dual coding theory: Retrospect and current status. *Canadian Journal of Psychology, 45*, 255-287.

Palmiter, S., & Elkerton, J. (1991). An evaluation of animated demonstrations for learning computer-based tasks. In S. P.Robertson, G. M. Olson, & J. S. Olson (Eds.), *CHI'92 Conference Proceedings* (pp.257-263). Reading, MA: Addison-Wesley.

Palmiter, S., & Elkerton, J. (1993). Animated demonstrations for learning procedural computer based tasks. *Human-Computer Interaction, 8*, 193-216.

Park, O., & Hopkins, R. (1993). Instructional conditions for using dynamic visual displays: a review. *Instructional Science, 21*, 427-449.

Plass, J., Chun, D., Mayer, R., & Leutner, D. (1998). Supporting visual and verbal learning preferences in a second-language multimedia learning environment. *Journal of Educational Psychology, 90*(1), 25-36.

Poole, M. E., Neilsen, P., & Langan-Fox, J. (1998). Learning to be competent: Important skills for Australian professional and managerial women in the context of educational reform. *International Journal of Lifelong Education, 17*(2) 172-182.

Proctor, R. W., & Van Zandt, T. (1994). *Human Factors in Simple and Complex Systems*. Boston: Allyn & Bacon.

Quealy, J., & Langan-Fox, J. (1998). Attributes of delivery media in computer assisted instruction. *Ergonomics, 41*(3), 257-279

Rayner, S., & Riding, R. (1997). Towards a categorisation of cognitive styles and learning styles. *Educational Psychology, 17*(1-2), 5-27.

Reeves, T. C. (1986). Research and evaluation models for the study of interactive video. *Journal of Computer-Based Instruction, 13*(4), 102-106.

Richardson, A. (1977). Verbalizer-visualizer: A cognitive style dimension. *Journal of Mental Imagery, 1*, 109-126.

Riding, R. J. (1997). On the nature of cognitive styles. *Educational Psychology, 17*(1-2), 29-49.

Riding, R., & Cheema, I. (1991). Cognitive styles-an overview and integration. *Educational Psychology, 11*(3-4), 193-215.

Riding, R., & Douglas, G. (1993). The effect of cognitive style and mode of presentation on learning performance. *British Journal of Educational Psychology, 63*, 297-307.

Riding, R. J., & Grimley, M. (1999). Cognitive style, gender and learning from multimedia materials in 11-year-old children. British Journal of Educational Psychology, 30, 43–56.

Riding, R. J., & Rayner, S. G. (1998). *Cognitive Styles and Learning Strategies*. London: David Fulton Publisher.

Riding, R., & Sadler-Smith, E. (1992). Type of instructional material, cognitive style and learning performance. *Educational Studies, 18*(3), 323-339.

Rieber, L. (1990). Using computer animated graphics with science instruction with children. *Journal of Educational Psychology, 82*, 135-140.

Rieber L. P. (2000). *Computers, graphics & learning*. Madison, WI: Brown & Benchmark.

Rowland, P., & Stuessy, C. (1988). Matching mode of CAI to cognitive style: An exploratory study. *Journal of Computers in Mathematics and Science Teaching, 7*(4), 36-40, 55.

Sadoski, M., Goetz, E.T., & Rodriguez, M. (2000). Engaging texts: effects of concreteness on comprehensibility, interest and recall in four text types. *Journal of Educational Psychology, 92*(1), 85-95.

Samaras, H., Giouvanakis, T., Bousiou, D., & Tarabanis, K. (2006). Towards a new generation of multimedia learning research. *AACE Journal, 14*(1), 3-30.

Schofield, N. J., & Kirby, J. R. (1994). Position Location on Topographical Maps: Effects of Task Factors, Training, and Strategies. *Cognition and Instruction, 12*(1), 35-60.

Sein, M. K., & Robey, D. (1991). Learning style and the efficacy of computer training methods. *Perceptual and Motor Skills, 72*, 243-248.

Sewell, E. H., & Moore, R. L. (1980). Cartoon embellishments in informative presentations. *Educational Communication and Technology Journal, 28*, 39-46.

Shih, Y., & Alessi, S.M. (1996). Effects of Text versus Voice on Learning in Multimedia Courseware. *Journal of Educational Multimedia and Hypermedia, 5*(2), 203-218.

Sitko-Lutek, A., Rakowska, A., & Hill, J. (2000). "To match or not to match? The conundrum of management education for reflective-analytical Polish managers", in Armstrong, S., Francis, A., Graff, M., Hill, J., Rayner, S., Sadler-Smith, E., Spicer, D. (Eds),*Proceedings of the 5th Annual Conference of the European Learning Styles Information Network*, Business School, University of Hertfordshire,, Hatfield,, 26-27 June 2000, pp.261-77.

Skehan, P. (1998). *A Cognitive Approach to Language Learning*. Oxford University Press: Oxford.

Smith, C. L. (1985). Relationship of microcomputer-based instruction and learning style. *Journal of Educational Technology Systems, 13*, 265-270.

Sneddon, J., Settle, C., & Triggs, G. (2001). The effects of multimedia delivery and continual assessment on student academic performance on a level 1 undergraduate plant science module. *Journal of Biological Education 36*(1), 6-10.

Snow, R. E. (1978). Individual differences and instructional design. In J. Hartley & I. K. Davies (Eds.), *Contribtions to an Educational Technology (2ⁿᵈ Ed.)*, pp.96-103). London: Kogan Page.

Stanney, K. M., & Salvendy, G. (1995). Diversity in field-articulation and its implications for human-computer interface design. In G. Perlman, G. K. Green, & M. S. Wagalter (Eds.), *Human Factors Perspectives on Human-Computer Interaction: Selections from Proceedings of Human Factors and Ergonomics Society Annual Meetings, 1983-1994* (pp.306-406). Santa Monica, CA: HFES.

Stern, E., Aprea, C., & Ebner, H. (2003). Improving cross-content transfer in text processing by means of active graphical representation. *Learning and Instruction, 13*, 191-203.

Tennant, M. (1988). *Psychology and Adult Learning*. London: Routledge.

Thies, A. (2003). "Connections, neuropsychology, neuroscience, and learning style", in Armstrong, S., Graff, M., Hill, J., Rayner, S., Sadler-Smith, E., Spicer, D. (Eds). *Bridging Theory and Practice, European Learning Styles Information Network (ELSIN), University of Hull, Hull, 30 June-2 July 2003*, 608-12.

Travers, R. M. W. (1964). The transmission of information to human receivers. *AV Communication Review, 12*(6), 373-385.

Tulving, E. (1983). *Elements of Episodic Memory*. New York: Oxford University.

Tulving, E. (1985). On the classification problem in learning and memory. In L. Nilsson & T. Archer (Eds), *Perspectives on Learning and Memory*. Hillsdale NJ: Lawrence Erlbaum.

van Merrienboer, J. J., & Ayres, P. (2005a). Research on cognitive load theory and its design implications for E-Learning. [This special issue]. *Educational Technology Researhc & Development, 53*(3), 5-13.

Weller, H. G., Repman, J., Lan, W., & Rooze, G. (1995). Improving the effectiveness of learning through hypermedia-based instruction: The importance of learner characteristics. *Computers in Human Behavior, 11*(3-4), 451-465.

Whyte, M. M., Karolick, D. M., Nielsen, M. C., Elder, G. D., & Hawley, W. T. (1995). Cognitive styles and feedback in computer-assisted instruction. *Journal of Educational Computing Research, 12*(2), 195-203.

Wickens, C. D. (1992). *Engineering Psychology and Human Performance*. New York: Harper & Row.

Wickens, C. D., Sandry, D. L., & Vidulich, M. (1983). Compatibility and resource competition between modalities of input, central processing, and output. *Human Factors, 25*(2), 227-248.

Williams, C. J., & Brown, S. W. (1990). A review of the research issues in the use of computer related technologies for instruction: An agenda for research 1. *International Journal of Instructional Media, 17*(2), 95-117.

Witkin, H. A., Oltman, P. K., Raskin, E., & Karp, S. A. (1971). *A Manual for the Embedded Figures Test*. Palo Alto, CA: Psychologists Press.

In: Multimedia in Education and Special Education
Editors: O. Demir and C. Celik

ISBN 978-1-60741-073-7
© 2009 Nova Science Publishers, Inc.

Chapter 2

DO ILLUSTRATED INSTRUCTIONAL BOOKS PROMOTE MULTIMEDIA LEARNING?

Barbara Colombo, Maura Lissoni, Alessandro Antonietti[*]
Department of Psychology,
Catholic University of the Sacred Heart, Milano
Italy

ABSTRACT

The paper addresses the question whether the illustrations which are associated to texts in instructional books match the multimedia principles supported by empirical research. A sample of textbooks devised for primary school was analysed by classifying the quantity, type, and use of pictures. The choices which led to devise picture-text combinations failed to parallel completely the principles of multimedia learning, even though they seemed to reflect criteria consistent with the cognitive development of the children for whom books were designed. Findings allowed us to draw conclusions about multimedia learning tools which are not as negative as previously reported in literature, even if a more substantial awareness concerning cognitive processes might help book illustrators to structure text-pictures relationships more effectively and teachers to select and employ illustrated books according to multimedia principles.

Keywords: Multimedia; Learning; Multimedia learning; Illustrated textbook; Cognitive psychology

[*] Corresponding Author. Professor of Cognitive Psychology Head of the Department of Psychology Catholic University of the Sacred Heart Largo Gemelli 1 - 20123 Milano (Italy) phone: +39-02-72342909 fax: +39-02-72342280 email: alessandro.antonietti@unicatt.it website: www.antonietti.psycholab.net

INTRODUCTION

An illustrated book can be defined as a book "with a dual narrative, in which both the pictures and the text work interdependently to tell a story. It is a tale told in two media, the integration of visual and verbal art" (Bishop & Hickman, 1992, p. 2). Over the past four decades wordless picture books have become a distinct genre within the world of children's literature (Degler, 1979; Dowhower, 1997; Grasty, 1978; Lindauer, 1988; Stewig, 1988). Moreover, illustrations are widely used in instructional texts — where they are put besides text accomplishing several functions, such as depicting part of the text, decorating the page, explaining a process or adding some elements to the text. Hence we can assume that a large part of the books read by children and young people are illustrated books. It is therefore interesting to study the cognitive processes which form the base of this kind of multimedia fruition. But, since school instruction traditionally has emphasized verbal learning, interest in visual learning has lagged behind (Mandl & Levin, 1989; Tufte, 1983; Willows & Houghton, 1987). A notable exception has been the promising work on imagery mnemonics as aids to learning arbitrary paired-associates and lists (Levin, 1981, 1982; Levin, Anglin, & Carney, 1987; Levin & Mayer, 1993; McDaniel & Pressley, 1987; Paivio, 1971, 1986); however, corresponding work on using pictures to enhance meaningful learning from prose passages has been slow to develop (Holley & Dansereau, 1984; Novak, 1990).

Studying the text-picture relationship as a particular format of multimedia communication has a theoretical rationale, but has been neglected. More precisely, apart from Mayer's own studies (1993, 2001, 2005), we see how the role of imagery in making sense of text has its theoretical roots in the work of Allan Paivio and his colleagues (Clark & Paivio, 1991; Paivio, 1971, 1986; Sadoski, Paivio, & Goetz, 1991). From this perspective, knowledge is represented both verbally and nonverbally in what is referred to as a dual-coding system, including both verbal and nonverbal representations. Verbal representations are composed of words for objects, events, and ideas. The imagery or nonverbal system embeds knowledge in "nonverbal representations that retain some resemblance to the perceptions giving rise to them" (Pressley & McCormick, 1995, p. 71). The concept of dual coding — namely, the coding of knowledge in both verbal and nonverbal representations — suggests that the elements of both systems are deeply connected. This connection between the verbal and nonverbal coding systems allows us to create images when we hear words and to generate names or descriptions of things we see in pictures. In fact, there is some evidence that successful readers do this automatically and that the inability to make verbal and nonverbal connections quickly and efficiently is related to learning disabilities (Swanson, 1989).

Pictures themselves can serve many functions when used as adjuncts to text. Several researchers (e.g., Gombrich, 1972; Kennedy, 1974; Samuels, 1970; Vernon, 1953; Lee et al., 2005; Park & Lim, 2007) have pointed out the usefulness of pictures in arousing the interest of readers and motivating them to read. From a cognitive point of view, pictures, by their very nature, seem also particularly well suited to the depiction of spatial information (Johnson, 1999). In the teaching practice, illustrated books have been conceived as a means of promoting the concept of story structure (Reese, 1996), developing comprehension (Arthur, 1982; Carney & Levin, 2002), supporting children's attempts at storytelling (Avery, 1996), and teaching visual literacy (Cianciolo, 1984; Evans, 1992; Lindauer, 1988; Read & Smith, 1982; Stewig, 1988). But can this preference be intended as mirroring a specific awareness of the potentialities of the pictures when related to text? We can assume that those who choose or draw illustrations to be added to a specific textbook act on the basis of their naive theories concerning which pictures are more or less useful and why. Thus, pictures that we observe in a text mirror the illustrator's naive theories, so constituting a sort of "embedded" representation of his/her beliefs about the role of picture in promoting readers' comprehension. Are such theories adequate? Do they reflect psychological principles supported by research data?

In his studies, Mayer (2001; 2005) often referred to the "common sense theory" of multimedia. Such a theory can be defined as a theoretical perspective according to which people have passive information elaboration system, relying on a single unlimited processing channel. Mayer considered the assumptions of such theory as inadequate and to them opposes the principles on which his own cognitive theory is based. While researching on his multimedia principles, Mayer (2001; 2005) again made reference to the common sense theory, conjecturing that the naive theories that people, non expert in the specific field, develop concerning multimedia, its properties, uses, advantages, and disadvantages, are similar to it, and therefore opposite to his assumptions.

Is this hypothesis sound? Do people's opinions actually diverge from Mayer's theory, or do they tend to comply with it? Mayer never actually tested his conjectures about the common sense theory, focusing his researches on the experimentally-tested validity of his principles. Hence, studying naive conceptions can be seen, de facto, as a brand new empirical path in the field of multimedia learning. In such a path this investigation has its roots.

Mayer's (1993) research aimed at investigating naive conceptions about multimedia learning in textbooks was taken as a starting point. In this study, the author considered 6 sixth-grade science textbooks approved for adoption in California and randomly selected a 5% of the total pages. For each page, Mayer measured the actual amount of space respectively dedicated to text and pictures, noting number and type of illustrations too. Furthermore, to assess the exact typology of each image, Mayer referred to Levin's (1989) classification. In her taxonomy, based on the function performed by the images with reference to the text, Levin discriminated:

A. *Decoration images*, that is, pictures that are not directly relevant to the text;
B. *Representation images*, namely, illustrations that portray one element that is mentioned in the text;
C. *Organization images*, showing the relations among elements in the text;
D. *Interpretation images*, that explain how something (e.g., a system, a process, a mechanism) works;
E. *Transformation images*, useful to remember items, paired-associates, and lists.

While starting from this classification, Mayer made some adjustments. In particular, he kept the Decorative (Decoration, in original Levin's system of classification), Representational (Representation), and Organizational (Organization) categories, whereas the category defined as Interpretation was changed into Explanative. The Transformation category was left out, since Mayer declared he had never found it in his survey of science textbooks. Like Levin's taxonomy, also Mayer's classification was based on the function performed by the pictures with reference to the text. So, the illustrations categorized by the Mayer were defined as follows:

A. *Decorative*, which correspond to Levin's Decoration category: they fill space on page without enhancing message of passage;
B. *Representational*, corresponding to Levin's Representation category: they portray a single element of the text;
C. *Organizational*, corresponding to Levin's Organization category: they depict relations among elements;
D. *Explanative*, corresponding to Levin's Interpretation category: they explain how a system works.

What kind of implications do the categories have regarding the learning processes? In his cognitive theory Mayer identified three basic processes necessary to elaborate actively incoming multimedia information: *selection* of relevant information (paying attention to relevant pieces of information in the instructional materials and placing one or more pieces of information into short term memory); *organization* within short term memory (integration with pre-existing knowledge, with the implication of long-term memory); *integration* of information (building external connections between the incoming information and knowledge already in long-term memory and finding similarities between newly received knowledge and existing knowledge). In accordance with the author's cognitive theory, depending on what kind of category the images belong to, they may elicit different cognitive processes. More precisely:

A. *Decorative* pictures should not have any effect on any cognitive process[1], since they fill space on the page without enhancing the message of passage;
B. *Representational* illustrations should influence the process of selection, since they represent single relevant elements of the text;
C. *Organizational* pictures should influence the process of selection and organization, since they depict relations among elements;
D. *Explanative* illustrations should influence the process of selection, organization and integration, explaining functioning or development of the depicted systems.

According to such a theoretical perspective, Explanative pictures are the most instructive. In fact, they can affect all three levels of cognitive processing, with a subsequent positive effect on learning. On the other hand, Decorative images are the least instructive, since they are ineffective in enhancing cognitive processing during the study of the text.

In order to assess whether his cognitive assumptions were considered or not, Mayer (1993) carried out a survey aimed at analysing the distribution of such image typologies in the sample of science textbooks mentioned before. What were the results of Mayer's survey? Regarding the use of space, illustrations and text had approximately the same percentages (respectively, 55% and 45% text). Nevertheless, pictures did not appear to have been chosen on the basis of their greater power to enhance cognition, according to Mayer's graduation. The majority of pictures (85%) were, in fact, Representational (62%) or Decorative (23%), whereas only 5% of the examined pictures were Organizational, and 10% Explanative. In conclusion, such a survey of science textbooks pointed out the prevailing presence of pictures which are ineffective to enhance learning. In the books examined, almost half of the space intended for instruction was, actually, occupied by pictures which simply decorate the page or represent a single element of the whole text.

The above mentioned results have been explained by Mayer as the multimedia designers' inability to make the most of the potentials of graphic elements as an aid to learning. Indirectly, such a conclusion seems to confirm the accordance between the naïve theories of multimedia designers and the common sense theory. A similar negative picture was depicted, more recently, by the analysis of Spanish scientific textbooks carried out by Perales and Jiménez (2002).

From Mayer's results, replicated by Perales and Jiménez, the picture derived was a pessimistic one. The message was that most textbooks include illustrations which are not designed to promote effective learning.

The analysis of Mayer's survey (1993) raised several questions that have been the basis on which to develop a new investigation. The new inquiry claimed to answer the following questions.

1. What differences in the quantity, type, and use of the illustrations may be found in examining school textbooks devised for lower schools than the ones considered by Mayer? More precisely: is it possible that in textbooks designed for primary school, where a larger use of illustrations and a higher pedagogical awareness might be expected, there could be found a more "cognitively wise" choice and use of images?
2. In examining textbooks that do not just cover a single school grade but all the grades of primary instruction, do differences in type and use of illustrations emerge? It could be hypothesised that more images will be found in texts for the first grades of primary school, when children still cannot read, or are not fluent at reading, and therefore rely more on illustrations.
3. Does the use of illustrations differ from one discipline to another? Mayer only examined science textbooks. Is it possible that different subjects lead to a different use of images? It can be hypothesised that other topics (such as reading books, grammar textbooks, maths exercises, and so on) lead text designers to apply a more accurate choice of the illustrations.
4. What kind of text-picture relationship appears in textbooks devised in a country other than the U.S.? That is, can the results obtained by Mayer (1993) be considered general? And, if so, with what limits, if any?

To answer these questions, a research plan was developed, following the lines of Mayer's (1993) survey, to analyse Italian primary schools textbooks, based on a taxonomy accordant with Levin's (1989) and Mayer's (1993) categorizations. As will appear clearly from the description of the method, the aim of the research was to answer the questions listed above. Besides, there was also an attempt to extend and improve Mayer's method of analysis of illustrated textbooks.

METHOD

Textbook Selection

Whereas Mayer analysed sixth-grade textbooks, the present study focused on publications related to all primary school grades of the Italian instructional system (that is, from the first to the fifth grade). To select the textbooks to analyse, reference was made to the official classification[2] of the books most frequently chosen by Italian teachers during the year 2004/2005. Such a list should in fact reflect the actual preferences of Italian teachers: in Italy it is the teacher of each individual school who annually chooses the texts employed for the different grades. Textbooks for every single class of primary school were taken into account.

In Italian primary schools there is a difference between the structure of the first two grades (first cycle, where a more integrated structure of disciplines is planned) and the last three grades (second cycle, where, as a kind of transition to a more advanced grade, a differentiation between disciplinary subjects and reading activity is intended). Such a differentiation is reflected in the textbooks: whereas texts for the first two grades are conceived as a whole (even though they are sometimes made up of several volumes, for teachers' and pupils' convenience of use), texts for the last three grades are divided into two different units: disciplinary subjects (grammar, history, geography, maths, science) and reading activities (poems, tales, excepts from newspapers). The distinction is quite clear-cut especially for the last two years – when, to suit the increasing learning demands of the growing students, the different units are grouped in two different textbooks, so that often books from different publishing houses are chosen for the two areas in the same class. In the survey, both textbooks for disciplinary subjects and for reading activities were examined.

Considering the huge mass of books (a single title is often composed of several volumes), it was decided to categorize fully only the textbooks which were first in the official classification.

For the first grade, the textbook analysed was "Pepe e i suoi amici 1", composed of two volumes[3]. For the second grade, the textbook analysed was "Pepe e il suo mondo 2", composed of three volumes. For the third grade, the five volumes of "Amico sole 3" were classified. For the fourth grade, the reading textbook analysed was "Io amo leggere 4", while the disciplinary textbook analysed was "Perché 4". For the fifth grade the reading textbook analysed was "Una tira l'altra 5", while the disciplinary textbook analysed was "Sapere e saper fare 5".

Textbook Analysis

For each textbook, the space devoted, respectively, to pictures and text was quantified, while all the illustrations were classified.

In order to estimate the amount of space devoted respectively to text and pictures, each page analysed was subdivided into six parts. Depending on the extension of the illustrations on the page, a value between a 1/6 and 1 was assigned. More precisely, the fractions considered were: 1/6, 1/3, 1/2, 2/3, 5/6, 1. These fractions correspond to the following percentages of the total space of the page: 17%, 33%, 50%, 67%, 83% and 100%.

The image analysis was carried out on the basis of Mayer's (1993) classification. The functional classification, therefore, was based on the division of the iconic material into Decorative, Representational, Organizational and Explanative pictures. During a first pilot analysis, however, it was felt that some categories should be specified further. Particularly, while examining Decorative images, a significant difference was found between images with no reference at all to the text they were juxtaposed to (and which therefore have a pure embellishment function) and illustrations in which analogies or connections with the text — albeit weak and indirect – could be found. Thus, we decided to split the Decorative category in two distinct categories: first level and second level Decorative images. Examples of the first type of Decorative illustrations include all those elements that decorate the page, such as page frames and borders, or cartoon-like characters which often fill the empty spaces. Second level Decorative images, instead, are slightly more appropriate images, like the picture of children playing in the woods, close to a text referring to photosynthesis. The image does not represent any part of the text, but a weak reference to the general topic can be found.

Representational images were also subdivided into two more categories: images which actually represent parts of the text and illustrations that represent additional elements, that is elements that somehow enrich or integrate the text. An example of Representational images of the first type may be easily recognised in an illustrated tale: each image representing a scene of the story is a first level Representational image, since it shows a part of the text. A Representational image of the second type, instead, is an image that replaces the text or that add something to the text, like the photo or drawing of different types of leaves, with a detailed caption explaining the differences among them, close to a text explaining vegetal life, mentioning trees and leaves but without giving details on the types of leaves. Table 1 shows the classification that we employed to categorize the illustrations.

After the examination of each single textbook, the overall number of pages devoted to pictures was computed. This number was subtracted from the volume's total pages to obtain the number of pages dedicated to text. This information was used to compute the general amount of space devoted to texts and to pictures in each textbook analysed.

Table 1. Image classification used in the study, with the corresponding abbreviation

Type of illustration		Functional description	Abbreviation
Decorative	**First level**	no relation with text, pure embellishment function	D1
	Second level	weak and indirect analogies or connections with the topics in the text	D2
Representational	**First level**	represent parts or scenes of the text	R1
	Second level	represent parts or scenes of the text that stand in for the text	R2
Organizational		depict relations among elements	O
Explanative		explain functioning/ development	E

Concerning the functional categorisation, every single image inserted in the examined textbooks was ascribed to one of the above mentioned categories. In the case of several images belonging to the same category, and relative to the same activity (e.g., an exercise), occupying each a portion of space under a 1/6 of the page, an average of their total occurrence was performed by merging them in order to obtain a "usable" fraction (being 1/6 the smallest fraction considered).

Two judges — psychologists expert in multimedia learning in school settings — carried out the analyses of the selected textbooks. Before starting the actual analyses, both judges analysed together a series of different images derived from textbooks not employed in the current study and discussed together the classification, in order to establish a common procedure. In order to secure uniformity of analysis, the index of accord between the two judges was measured. Both categorised independently 20 pages, randomly chosen. The categorisations were compared and a 98% level of agreement emerged: it was considered satisfactory. The infrequent controversial cases which emerged during the independent classification procedure were nevertheless discussed between the judges.

RESULTS

Space Occupied by Illustrations in the Textbooks

If we consider the whole set of textbooks analysed, we may observe that texts occupied 56% of the typographic surface, against the 44% covered by illustrations. Such a result is quite different from to the one reported by Mayer (1993): in his survey pictures achieved the 55% of the total space versus the 45% of texts.

In order to deepen the analysis of the amount of space devoted to illustrations in school textbooks, we distinguished data according to the school grade and to the type of image. Table 2 reports the percentages of space occupied respectively by pictures and texts with reference to the total pages selected. In first grade textbooks space devoted to pictures was larger than that devoted to texts. Starting from the second grade, percentages reveal the opposite trend, with more space occupied by texts than by illustrations. The analysis of the distribution of space among textbooks proved that the amount of space occupied by pictures varied significantly across school grades, χ^2 (4, N = 836) = 109.96, p < .001.

Table 2. Percentages of space devoted to texts and pictures in the examined textbooks for the five grades

	Percentage of space devoted to texts	Percentage of space devoted to pictures
1st grade	44.91%	55.08%
2nd grade	61.85%	38.15%
3rd grade	57.12%	42.88%
4th grade	55.92%	44.08%
5th grade	57.48%	42.51%

The predominance of iconic elements seems to be consistent with the school level of the pupils: while children are still learning to read and write, illustrations play a role of support and motivation to comprehend and perform different activities, and coherently they were more present in first grade textbooks.

In the reading textbook analysed for the fourth grade, iconic pages (43%) and text pages (57%) were almost similar in number – despite a slight predominance of space devoted to text (and this is consistent with the grade the textbook refers to) – similarly to what we found in analysing the correspondent disciplinary textbook, where illustrations (45%) and text (55%) were seen to have similar percentages of space. Concerning the fifth grade, in the reading textbook, the amount of space occupied by illustrations (44%) and text (56%) was found to be almost analogous to the one resulting from the reading textbook used in the fourth grade, with the usual slight majority of textual pages. In the disciplinary textbook, once again, the space occupied by illustrations (41%) was close to the one ascribed to the text (59%).

We can conclude that editorial choices seem to recognise the importance of illustrations mostly when the children's competence in "decoding" the text is still rough. After this phase they do not tend to give a strong predominance either to iconic or textual elements. In disciplinary textbooks for the fifth grade, though, we can highlight a stronger predominance of the textual part: this may be read as being equivalent to the tendency of enhancing illustrations in the first grade. In the last grade, when facing disciplinary subject, children are conceived as being more able to focus on textual elements. Hence the mental model of the child as a textbook reader does not appear to be focused on his/her cognitive processing but on the scholastic competences in interpreting the codes.

Frequency of the Types of Illustrations in the Textbooks

The second kind of analysis which we performed was based on a count of the number of images reported in the pages of the selected textbooks. By recording the number of images included in each category, we found that the most frequently used images were first and second level Representational ones (respectively, R1 = 34%, R2 = 28%). They were followed by the Organizational pictures (14%), the two levels of the Decorative ones (respectively, D1 = 9%, D2 = 10%), and the Explanative illustrations (5%). To make a direct comparison with Mayer's (1993) results, the percentages referring to the two levels of Decorative and Representational pictures were combined (Table 3). The supremacy of Representational illustrations appeared clearly (62%). Considered as a whole, Decorative images (19%) overtook the Organizational (14%), whereas the Explanative ones were of course rearmost (5%).

As far as Decorative and Representational pictures are concerned, percentages recorded in the present study were rather similar to those recorded by Mayer (1993). The larger number of Organizational images in the present study was balanced by the decrease of the frequency of the Explanative ones. Once again, the generalizability of Mayer's (1993) statistics seems to be questionable. While the frequencies of the kinds of images which have no cognitive role (Decorative illustrations) and serve the simplest cognitive function — such as depicting an element of the text a in visual form (Representative illustrations) — were similar in the two surveys, the more elaborated types of images (Organisational and Explanative) were differently present in the textbooks considered in the two investigations. Explanative illustrations were more frequent than Organisational pictures in Californian scientific textbooks for a higher grade of the primary school, whereas the opposite was true in Italian textbooks for lower grades. Thus, the choice to include in textbooks certain genders of images appears to be context-dependent.

In order to understand better how the different types of images were employed in textbooks, the frequencies of each kind of illustrations were analyzed separately within each school grade (Table 4). As far as *first grade* textbooks were concerned, significant differences emerged in the distribution of the frequency of each kind of images, χ^2 (5, N = 642) = 777.40, p < .001. The predominant image typology was actually the second level Representational one (52%), which corresponds to pictures which integrate the text. On a global scale, considering the total number of images present in the textbook, Representational images were the most frequent (R1 = 30%[4], R2 = 52%, total R = 82%). Decorative images followed (D1 = 8%, D2 = 2%, total D =10%) and, lastly, Explanative (6%; mostly as illustrated instructions to perform activities) and Organizational (2%).

Table 3. Number of images (in percentage) of each category in Mayer's (1993) survey and in the present study

Type of illustration	Percentages of illustrations	
	Mayer's study	Present study
Decorative	23%	19%
Representational	62%	62%
Organizational	5%	14%
Explanative	10%	5%

Table 4. Frequencies of images of different functional categories across the five grades

	1st grade	2nd grade	3rd grade	4th grade		5th grade	
				Reading	Disciplinary	Reading	Disciplinary
D1	54	126	59	86	52	22	27
D2	11	41	111	48	89	90	83
R1	190	202	418	163	229	222	134
R2	333	330	148	24	190	51	246
O	13	152	216	30	134	10	101
E	41	47	76	0	44	3	41

Also in *second grade* textbooks the various kinds of pictures showed different distributions, χ^2 (5, N = 898) = 389.69, p < .001. It was noticed that the frequency of the Representational pictures decreases (R1 = 22%, R2 = 37%, total R = 59%), whereas the frequency of the Organizational (17%, mostly as maths graphs) increases. The frequency of the Decorative images increases, too (D1 = 14%, D2 = 5%, total D = 19%). Pictures related to this category were seen to be mostly graphical elements with a distracting function, such as repeated characters (children or anthropomorphic objects) which are placed beside the text without any specific link to it. Besides, a considerable number of Decorative pictures could be identified as having a "missed representational" nature. These are illustrations portraying elements only vaguely related to text (often poetic or descriptive)[5]. The percentage of Explanative images was quite similar to one in the examined textbook for the first grade (5%).

Significant differences in the distribution of the types of images occurred also in *third grade* textbooks, χ^2 (5, N = 1028) = 517.89, p < .001. The most frequent iconic typology was, again, the Representational (R1 = 41%, R2 = 14%, total R = 55%). An inversion between Representational illustrations of first and of second level appeared: it might be due to different publishing choices. We can hypothesise that editors decided to give more importance to the representation of the text, than to trying to integrate with appropriate illustrations the information given by text, basing this choice on an ineffective mental model of cognitive processing or on a more easily achievable editorial practice. Against the second grade categories, both Explanative (7%) and Organizational (21%) illustrations showed to be more employed. More precisely, Organizational pictures surpassed the Decorative (D1 = 6%, D2 = 11%, total D =17%), whose number was overall analogous to the ones for the previous grade.

Distributions of pictures in *fourth grade* reading textbooks varied according to the kinds of illustrations, χ^2 (5, N = 351) = 186.68, p < .001. The most frequent pictures were first level Representational images (45%). A reading textbook, as a matter of fact, mainly comprises narrative texts to which are juxtaposed images that aptly represent them. It is important to notice, though, that the pictures did not always belong to this category: quite often, these illustrations served as pure ornaments to the page, as clearly appears from the high percentage of Decorative images (the majority of which are of first level; D1= 25%, D2 = 14%, total D = 39%). As was foreseeable, Explanative images were not used, while small occurrences of Organizationa Images (9%) were found. In the disciplinary textbooks (χ^2 (5, N = 738) = 229.95, p < .001), Representational images were the most recurring (R1= 31%, R2 = 26%, total R = 57%). Given the kind of textbooks being referred to, the number of second level Representational images is greater than in the reading text. The second level Representational images were mostly pictures and photos which, with a proper caption, integrate texts of science, geography, and history. In this case, illustrations widened the contents of the text and were not just limited to embellishing the text – as often happened within narrative texts. Organizational (18%) and Explanative (6%) images, while not having a greater percentage of frequency here as compared to their use in previous grades, were found to maintain the same levels. The same was found to be true for Decorative illustrations, too (D1= 7%, D2 = 12%, total D = 19%).

Finally, in *fifth grade* reading textbooks images were distributed differently according to their kind, χ^2 (5, N = 398) = 515.24, p < .001. First level Representational images (55% against 13% of R2) were found to predominate, followed by second level Decorative (22% against 6% of D1) – that is, those considered, as mentioned above, as having a "missed representational" nature. Organizational (3%) and Explanative (1%) illustrations were found to have very low percentages. Yet, it is important to stress that here reading textbooks were being considered, with the majority of texts being narrative, and thus requiring only linguistic activities. Data relative to the disciplinary textbooks (χ^2 (5, N = 632) = 298.11, p < .001) mirrored the ones that emerged for fourth grade disciplinary textbooks. The only noteworthy fact was an increase in second level Representational images (40%), and a correspondent decrease in first level Representational images (21%). This can be ascribed to an open attempt to use more iconic documents to transmit information, since Representational images of second level are used to represent parts or scenes of the text that stand in for the text, while the Representational images of first level simply depict part of the text. Comparing disciplinary with reading textbooks, an increase in Organizational (16%) and Explanative (6%) illustrations, and a parallel decrease in Decorative images (D1 = 4%, D2 = 13%, total D = 17%), occurred, just as it was noticed in the fourth grade.

Table 4 can be analysed also by considering the distribution of the same kind of images across the school levels. The steady prevalence of *Representational* images can be noticed. The first level Representational pictures showed a peak in correspondence with the third grade, whereas they were settled at similar levels for the other grades, χ^2 (4, N = 1558) = 149.41, p < .0001. A more indented course, conversely, was outlined by second level Representational images, χ^2 (4, N = 1332) = 98.95, p < .0001. They appeared to be particularly numerous in the first and second grade, that is during the beginning of literacy, when images play a supporting role for the texts. They decreased in the third grade, when it is likely that the enhanced children's literary competence led to the choice to apply first level Representational images or second level Decorative ones (both increasing in this grade). In the fourth and fifth grade the number of second level Representational illustrations depended on the type of textbook: whereas it decreased in reading books, it increased significantly in disciplinary (i.e. historical, geographical or scientific) texts.

Decorative illustrations, despite some variations across different grades (D1: χ^2 (4, N = 426) = 87.12, p < .0001; D2: χ^2 (4, N = 473) = 191.07, p < .0001), maintained the same values: never as numerous as the Representational, but nevertheless conspicuous if compared with other categories.

Organizational images were characterised by some significant variations, χ^2 (4, N = 656) = 175.90, p < .0001. They were almost missing in the first grade and increased progressively during the second and third grades. This can be related to the children's cognitive development as they become stronger and stronger in reading and understanding schemata and graphs. After this increase, the number of Organizational pictures remained high in the disciplinary textbooks of the following grades, and, predictably, decreased sensibly in reading books.

Explanative illustrations (χ^2 (4, N = 252) = 16.61, p < .005), though less numerous than the other categories, followed a course analogous to the Organizational ones.

To clarify the emerging differences between reading and disciplinary textbooks in Figure 1, data from the fourth and fifth grades have been summed up according to the editorial (reading vs. disciplinary) category. Differences in the distributions of image typologies within the same book clearly emerged (Reading textbooks: χ^2 (5, N = 749) = 742.42, p < .001; Disciplinary textbooks: χ^2 (5, N = 1370) = 470.03, p < .001). As appears, Representational illustrations were, in both textbooks, the most chosen. First level Representational images remained on similar levels, with a slight majority in reading texts. Here, in fact, illustrations mostly represented narratives, or decorated them through faint references to the main topic (Decorative illustrations of second level). Whereas Decorative pictures remained relatively stable in both textbooks, the second level Representational ones changed considerably. In particular, they were the largest category regarding disciplinary texts. As anticipated, they were mostly made up of photos, accompanied by an opportune caption, which integrates information provided by the text. Organizational and Explanative pictures showed a different distribution in the two typologies of textbooks: they were definitely more used in disciplinary texts than in reading ones.

DISCUSSION AND CONCLUSIONS

As put forward in the methodological section, during the first analysis of the textbooks, taking Levin's and Mayer's functional categorizations as a starting point, the requirement for a further specification of the Decorative and Representational categories emerged, leading us to define two sub-categories for each of them: first and second level Decorative and first and second level Representational pictures. Such a distinction proved to be useful during the actual analysis of the chosen textbooks. As seen previously, discussing differences in the use of illustrations through different grades, a significant difference in the use of Representational images in the first and second grades emerged. Moreover, in reading texts the percentages of second level Decorative images were similar to that of first level Representational ones, if not greater. This can be ascribed to the fact that a considerable number of Decorative pictures might be identified as having a "missed representational" nature, due to a misled attempt to insert a first level Representational image. This element highlights a possible confusion in the choice of the illustrations according to their ideal function: it is likely that the cognitive properties of the images are often overrated by the book designers. In conclusion, a first outcome of the present study consisted in having devised a system of classification of pictures included in textbooks which is different form the existing ones, in having tested its applicability, and in having showed that it allows us to highlight detailed distinctions concerning the functions played by textbook pictures.

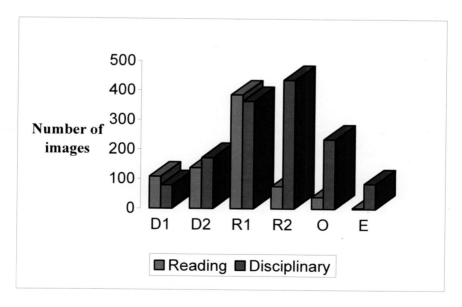

Figure 1. Image categories in reading and disciplinary textbooks (fourth and fifth grade).

The study was also aimed at assessing to what extent Mayer's (1993) findings can be generalized. The present survey, examining Italian textbooks, makes it actually possible to compare choices concerning text illustrations in two different countries, so allowing us to test to what extent the situation described by Mayer is replicated in another context. With reference to type, quantity, and use of the illustrations found in primary school textbooks, some differences emerged if we compare our data to those collected by Mayer (1993). Mayer analysed sixth grade school textbooks, whereas we considered textbooks adopted in first to fifth grades. Considering the grade of primary school textbooks examined, a larger use of illustrations in our set of books had been expected: it might be reasonable that the amount of pictures decreases as the reader's ability to comprehend texts and to deal with abstract concepts increases along the curriculum. On the contrary, a difference can be found in the percentages of space devoted to text and pictures between the present data and Mayer's ones: more space was devoted to pictures in sixth grade science textbooks than in all primary school textbooks. In fact, the percentage of space devoted to illustrations in the present was lower than that reported by Mayer. The inversion of tendency might be due to several factors: the fact that Mayer (1993) considered a single disciplinary field (it is likely that scientific notions hint at visualizing more than contents of different domains) or to differences existing between the American and Italian educational system and culture. This datum might be ascribed also to different Italian and American editorial choices (a different choice of the editorial board concerning the total space to be devoted to text and picture). Finally, we can not discard historical factors (more than one decade separates the two studies). In any case, doubts might be cast about the possibility to generalise Mayer's (1993) findings.

If we move to consider more in detail the importance attributed to the different kinds of images in editing school textbooks by comparing the results of our investigation to those of Mayer's (1993 survey, we observe similar percentages of space devoted to Decorative and Representational pictures, but different trends concerning the presence of Organizational and Explanative illustrations (more precisely, showing an increase of Organizational images in the present study, balanced by a correspondent decrease in Explanative illustrations). The comparison between the two studies suggests that the choice of pictures seems to rely, on the one hand, on the same criteria regards to page decoration and representation of single elements mentioned in the texts, but, on the other hand, on different assumptions associated to (presumably implicit) beliefs about the cognitive activity elicited by different types of illustrations in the readers' head.

In our study, as well as in Mayer's (1993), a considerable part of the pages of primary school textbooks is covered by illustrations which play a minor role in facilitating understanding. Decorative and Representational images might serve as embellishments enhancing readers' curiosity and motivation and, at most, increase the memorability of some contents thanks to the impressive characters of some visual devices. In some occasions, the presence of such "embellishments" seems to render the page too rich with stimuli, with the risk of confusing children's ideas and deflecting their attention from more significant elements (such as Organizational and Explanative illustrations). In this sense, the conclusion that illustrators share a deceptive naïve theory of multimedia learning is supported by both investigations. However, in the present investigation Organizational images appeared to be used more than in Mayer's survey, whereas the opposite was true for the Explanative images. It might be that scientific contents need more, or are more suitable to, graphic representations consisting in visualising the steps of a process (as occurs in Explanative pictures).

Alternatively this difference might be ascribed to cultural factors concerning the criteria employed by illustrators to select pictures to be included in textbooks. Italian book designers seemed to believe Organizational pictures are more effective than the Explanative ones, whereas the opposite was true for the Americans. It might be that in Italian textbooks more importance was give to the organization of the given information, assuming that a global view facilitates the learning process, while in the American textbooks it was believed to be more important to explain the way something works – stressing the importance of a procedural processing of the information in the learning process.

Whereas previous investigations were focused only on one school grade and one typology of textbooks, the present study considered the full range of (Italian) primary school grades and all the kinds of textbooks adopted in the classes. This allowed us to assess whether the use of illustrations varies according to the school level and to the textbook contents, so contributing to a better understanding of the implicit theories of multimedia learning underpinning the use of visual cues by illustrators. As far as possible differences in the type and in the use of illustrations across the five grades of primary school are concerned, it was hypothesised that more meaningful images would be found in textbooks used in the first grades, when children still cannot read, or are not fluent at it, and therefore rely more on illustration. Results pointed out that, though a steady prevalence of Representational images can be found through the grades, second level Representational pictures (those that substitute the text or integrate it) appeared to be particularly numerous in the first and second grades, that is, when, given the still poor proficiency of children at reading, the images do play a fundamental supporting role for the text. In the following grades they decreased, whereas the first level Representational and second level Decorative of images (supposing a more advanced literary competence) increased. Organizational and Explanative illustrations were almost missing in the first grade and increased progressively during the subsequent years. This can be obviously related to children's cognitive development, assuming that they get better at reading and at understanding schemata and graphs. In the upper grades, as will be explained in more detail below, the use of different types of illustrations changes also according to the type of discipline.

The relative different amount of the different categories of images across the five grades of the primary school seems to reveal implicit assumptions by illustrators about the cognitive development of children. Illustrators addressed above all Representational pictures to the youngest pupils, reserving more complex images – involving abstract concepts, as well the understanding of iconic conventions such as boxes and arrows included in flow charts – to the oldest ones, who possess the capacity to take full advantage of the "cognitive opportunities" provided by Organizational and Explanative illustrations. Such assumptions, even though naïve, are consistent with the description of the cognitive development provided by experts, so showing that the beliefs shared by illustrators (and by teachers, when they choose to adopt a certain textbook) and "embedded" in the pictures that they draw are not misleading.

Since Mayer focused his survey on science textbooks only, the present study, focused on examining all the subjects of the first five grades, also aimed at investigating the possibility that different subjects motivate a different use of images. It was hypothesised that other topics (such as those included in reading books) might lead text designers to make a different selection of illustrations. By comparing images used in reading books with those employed in disciplinary texts, it was noticed that the number of second level Representational illustrations depended on book typology: whereas it decreased in reading books, it increased significantly in disciplinary texts (e.g. historical, geographical, or scientific). Also Organizational and Explanative images showed a different distribution in the two typologies of textbooks: as might have been expected, they were definitely more used in disciplinary texts than in reading ones. It is worthwhile noticing that also the typology of Organizational and Explicative images employed in the two kinds of book changed. Whereas in the disciplinary texts the Organizational illustrations were usually images provided with captions which denominate different parts of something and show relations among them, in the reading books they were inserted as conceptual maps. Explanative images, instead, were usually employed in disciplinary texts to show the different steps of processes or to help retrace phases described in the text. For instance, some scientific processes, such as photosynthesis, were often accompanied by Explanative images, which described different steps and helped to retrace the phases described in the text. On the other hand, when inserted in reading books, Explanative images were instructions for manual activities. Thus, we can conclude that the naïve theory of multimedia learning shared by illustrators (as can be derived by the kinds of images they drew) - and by teachers (as can be revealed by the decision to adopt a textbook which includes certain types of illustrations) – led to differentiate pictures according to the activities and topics handled by the textbooks. Illustrators (and teachers) perceive that in disciplinary books (devoted to maths and to science) students may benefit from the use of schemata and iconic explanations. In reading books, on the contrary, the scarce Explanative images were, generally, illustrated instructions for manual activities, whereas Organizational ones were often inserted as conceptual maps. Also in this case, as far the use of illustrations is concerned, the naïve theory "embedded" in the textbooks appears to reflect some principles supported by cognitive research.

Some general conclusions concerning the naïve theories of multimedia learning can be derived, as they indirectly emerge from the choice of images, and the management of space in textbooks for primary schools. It can in fact be hypothesised that the type and number of illustrations chosen by book designers mirror their implicit beliefs concerning the function of illustrations and their utility to promote learning. Moreover, examining the textbooks that are more frequently chosen by Italian teachers (we had access to those books whose graphical organization seemed to be optimal to the teachers who chose them) our data outline a complex picture. On the one hand, the choice of illustrations does not seem to exploit the cognitive potentialities of pictures: in fact the most frequently employed images were Representational and Decorative that, according to Mayer's cognitive theory, do not serve prominent cognitive functions. On the other hand, by comparing the use of illustrations in the different grades and disciplines, consistent implicit theories seem to emerge: the cognitive development and the reading proficiency of children was taken into consideration in the choice of pictures (especially, as mentioned earlier, in the use of second level Representational images and in the progressive introduction of Organizational and Explanative ones). Moreover illustrations appear to be wisely distinguished among different disciplines.

What implications can be derived? Naïve theories, as they indirectly emerge from this survey, while not completely consistent with cognitive principles of multimedia processing and elaboration, seem to reflect underlying principles consistent with the cognitive development of the children for whom books are designed. Within this frame - that is not as negative as Mayer hypothesised when he opposed his cognitive theory to a "common sense theory" that was supposed to be far from cognitive principles than what our data leads one to believe - it may be that a more substantial awareness concerning cognitive processes might help book designers to structure text-pictures relationships more effectively and teachers to select and use such books with cognitive proficiency. In any case, the naïve theory includes a relevant background, which is in line with some general notions of cognitive psychology, in which more technical details about the principles of multimedia learning can be nested. Illustrators and teachers seem to need to be taught about specific notions rather than to be convinced to reject totally their beliefs in order to assume a completely different point of view.

Even if the pessimistic claims about the unwise use of illustrations in school textbooks were not supported by the present survey, there is, however, space to improve illustrators' and teachers' awareness of the mechanisms underlying multimedia learning so as to lead them to make an even more "cognitively wise" choice and use of images. Being able to identify the hidden structure of the relationship between text and pictures and to point it out clearly can lead to structure training paths for teachers and illustrators. Illustrators will gain a higher metacognitive awareness concerning the cognitive role of their work and be then more able to better define and realize appropriate illustration for the texts they have to work on. Teachers will be able to choose their textbooks more intentionally and will lead the student to recognise and use, in a proper way, the more cognitively useful illustrations.

ENDNOTES

[1] This is Mayer's statement, though it could be hypothesised, coherently both with the author's cognitive theory and with the cognitive load theory, that such images can actually act on the cognitive processes, by way of interfering with information analysis and by overloading the cognitive system.

[2] This classification was compiled by the Publishing Houses based on the choices made by teachers and communicated to them.

[3] Textbooks composed of more volumes were considered as a whole, by summing the pages of the different volumes.

[4] The percentage refers to the total number of images.

[5] For example, a photo of sunflowers close to a text about summer holidays. At a glance such an illustration could be categorised as Representational; only after having read the text, though, does it become clear that, unexpectedly, it is about seaside and sand games, with no reference at all to sunflowers.

REFERENCES

Arthur, S. V. (1982). What can you do with a book without words? *The Reading Teacher, 35,* 738-740.

Avery, N. (1996). The wordless picture book: a view from two. *Reading Improvement, 33,* 167-168.

Bishop, S. R., & Hickman, J. (1992). Four or fourteen or forty: Picture books are for everyone. In S. Benedict & L. Carlisle (Eds.), *Beyond words: Picture books for older readers and writers* (pp. 1-10). Portsmouth, NH: Heinemann.

Carney, R. N., & Levin, J. R. (2002). Pictorial illustrations still improve students' learning from text. *Educational Psychology Review, 14*, 5-26.

Cianciolo, P. J. (1984). Use wordless picture books to teach reading visual literacy and to study literature. In P. P. Barron & J. Burley (Eds.), *Jump over the moon: Selected professional readings* (pp. 138-144). New York: Holt, Rinehart, and Winston.

Clark, J.M., & Paivio, A. (1991). Dual coding theory and education. *Educational Psychology Review, 3*, 149-210.

Degler, L. S. (1979). Putting words in wordless books. *Reading Teacher, 32*, 399-402.

Dowhower, S. (1997). Wordless books: Promise and possibilities, a genre comes of age. In K. Camperell, B. L. Hayes & R. Telfer (Eds.), *Yearbook of the American Reading Forum, 17*, 57-79.

Evans, D. (1992). Wordless picture books--The medium is the message. *Book Links, 1*, 46-49.

Gombrich, E. H. (1982). *The image and the eye: Further studies in the psychology of pictorial representation.* Ithaca, NY: Cornell University Press.

Grasty, P. E. (1978). The status of wordless picture books, 1960-1976. (Doctoral dissertation: Temple University) *Dissertation Abstracts International, 39*.

Holley, C. D., & Dansereau, D. F. (1984). *Spatial learning strategies.* New York: Academic Press.

Johnson, G. (1999). Multiple readings of a picture book. *Australian Journal of Language and Literacy, 2*, 176.

Kennedy, J. M. (1974). *A psychology of picture perception.* Washington, DC: Jossey-Bass.

Lee, Y., Park, S., Kim, M., Son, C., & Lee, M. (2005). The effects of visual illustrations on learners' achievement and interest in pda- (personal digital assistant) based learning. *Journal of Educational Computing Research, 33*, 173-187.

Levin, J. R. (1981). On functions of pictures and prose. In F. J. Pirozzolo & M. C. Wittrock (Eds.), *Neuropsychological and cognitive processes in reading* (pp. 203-228). New York, NY: Academic Press.

Levin, J. R. (1982). Pictures as prose-learning devices. In A. Flammer & W. Kintsch (Eds.), *Discourse processing* (pp. 412-444). Amsterdam: North-Holland.

Levin, J. R., Anglin, G. J., & Carney, R. N. (1987). On empirically validating functions of pictures in prose. In D. M. Willows & H. A. Houghton (Eds.), *The psychology of illustrations: Basic research* (Vol. 1, pp. 51-85). New York: Springer-Verlag.

Levin, J. R., & Mayer, R. E. (1993). Understanding illustrations in text. In B. K. Britton, A. Woodward & M. Binkley (Eds.), *Learning from textbooks: Theory and practice* (pp. 95-119). Hillsdale, NJ: Erlbaum.

Lindauer, S. L. K. (1988). Wordless books: An approach to visual literacy. *Children's Literature in Education, 19*, 136-142.

Mandl, H., & Levin, J.R. (1989). *Knowledge acquisition from text and pictures.* Amsterdam: North-Holland.

Mayer, R. E. (1993). Illustrations that instruct. In R. Glaser (Ed.), *Advances in instructional psychology* (vol. 4, pp. 253-284). Hillsdale, NJ: Erlbaum.

Mayer, R. E. (2001). *Multimedia learning.* Cambridge, UK: Cambridge University Press.

Mayer, R. E. (2005). *The Cambridge handbook of multimedia learning*. Cambridge, UK: Cambridge University Press.

McDaniel, M. A., & Pressley, M. (1987). *Imagery and related mnemonic processes: Theories, individual differences, and applications*. New York: Springer.

Novak, J. D. (1990). Concept maps and vee diagrams: Two metacognitive tools to facilitate meaningful learning. *Instructional Sciences, 19*, 29-52.

Paivio, A. (1971). *Imagery and verbal processes*. New York, NY: Rineheart and Wiston.

Paivio, A. (1986). *Mental representations: A dual coding approach*. Oxford, UK: Oxford University Press.

Park, S., & Lim, J. (2007). Promoting positive emotion in multimedia learning using visual illustrations. *Journal of Educational Multimedia and Hypermedia, 16*, 141-162.

Perales, F. J., & Jiménez, J. d. D. (2002). Las ilustraciones en la enseñanza-aprendizaje de las ciencias. análisis de libros de texto [Illustrations in the teaching-learning of science: Analysis of textbooks]. *Ensenañza de las Ciencias. Revista de Investigacíon y Experiencias Didácticas, 20)*, 369-386.

Pressley, M., & McCormick, C. (1995). *Advanced educational psychology*. New York, NY: Harper Collins.

Read, D., & Smith, H. M. (1982). Teaching visual literacy through wordless picture books. *The Reading Teacher, 35*, 928-933.

Reese, C. (1996). Story development using wordless picture books. *The Reading Teacher, 50*, 172-173.

Sadoski, M., Paivio, A., & Goetz, E. T. (1991). A critique of schema theory in reading and a dual coding alternative. *Reading Research Quarterly, 26*, 463-484.

Samuels, S. J. (1970). Effects of pictures on learning to read, comprehension, and attitudes. *Review of Educational Research, 40*, 397-407.

Stewig, J. W. (1988). *Children and literature* (2nd ed.). Boston: Houghton Muffin.

Swanson, H. L. (1989). Verbal coding deficits in learning-disabled readers: A multiple stage model. *Educational Psychology Review, 1*, 235-277.

Tuft, E. R. (1983). *The visual display of quantitative information*. Cheshire, CT: Graphics Press.

Vernon, M. D. (1953). The value of pictorial illustration. *British Journal of Educational Psychology, 23*, 180-187.

Willows, D. M., & Houghton, H. A. (Eds.) (1987). *The psychology of illustration: Vol. 1. Basic research*. Berlin: Springer.

In: Multimedia in Education and Special Education
Editors: O. Demir and C. Celik

ISBN 978-1-60741-073-7
© 2009 Nova Science Publishers, Inc.

Chapter 3

THE RISE OF THE COMPUTER AS AN ASSISTIVE TECHNOLOGY FOR EDUCATION IN CHRONIC MUSCULOSKELETAL DISEASE

Andrew S. Wilson[1] and Stephen P. Young[2]

[1]School of Computing, Telecommunications and Networks, Birmingham City University, Millennium Point, Curzon Street, Birmingham B4 7XG, United Kingdom
[2]School of Immunity and Infection, College of Medical and Dental Sciences, University of Birmingham, Birmingham B15 2TT, United Kingdom

ABSTRACT

Musculoskeletal diseases such as rheumatoid and osteo- arthritis are some of the major causes of chronic disability. Their incidence is predicted to increase as the proportion of elderly people in the population increases. These conditions can result in long-term and variable effects on the sufferer. Education is considered to be an integral part of their treatment equipping patients to cope with the different stages of these progressive diseases.

The range and complexity of information needed has seen the medical discipline of rheumatology embrace technology in support of a wide variety of educational interventions. Early pioneers demonstrated how computer assisted learning could benefit both patients and medical students by increasing their knowledge about these conditions. The establishment of the Internet has provided a new medium for wide spread dissemination of information. As this digital evolution continues there is increasing interest in how video games might be used to stimulate learning in younger generations who have grown up with this type of media.

These educational initiatives have proven to be measurably successful. Patients have access to a broad knowledge base from which they are able to increase their understanding of their illness, resulting in beneficial changes in behaviour. Medical students and qualified doctors have ready access to current research and best practise. The flexibility of the delivery medium supports more adaptable and distance modes of study whilst encouraging students to be more self-sufficient learners.

Computer assisted education has established itself as an invaluable resource in support of medical teaching and learning. But it will not appeal to everyone. Given the challenges facing each individual in education, these resources can only be commended, with learners now having access to a range of resources from which they can meet their educational needs. Continued development and innovative use of new media is likely to broaden their appeal and enhance their educational efficacy.

INTRODUCTION

Chronic (long term) conditions such as rheumatoid and osteo- arthritis are some of the most significant causes of disability in the United Kingdom (UK). These musculoskeletal conditions affect hundreds of millions of people of all ages world-wide [1] and, despite modern drug treatments, they cannot be cured.

Sufferers experience severe pain, general ill health and functional disabilities, all of which have major impacts on them and their families. A study by the Arthritis Research Campaign (ARC) in the UK highlighted the economic cost of arthritis and related connective tissues diseases. Between 1999 and 2000 these conditions resulted in significant impacts on loss of working days, major payments in incapacity benefit and financial burden on health services [2]. A similar situation exists in the USA and in other developed countries [1] .

The general consensus is that average life expectancy in the Western world is rising. With a higher proportion of elderly people in the population it is expected that there will be a corresponding increase in the prevalence of musculoskeletal disease [2,3].

The management of these conditions involves interactions between the patient, a range of health care professionals, as well doctors. Yet the provision of rheumatology training for both undergraduate health care professionals and in the undergraduate medical curriculum is perhaps not what it should be with very limited time devoted to these topics [1, 4-6]. A large proportion of undergraduate medical students will take up their profession in general practice and so become the first line of management for many patients with musculoskeletal disease [7]. If these future doctors are not equipped to optimally manage these conditions then there will be a need for appropriate mechanisms to communicate current knowledge and best practice into primary care.

Patient education is considered to be an important part of the treatment process for chronic arthritis. Its objectives are to promote in patients a range of knowledge, skills and attitudes. These include an understanding the disease process and its management, the role of drugs, diet, exercise and joint protection. They need to learn techniques for managing pain, stress relief, improve self care, problem solving, as well as ways of enhancing their psychological well-being, maintaining their social interactions and employability [8-10].

Patients want to be informed about their condition and the impact it will have upon them, so that they can make meaningful decisions. They do not want to feel isolated or to be an exception. They want to be able to communicate effectively and understand what their doctor is telling them. However, the doctor/patient dialogue is not always effective. The patient may not fully understand or remember what was said [11]. This may occur for various reasons. If the patient has only just been diagnosed with the condition, the information given may conflict with their preconceptions and lay beliefs, it may have been communicated by a well educated doctor and was beyond their knowledge level or merely that there was insufficient time available with the doctor to discuss their concerns [10,12,13].

The educational needs are therefore complex. They encompass those required by doctors and health care professionals, the information that they need to impart as part of their patient care as well as what the patient wants to know. This has prompted the exploration of novel teaching methods, many of which use a range of computer-based technologies.

COMPUTER ASSISTED LEARNING

The use of computers in education is not new. It has appeared in many guises with names like computer based (assisted or aided) teaching, learning, education or instruction. At a time when personal computers were only just finding their way into peoples homes and public life its potential was being explored in patient education [14,15]. Given the nature of arthritis with its highly variable impact on a person and their lifestyle determining the amount and complexity of information that they would need to know, there was uncertainty as to the effectiveness of the educational potential of computers [14]. However, studies showed that patients accepted and enjoyed using computers, with positive benefits being demonstrated from their use, including increases in knowledge and self-reported behavioural change [14,15].

Some of the most computer literate people are children. They too can suffer from arthritis and have no less of a requirement for education. The impact of juvenile idiopathic arthritis (JIA) is wide-ranging affecting the child, family and home environment. Lifestyle and behavioural issues are likely to change as the child grows older. Kidzone was a collaborative project between Birmingham Children's Hospital, Birmingham and Coventry Universities (UK). It was aimed at evaluating and comparing the educational benefits of a video and computer program whose content was specifically aimed at helping children and family understand JIA. Both forms of media were well received by the users, the interactive nature of the computer program allowed the children to control what they wanted to learn, its built-in quizzes supporting consolidation of their knowledge and its information being relevant throughout the course of their illness [unpublished data].

Interactive computer programs have also been used as a supplement in undergraduate rheumatology education. These tools provide information, in the form of multimedia, on rheumatic diseases as well as instruction in essential clinical skills [16,17]. The "interactive rheumatology tutor" [17] includes media explaining history taking, physical examinations and local injections. Quizzes are incorporated to test knowledge and simple artificial intelligence can be implemented which can generate diagnostic hypotheses. Other computer programs have used simulations based upon the processes involved in patient diagnosis and treatment [18]. Students find computer assisted learning to be a useful supplement to their traditional studies [19 cited in 20].

THE INTERNET

Arguably one of the biggest impacts of technology on information, knowledge transfer and education has resulted from the establishment of the Internet. There has been a shift from it being a privilege of a few to one where nearly everyone has access, either at home or work.

At the beginning of 1998 a search of the Internet for 'rheumatology' returned 1912 sites; by the end of that year there was a three fold increase in their number [21,22]. Ten years later, entering the same term into Google, produces several million results. Many of the early web sites were aimed at the medical professions with little focus on patient education [21]. This soon changed but with little regulation, questions were raised over the quality and accuracy of the information [21-23]. This saw the development of guidelines so that people could evaluate the credibility of the websites [24]. Organisations, for example the International League of Associations for Rheumatology (ILAR), Arthritis Research Campaign, and Arthritis Care, as well as academic rheumatology institutes, started to develop their own web sites in order to provide information from reputable sources. ArthritisHelp, LupusHelp and Kidzone were three websites developed by the staff and doctors in the department of Rheumatology, University of Birmingham (UK).

Online questionnaire and web site usage statistics were used to generate a profile of the people visiting these sites and evaluate what information they were looking for [25]. The findings indicated that they were either suffering from, or knew someone who was suffering from, arthritis or related conditions. Another large group of visitors were medical staff or health care providers. At the time of the study it was not surprising that the majority of visitors were from the USA where public access to the Internet had been established longer than in the UK and Europe. Users indicated that they were visiting the web sites in order to collect as much information as they could, a situation which has been reported by other investigators [26]. By actively engaging with patients, educational web sites can be developed which specifically address the needs of patients and can have measurable effects on their knowledge [27]. However, despite access to this wealth of information not all patients are prepared to discuss with their doctor what they have found [28].

Responses to our questionnaires indicated that the surfers were also looking for mutual support or contact details of care providers, an observation which subsequent studies have corroborated [29].

There is a current philosophical shift in the way the users of the Web are trying to shape it. Web 2.0 is the concept of a social web where ideas and technologies focus on how the Internet can be used more collaboratively. This may have a role in health care education [30], providing the means for the mutual support that patients have been looking for.

Rheumatologists, like most medical specialists, actively engage in research and the many new ideas and information often make it difficult for clinicians to keep up to date [6]. Large numbers of doctors use the Internet to locate and seek information. Curran and Fleet [31] suggest that a significant proportion of Internet use by doctors results directly from questions arising from patient care. A more structured use of the Internet in education has seen academic institutions embrace what has now commonly become known as e-learning. Medical education was quick to realise its potential [32] due to increasing student numbers requiring more flexible patterns of study and often the need to study remotely from their institutes.

The introduction of e-learning into undergraduate rheumatology education at the University of Birmingham (UK) was cautiously accepted by students. However, many did realise its potential as it provides a centralised resource for a range of course specific material in support of their studies [33]. Over time e-learning has become commonplace in medical education [34,35]. Online teaching material for rheumatology includes lectures, videos, quizzes as well as sophisticated online virtual patients [33,36,37]. With the latter students perform simulated clinical consultation. They collect relevant data including patient history, make clinical examinations and select appropriate tests, all of which form the basis of the core skills required in clinical practice [7]. This patient case-based approach to teaching has been suggested to provide a stronger sense of the patient as a person, promoting clinical communication and clinical reasoning skills [38].

COMPUTER GAMES

Computer (video) games are now one of the most significant forms of entertainment. As a result of their widespread appeal there is a growing interest in their use in education in what is now being termed "serious gaming".

Games are of interest to educationalists because of their inherent mix of goals, challenges, competition and feedback. Each time a game is played it gives the player different perspectives and experiences. A successful game is entertaining, immersive and engaging. This offers the potential for creating fun educational environments that can be used to facilitate active participation in learning. Students can construct knowledge at their own pace and under their control. They can experiment in risk free environments that allow for trial and error, where mistakes can be made and that result in meaningful and measurable learning experiences.

As early as 1985, Winter and colleagues [39] suggested that, because games were becoming an accepted part of computer use, they could have a role in the support of occupational therapy and patient rehabilitation. Positive effects were demonstrated when computer games were used as a means of distraction and in pain management [40].

Currently there appears to be little work on the use of games in education and in the management of arthritis and musculoskeletal disease, perhaps because of the older age groups predominantly affected. However, other chronic conditions including asthma, diabetes and cancer have evaluated them as educational interventions for children and adolescents [41]. Their use has been shown to improve attitudes and behaviour including quality of life, self-efficacy for self-care, adherence to prescribed medicine and increased knowledge about cancer [41,42]. Similar improvements in behaviour and knowledge have been found in their use in juvenile diabetes and asthma [43,44].

More traditional (non digital) games have been used in support of teaching medical professionals [45-49]. It is believed that their use helps to reduce stress and generate an enthusiasm for learning where it has been difficult to communicate boring, tedious or difficult concepts [45,46]. Computer games for medical education range in their complexity from interactive quizzes [50,51] to sophisticated simulations and video games used to train surgeons [52,53].

There are negative connotations associated with video game use, including the promotion of violence; injuries resulting through overuse; and potential addiction. Pedagogically concerns about the use of any form of game in education arise from the notion that the game itself may end up being a more memorable experience than the information it was trying to communicate [54]. The freedom for learning that games offer should not result in the student misunderstanding the educational intent of the game resulting in them not achieving the desired learning objectives [55]. Importantly, games should not trivialise or devalue the importance of the medical issues that they are dealing with [47].

The amalgamation of video game technology, simulations and virtual reality has seen the emergence of complex online digital 3D worlds which can be simultaneously inhabited by thousands of "players". The genre includes massively multiplayer online role paying games (MMORPG) and social environments such as Second Life. Participants inhabit these worlds as digital representations (avatars) of themselves or they assume the role of a character in the game world (MMORPG). These virtual worlds are diverse, changing and evolving as a result of the interactions between the many players. Their focus on creating and fostering social interactions means that there is current interest in their potential for collaborative learning [56], research [57] and as a way of combating social isolation and loneliness [58]. Given their potential, they may find important roles in promoting the well-being of patients affected by chronic disabling diseases.

CONCLUSION

Education is considered to be an important part of the treatment process in the management of arthritis and musculoskeletal conditions. Improving patients' knowledge forms the basis for behaviour change and computer technology has frequently been used in support of this. Studies have demonstrated that its use can help to increase patient knowledge, have positive effects on behaviour. However, these can be limited, dependent on the educational approach used, and short-lived [8-10, 59, 60]. Behaviour change is important but can be confounded by the patient's beliefs, lifestyle and willingness to change. Therefore, reinforcement plays an important part in maintaining positive effects [8], and this is a prime role that computers can play.

Even though people with conditions like arthritis will use computers in their quest for information, it should not be forgotten that the functional disabilities experienced by these individuals may pose barriers to the use of computers. Further work is warranted into better ways for these people to interact with this kind of technology. Fortunately new opportunities are presenting themselves with the development of innovative game controllers (e.g. Wiimote) and gesture control systems.

The evolution of computer technology has provided a means for more effective knowledge transfer. Qualified doctors can be kept informed of current research and best practise. Trainee doctors are exposed to a wide range of resources which support the more flexible approach to learning that is now being required by academic institutes. The diversity of resources also being used encourages undergraduates to be more self-sufficient learners.

As computer technology advances the opportunities for more sophisticated digital learning improve. Developing more engaging educational media may become more important in future if the observations of Prensky [61] are correct. He proposes that younger generations are now exposed to far more technology and digital stimuli in their lives than their parents. As a result they have developed different cognitive skills and learn in less formal or in less traditional patterns than their predecessors, embracing technology as friend rather than as a foe.

Education is multifaceted; people are known to have different styles and ways of learning. Computer-based education has established itself as a flexible and useful approach that can be used to stimulate, engage and support learning. It will appeal to some and not to others. Its future development will result from the creativity of the teacher, the collaborations formed between the clinician, educators and technologists in order to realise the potential. Given the challenges and complexities facing education, the availability of a broad spectrum of teaching resource can only be commended.

REFERENCES

[1]   Dequeker, J; Rasker, JJ and Woolf, AD. Educational issues in rheumatology. *Baillière's Clinical Rheumatology,* 2000, 14(4), 715-729.
[2]   Arthritis the big picture. A report commission by the ARC from MORI and the ARC Epidemiology Unit [on line]. 2002. Available from: URL: http://www.arc.org.uk/ arthinfo/documents/BigPic.pdf
[3]   Meenan, R; Callahan, LF, and Helmick, CG. The National Arthritis action plan: a public health strategy for a looming epidemic. *Arthritis Care Research,* 1999, 12, 79-81.
[4]   Almeida, C; Clarke, B; O'Brien, A; Hammond, A; Ryan, S; Kay, L; Hewlett, S. Current provision of rheumatology education for undergraduate nursing, occupational therapy and physiotherapy students in the UK. *Rheumatology (Oxford),* 2006, 45(7), 868-73.
[5]   Kay, LJ; Deighton, CM; Walker, DJ; Hay EM. Undergraduate rheumatology teaching in the UK: a survey of current practice and changes since 1990. Arthritis Research Campaign Undergraduate Working Party of the ARC Education Sub-committee. *Rheumatology (Oxford),* 2000, 39(7), 800-3.
[6]   Dacre, J; Griffith, SM and Jolly, BC. Rheumatology and Medical Education in Great Britain. *British Journal of Rheumatology,* 1996, 35, 269-274.
[7]   Thompson, PW. Undergraduate education. *Annals of the Rheumatic Diseases,* 1991, 50, 445-448.
[8]   Daltroy, LH and Liang, MH. Advances in patient education in rheumatic disease. *Annals of the Rheumatic Disease,*1991, 50, 415-417.
[9]   Tucker, M and Kirwan, JR. Does patient education in rheumatoid arthritis have therapeutic potential? *Annals of the Rheumatic Disease,* 1991, 50, 422-428.
[10] Mäkeläinen, P; Vehviläinen-Julkunen, k and Pietilä, A-M. Rheumatoid arthritis patients' education – content and methods. *Journal of Clinical Nursing,* 2007, 16 (11C), 258-67.
[11] Wright, V; Hopkins, R and Burton, K. How long should we talk to patients? A study in doctor-patient communication. *Annals of the Rheumatic Disease,* 1982, 41, 250-252.

[12]   Donovan, J. Patient education and the consultation: the importance of lay beliefs. *Annals of the Rheumatic Disease,* 1991, 50, 418-421.

[13]   Maycock, JA. Role of health professionals in patient education. *Annals of the Rheumatic Disease,* 1991, 50, 429-434.

[14]   Wetstone, SL; Sheehan, TJ; Votaw, RG; Peterson, MG; Rothfield, N. Evaluation of a computer based education lesson for patients with rheumatoid arthritis. *Journal of Rheumatology,* 1985, 12(5), 907-12.

[15]   Rippey, RM; Bill, D; Abeles, M; Day, J; Downing, DS; Pfeiffer, CA; Thal, SE; Wetstone, SL. Computer-based patient education for older persons with osteoarthritis. *Arthritis and Rheumatism,* 1987, 30(8), 932-5.

[16]   Rheumatology Ed. Klippel, JH and Dieppe, PA. London: Mosby; 1998.

[17]   Armstrong, R. Interactive Rheumatology Tutor: A Multimedia Guide to Clinical Rheumatology on CD-ROM: A Multimedia Guide to Clinical Rheumatology on CD ROM (CD-ROM). Cambridge University Press; Cdr edition; 1997.

[18]   Schewe, S. RheumaTutor. A case-based rheumatological training program. ISBN 3-86126-934-1.

[19]   Schewe, S; Reinhardt, B; Betz, C. Experiences with a knowledge-based tutoring system for student education in rheumatology [Online]. 1998. Available from: URL: http://ki.informatik.uni-wuerzburg.de/forschung/publikationen/lehrstuhl/Reinhardt-XPS-99/XPS-99.pdf

[20]   Bernelot Moens, HJ. Two interactive rheumatology tutors on CD-ROM. *Annals of the Rheumatic Disease,* 2000, 59, 328-329.

[21]   Tench, CM; Clunie, GPR; Dacre, J and Peacock, A. An insight into rheumatology resources available on the world wide web. *British Journal of Rheumatology,* 1998, 37,1233-1235.

[22]   Armstrong, R; Rasker, H and Dequeker, J. An insight into rheumatology resources available on the World Wide Web (http://www.ilar.org). *Rheumatology (Oxford),* 1999, 38(10),1028-9.

[23]   Impicciatiore, P; Pandolfini, C; Casella, N and Bonati, M. Reliability of health information for the public on the World Wide Web: systematic survey of advice on managing fever in children at home. *British Medical Journal,* 1997, 314, 875–81.

[24]   Kim, P; Eng, TR; Deering, MJ and Maxfield, A. Published criteria for evaluating health related web sites: review. *British Medical Journal,* 1999, 318(7184), 647-649.

[25]   Wilson, AS; Kitas, GD; Llewellyn, P; Carruthers, DM; Cheseldine, DC; Harris, S; Huissoon, AP; Bacon, PA; Young SP. Provision of Internet-based rheumatology education (http ://rheuma.bham.ac.uk). *Rheumatology (Oxford),* 2001, 40(6), 645-651.

[26]   Gordon, MM; Capell, HA and Madhok, R. The use of the Internet as a resource for health information among patients attending a rheumatology clinic. *Rheumatology (Oxford),* 2002, 41(12), 1402-1405.

[27]   Young, SP; Henderson, E; Cheseldine, DL; Wilson, AS; Skan, J; Heaton S; Bowman, SJ; Situnayake, D; Bacon, PA; Southwood, TR; Gordon C. Development and assessment of a World Wide Web site for systemic lupus erythematosus patient information. *LUPUS,* 2002, 11(8), 478-484.

[28]   Hay, MC; Cadigan, RJ; Khanna, D; Strathmann, C; Lieber, E; Altman, R; Mcmahon, M; Kokhab, M; Furst, DE. Prepared patients: Internet information seeking by new

rheumatology patients. *Arthritis & Rheumatism-Arthritis Care & Research*, 2008, 59(4), 575-582.

[29]   Van Lankveld, WGJM; Derks, AM; van den Hoogen, FHJ. Disease related use of the Internet in chronically ill adults: current and expected use. *Annals of the Rheumatic Diseases*, 2006, 65(1), 121-123.

[30]   Kamel Boulos, MN and Wheeler, S. The emerging Web 2.0 social software: an enabling suite of sociable technologies in health and health care education. *Health Information and Libraries Journal*, 2007, 24(1),2-23.

[31]   Curran, V and Fleet, L. A review of evaluation outcomes of web-based continuing medical education. *Medical Education*, 2005, 39, 561-567.

[32]   Greenhalgh, T. Computer assisted learning in undergraduate medical education. *British Medical Journal*, 2001, 322, 40-4.

[33]   Wilson, AS; Goodall, JE; Ambrosini, G; Carruthers, DM; Chan, H; Ong, SG; Gordon, C; Young, SP. Development of an interactive learning tool for teaching rheumatology - a simulated clinical case studies program. *Rheumatology (Oxford)*, 2006, 45(9), 1158-1161.

[34]   Ruiz, JG; Mintzer, MJ and Leipzig, RM. The impact of e-learning in medical education. *Academic Medicine*, 2006, 81 (3), 207-212.

[35]   Le Beux, P and Fieschi, M. Virtual biomedical universities and e-learning. *International Journal of Medical Informatics*, 2007, 76(5-6), 331-335.

[36]   Barraclough, D. e-Rheumatology and medical education. *Clinical Rheumatology*, 2003, 22(3), 177-180.

[37]   Ng, MH; Armstrong, R; Hall, W; Maier P. JointZone: An Adaptive Web-based Learning Application. Technical Report. University of Southampton (UK), Report No.: ECSTR-IAM02-002; 2002.

[38]   Bearman, M; Cesnik, B and Liddell, M. Random comparison of 'virtual patient' models in the context of teaching clinical communication skills. *Medical Education*, 2001, 35, 824-832.

[39]   Winter, J; Newell, AF and Arnott, JL. The therapeutic application of computerised games. *International Journal of Bio-Medical Computing*, 1985, 17, 285-293.

[40]   Griffiths, M. Video games and health - Video gaming is safe for most players and can be useful in health care. *British Medical Journal*, 2005, 331 (7509), 122-123.

[41]   Beale, IL; Kato, PM; Marin-Bowling, VM; Guthrie, MS and Cole, SW. Improvement in cancer-related knowledge following use of a psychoeducational video game for adolescents and young adults with cancer. *Journal of Adolescent health*, 2007, 41, 263-270.

[42]   Kato, PM; Pollock, BH; Dahl, GD; Baggott, CR; Beale, IL; Marin-Bowling, VM and Cole, SW. The effect of a video game on self-care and quality of life among adolescents and young adults with cancer: A randomized controlled trial. Teenage Cancer Trust Fourth International Conference on Teenage and Young Adult Cancer Medicine (April). London; 2006.

[43]   Brown, SJ; Lieberman, DA; Gemeny, BA; Fan, YC; Wilson, DM and Pasta, DJ. Educational video game for juvenile diabetes: Results of a controlled trial. *Medical Informatics*, 1997, 22(1), 77-89.

[44]   Shegog, R; Bartholomew, LK, Parcel, GS; Sockrider, MM; Masse, L and Abramson, SL. Impact of a computer assisted education program on factors relating to asthma

self-management behavior. *Journal of the American Medical Informatics Association*, 2001, 8, 49-61.

[45]   Resko, D and Chorba, M. Enhancing learning through the use of games. *Dimensions in Critical Care Nursing*, 1992, 11, 173-7.

[46]   Barnett, L. Teaching through games. *Tropical Doctor*, 1993, 23(3), 97-98.

[47]   Fukuchi, ST; Offutt, LA; Sacks, J and Mann, BD. Teaching a multidisciplinary approach cancer treatment during surgical clerkship via an interactive board game. *American Journal of Surgery*, 2000, 179(4), 337-340.

[48]   Steinman, RA and Blastos, MT. A trading-card game teaching about host defence. *Medical Education*, 2002, 36, 1201-1208.

[49]   LeCroy. C. Games as an innovative teaching strategy for overactive bladder and BPH. *Urologic Nursing*, 2006, 26, 381-5

[50]   Mooney, GA and Bligh, JG. CyberIST (c): a virtual game for medical education. *Medical Teacher*, 1998, 20 (3), 212-216.

[51]   Smith-Stoner, M. Innovative use of the internet and intranets to provide education by adding games. *CIN: Computers, Informatics, Nursing*, 2005, 23(5), 237-241.

[52]   Gomoll, AH; O'Toole, RV; Czarnecki, J and Warner, JJP. Surgical experience correlates with performance on a virtual reality simulator for shoulder arthroscopy. *American Journal of Sports Medicine*, 2007, 35(6), 883-888.

[53]   Rosser, JC; Lynch, PJ; Cuddihy, L; Gentile, DA; Klonsky, J and Merrell, R. The impact of video games on training surgeons in the 21st Century. *Archives of Surgery*, 2007, 142(2), 181-186.

[54]   Allery, LA. Educational games and structured experiences. *Medical Teacher*, 2004, 26(6), 504-505.

[55]   Rieber, LP. Seriously considering play: Designing interactive learning environments based on the blending of microworlds, simulations and games. *ETR&D-Educational Technology Research and Development*, 1996, 44(2), 43-58.

[56]   De Freitas, S and Griffiths, M. Online gaming as an educational tool in learning and training. *British Journal of Educational Technology*, 2007, 38(3), 535-537.

[57]   Bainbridge, WS. The scientific research potential of virtual worlds. *Science*, 2007, 317 (5837), 472-476.

[58]   Kamel Boulos, MN; Hetherington, L and Wheeler, S. Second Life: an overview of the potential of 3-D virtual worlds in medical and health education. *Health Information and Libraries Journal*, 2007, 24, 233-245.

[59]   Lindroth, Y; Bauman, A; Barnes, C; McCredie, M and Brooks, PM. A controlled evaluation of arthritis education. *British Journal of Rheumatology*, 1989, 28, 7-12.

[60]   Riemsma, RP; Taal, E; Kirwan, JR and Rasker, JJ. Patient educational programmes for adults with rheumatoid arthritis. *British Medical Journal*, 2002, 325, 558-559.

[61]   Prensky M. Digital game-based learning. New York: McGraw-Hill; 2001.

In: Multimedia in Education and Special Education
Editors: O. Demir and C. Celik

ISBN 978-1-60741-073-7
© 2009 Nova Science Publishers, Inc.

Chapter 4

RELATIONAL FRAME THEORY AND BEHAVIORAL INTERVENTIONS FOR YOUNG CHILDREN WITH AUTISM AND OTHER DEVELOPMENTAL DISABILITIES

Robert F. Gulick, Danielle L. Cotterill and Phillip J. Belfiore
Mercyhurst College, PA USA

ABSTRACT

The past ten to fifteen years have seen a rapid resurgence of behavioral approaches in the teaching of language and social skills to young children with developmental delays. Particularly in the area of autism, this has been most evident with the advent of Early Intensive Behavioral Intervention (EIBI) programs in both home and Special Education settings. These "traditional" EIBI programs are often criticized, however, for fostering a rather rigid use of language. Learners who have participated in EIBI are often seen to demonstrate highly formal or "robotic" conversational skills. While these children respond very well to the contrived stimulus conditions that characterize many EIBI programs and clearly benefit from their ability to master rote skills such as verbal imitation, labeling, and receptive language, they often fall short in generating novel language responses. Moreover, the current evidence-based methods found in EIBI programs (discrete trial instruction and incidental teaching), are often found lacking in their ability to consistently produce the kind of flexibility in language and social skill repertoires that is necessary for these children to be successfully integrated with their peers in the classroom and on the playground.

Alternatively, relational frame theory and its formulation of derived relational responding may provide a conceptual framework on which to build a line of applied research to develop and test interventions that will bolster existing EIBI programs in these areas of generality and flexibility of language skills. Derived relational responding refers to an individual's ability to discriminate and respond psychologically to the relationships between stimuli without having those relationships directly taught. The following study, representing some of the early work being done in this new area of applied research, investigated the possibility of children with autism acquiring and demonstrating novel mands without direct teaching. The results indicated success on several levels. The study replicated previous findings that the establishment of an equivalence class through conditional discrimination training is a viable means to facilitate the derived transfer of mand function. Secondly, by addressing the conversational use of complex mands, the present study extended previous findings beyond basic manding for tangible reinforcers to more advanced applications, such as manding for information. Finally, this work can be seen as a positive step toward improving the current teaching technology so that it may eventually foster more natural, flexible language repertoires for young children with autism and other developmental delays.

INTRODUCTION

The History of Early Intensive Behavioral Intervention

The autobiographical account of a mother's search for effective treatment for her two children diagnosed with autism in Catherine Maurice's book *Let Me Hear Your Voice* (1993) promoted Applied Behavior Analysis (ABA) into the popular spotlight of autism intervention in the mid 1990's. It described how a behavioral approach to language and social skills training could significantly improve the functioning of children previously viewed as un-teachable. It also brought into the public eye the ground-breaking work of O. Ivar Lovaas and the UCLA Young Autism Project who had selected some of the basic procedures that had been developed and researched within the field of ABA – such as shaping and differential reinforcement as well as the visual analysis of data produced from these procedures, and applied them to language instruction for this population of children. The results of these interventions were very promising. Lovaas' culminating 1987 study suggested improvement in 47% of the test group to the point where they functioned within the normal range in terms of IQ and other standardized cognitive measures.

During the past two decades, the technology of Early Intensive Behavioral Intervention (or EIBI) has been refined to the point where very specific instructional methodologies and curricula have been developed to service children with Autism Spectrum Disorder (ASD) diagnoses. Consultative services in EIBI conducted by Board Certified Behavior Analysts are now available worldwide. Furthermore, parents are becoming more and more vocal in their advocacy for these services both as an early intervention option within the child's home and as part of school district-funded programs within the public schools.

In *Effective Instruction for Individuals with Autism*, Gulick and Kitchen (2007) identified 3 critical components of a good EIBI program. These components are:

1) *A behavioral approach to teaching language and social skills* - viewing language as behavior that is sensitive to environmental contingencies. So, if we want to be successful in teaching language to a young child, we must effectively engineer the environment so that the language responses that we are targeting are strengthened. This typically involves breaking complex language down into small, teachable units and then, via shaping or differential reinforcement procedures, systematically teaching them to the child.

2) *Intensity* – providing the child with ample opportunity to practice the language or social skill. With some methodologies such as the early phases of *discrete trial instruction* (DTI), this involves the instructor presenting mass trials of a single skill until prompts can be faded and the child begins responding to the instructional cue without assistance. Well-constructed EIBI programs do not limit instructional opportunities to contrived DTI sessions but rather view the child's entire day as the stage upon which teaching is carried out. Many EIBI consultants recommend that even very young children (age 2-3 years) receive 20 to 30 hours per week of such intervention. With older children (age 4-6) the optimum intensity is at least 30 hours per week (Green, 1996).

3) *Data-based decision making* – taking objective data on the child's responses to the intervention and then using those data to determine skill mastery and to drive curricular decisions. One of the hallmark characteristics of ABA is its reliance on the visual analysis of data to determine a functional relation between the dependent and independent variables. EIBI, if done well, embraces this foundational principle of ABA.

SKINNER'S ANALYSIS OF VERBAL BEHAVIOR

In 1998, two behavior analysts, James Partington and Mark Sundberg, played a pivotal role in introducing the EIBI world to B.F. Skinner's analysis of verbal behavior with the publication of two very important works - *The Assessment of Basic Language and Learning Skills (ABLLS)* (Partington & Sundberg, 1998) and its companion text *Teaching Language to Children with Autism and Other Developmental Disabilities* (Sundberg & Partington, 1998).

Partington and Sundberg's assessment tool and teaching text were based on B.F. Skinner's treatment of human language in *Verbal Behavior*. Published in 1957, *Verbal Behavior* approached language as behavior that can be functionally analyzed and categorized according to the antecedent and consequent variables that are part of the external, environmental contingencies surrounding its display. Skinner clearly differentiated *verbal* from nonverbal behavior by defining verbal behavior as behavior that operates on the environment through the mediation of another person (Skinner, 1957). Turning on a light switch would be nonverbal behavior. Asking someone to turn on the light switch would be verbal behavior. Although both responses result in the same environmental change – the light gets turned on; the former involves the individual directly operating on the environment while the latter involves the mediation of another person – meeting the criterion for verbal behavior.

Skinner's theoretical account categorized language into functional types that he referred to as *verbal operants*. These were differentiated by the function of the particular operant according to the antecedent and consequent variables associated with it. This formulation was a significant departure from the traditional receptive/expressive language dichotomy utilized in more traditional conceptualizations of language.

For our purposes, we will limit the discussion to four of the basic verbal operants that routinely come into play in the teaching of language to children with autism and other developmental disabilities. This can be best illustrated if we consider how a single word such as "water" can, depending on the context and how it is used, function as each of the different verbal operants.

If a thirsty child says the word "water" and receives a drink of water from his mother, then the word "water" functions as a *mand*. Skinner chose the term mand to describe a specific type of verbal behavior that is under the antecedent control of a motivational operation – in this case water deprivation (Skinner, 1957). From a consequence standpoint, the child's use of the word "water" is reinforced by the item that the word specifies – i.e., saying "water" gets me water.

Since the mand is tied so closely to motivation, it is often the easiest of the verbal operants to teach to our young children with ASD or other disabilities. Contriving or capturing naturally occurring motivational operations can set the stage for the effective teaching of mands. Simple mands can be used to obtain objects, activities, or the actions of others while more complex mands can be used to obtain social attention, information, or consent. All question-asking behavior would fall within the definition of mands.

Now, if that same word, "water," is spoken following an instruction to "Say "water"", then it would function as an *echoic*. The echoic is the verbal operant that is under the antecedent control of a verbal model that has point-to-point correspondence with the response (Skinner, 1957). In other words, the child's response "water" is identical to the instructor's model "water." The consequence for echoic responding is some form of non-specific reinforcement. With a typically developing toddler, a response of "mama" after being asked to "Say mama" is followed by enthusiastic social praise and attention – particularly if it is the first time that the child says "mama" in that context.

The generalized behavior of verbal imitation and the ability to respond to imitative prompts are critical elements in language instruction – regardless of the theoretical orientation of the program. The echoic therefore plays a central role in EIBI programs. Much of the early skill instruction in EIBI focuses on motor imitation which, while not echoic behavior, serves as a prerequisite for future echoic development. The child is often taught to first imitate instructor actions with simple objects (placing a block in a bucket, shaking a rattle, pushing a toy car). Once generalized imitation of actions with objects has been displayed, the instruction advances to require the child to imitate gross motor movements modeled by the instructor – without objects (clapping hands, stomping feet, waving bye-bye). Progression to the imitation of fine motor movements and oral motor movements (opening mouth wide, sticking out tongue, blowing kisses,) then follows. Once the child has demonstrated generalized imitation skills (i.e., the ability to readily imitate novel actions) among all of these nonverbal behaviors, the instruction might advance to include vocal or verbal imitation training where true echoic behavior would be taught.

A child's ability for echoic responding is essential to the success of future training when more complex verbal behavior is taught – such as labeling in full sentences, asking or answering questions, reciprocating social information, etc. All of these advanced language skills are generally taught using verbal modeling prompts. A strong foundation in echoic responding is necessary for verbal models to be effective teaching prompts.

Returning once again to the basic verbal operants, if the child observes water spilled on the floor and, pointing to it, says to her mother "water," then the word "water" is functioning as a *tact*. The tact is the verbal operant that is under the antecedent control of a nonverbal stimulus that is present in the immediate environment (Skinner, 1957). This nonverbal stimulus could be an object, an action, or some other characteristic that is present for the child to observe. Like the echoic, the consequence that follows the tact is non-specific reinforcement – often social praise or attention. In the case of our example, the mother might respond "Yes, there's water on the floor. Thank you for telling me." Unlike the mand where the child says "water" because she wants water, this example of a tact illustrates a situation where the child does not *want* water but merely wants to engage in social commenting with her mother – a behavior that has been previously rewarded with attention and praise.

Because of its link to social reinforcement, teaching tacts to our children with ASD often carries with it considerable motivational difficulties. In contrast, the nature of the *mand* involves a built-in motivation for the child to respond, again making it the most straightforward of the verbal operants to teach. If the child is thirsty, she is more apt to respond in a manner that results in getting a drink – i.e., by saying "water". On the other hand, if a child with autism sees water, she may not be as motivated to say "water" when historically such comments (tacts) have been followed only by attention and praise – two secondary social reinforcers that typically do not hold significant value to this population of children. Pairing of more valued primary reinforcers such as food or access to toys with the social praise that follows tact responses is often the means of bridging this motivational gap and establishing social praise and attention as effective reinforcement for these children.

Our fourth basic verbal operant might involve a situation where the word "water" is now spoken in response to a question such as "What do dogs drink?" The child's response "water" in this case functions as an *intraverbal*. Antecedent control of an intraverbal is the verbal behavior of another person – the question "What do dogs drink?" As with echoics and tacts, the consequence for an intraverbal is non-specific reinforcement – quite often verbal praise ("That's right! Dogs drink water.") or some other form of positive social attention. Unlike tacts however, for a verbal response to be considered an intraverbal, the antecedent condition must not include the nonverbal stimulus. For the response to be considered a pure intraverbal, no actual water or visual reference to water would be present when the question is posed to the child. Her response to the question is under the antecedent control of the verbal stimulus (the question) presented by another person.

Furthermore, in contrast with the echoic, the antecedent verbal stimulus does not possess point-to-point correspondence with the response (Skinner, 1957). While with the echoic, the instructor models the exact word or words that the child is to repeat, with the intraverbal, the instructor's question ("What do dogs drink?") is structurally very different from the child's response ("water").

As with tacts, the motivation for engaging in intraverbal responding often requires a certain amount of contrivance on the part of the instructor. Pairing intraverbal responses with more salient primary reinforcers might need to be first established and then systematically faded. Additionally, the tendency for children with ASD to rely on visual cues in their environment to respond to instruction puts them at a clear disadvantage when they are being asked to respond strictly to an auditory stimulus such as a teacher's question. Considerable success has been realized by the authors in utilizing visual materials (e.g., photo's or written words) as stimulus prompts during intraverbal training and then transferring stimulus control from the nonverbal/visual stimulus to the verbal/auditory stimulus. In our example above, the instructor might simultaneously present a photograph of a dog drinking water from a dish (nonverbal stimulus) as she poses the question "What do dogs drink?" (verbal stimulus). Over subsequent teaching trials, the visual stimulus would be gradually covered up or perhaps presented for shorter periods of time until the child's responses were being accurately made in the sole presence of the instructor's question.

This brief explanation of just four of Skinner's verbal operants should be sufficient, however, to illustrate how a behavioral approach to language can enhance the teaching of functional communication skills to children with autism or other developmental disabilities. Rather than limiting our view to the traditional receptive/expressive dichotomy of language, the Skinnerian view allows for a more balanced approach across the functional nuances of human language. Of particular utility to those designing language instruction for these children is the fact that both antecedent and consequent variables play important roles in the establishment of the various verbal operants and that these variables can be manipulated in very precise ways so that 1) language happens and 2) that those instances can be reinforced. The following table (Figure 1) gives a quick summary of the four basic verbal operants and their controlling variables.

Going beyond our ability to engineer language environments where the critical antecedent and consequent variables can be manipulated to evoke a specific verbal operant, Sundberg and Partington (1998) suggest that an established operant can be used to teach previously nonexistent operant repertoires for a given child. This can be accomplished by transferring the stimulus control for the language response from one set of antecedent conditions to another. For example, perhaps the child in our earlier example is adept at manding (requesting) water using the spoken word "water" when she is thirsty, but has limited ability to label water when asked "What is it?" in the presence of water (a mixed tact/intraverbal). A transfer of stimulus control from a mand to a tact might be possible by systematically changing both the antecedent and consequent conditions over time. Instructional trials would begin with standard mand training trials where the MO for water (thirst) is high and the instructor consistently provides small amounts of water for each correct response of "water" by the child. As the session progresses and the consumption of water serves as an MO to abolish the value of water (i.e., the child's thirst is quenched), the antecedent condition can then be changed to that of a tact trial – namely by introducing a nonverbal stimulus (e.g., a glass of water) and the verbal prompt "What is it?" During these tact trials, consequences for the child's response of "water" would likewise change from the specific reinforcement of receiving a drink of water to a non-specific reinforcer such as verbal praise, a food item or access to a highly preferred toy. In this manner, a previously nonexistent or poorly developed tacting repertoire could be established or strengthened by linking it to the formerly mastered skill of manding (Sundberg & Partington, 1998).

The marriage of the evidence-based teaching strategies inherent in ABA with a Skinnerian analysis of verbal behavior has contributed to EIBI programs around the world – both in assessing language problems in children diagnosed with autism and other developmental disabilities and in making inroads into treating those children.

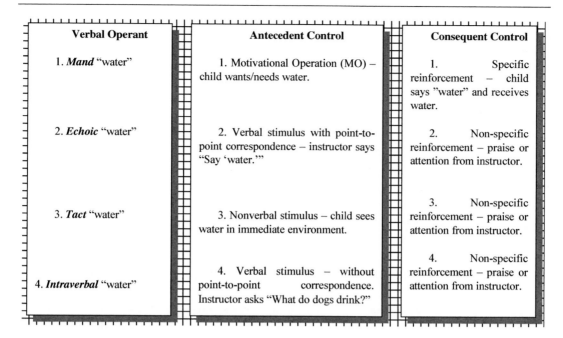

Verbal Operant	Antecedent Control	Consequent Control
1. *Mand* "water"	1. Motivational Operation (MO) – child wants/needs water.	1. Specific reinforcement – child says "water" and receives water.
2. *Echoic* "water"	2. Verbal stimulus with point-to-point correspondence – instructor says "Say 'water.'"	2. Non-specific reinforcement – praise or attention from instructor.
3. *Tact* "water"	3. Nonverbal stimulus – child sees water in immediate environment.	3. Non-specific reinforcement – praise or attention from instructor.
4. *Intraverbal* "water"	4. Verbal stimulus – without point-to-point correspondence. Instructor asks "What do dogs drink?"	4. Non-specific reinforcement – praise or attention from instructor.

Figure 1. Basic Verbal Operants Taught in EIBI Programs

Advanced Language, Stimulus Equivalence, and Relational Frame Theory

While early mand training focuses on teaching the child to ask for preferred tangibles, activities, or actions, more advanced training programs might involve teaching the child to mand for permission, assistance, or information. So, if the mand is under the control of the motivational operation (MO), these more complex forms of manding would likewise demonstrate MO control. Where previously the need for a cookie served as the MO for the mand "cookie", now the need for information such as "What time is it?" serves as the MO for a more complex mand - assuming that the information (the correct time) is valuable to the child. The problem faced with teaching complex mands to children with autism is that these children do not typically value verbal information This typically requires contriving or "capturing" MO's to drive up the value of information for the child (Sundberg & Michael, 2001).

Even when many complex questions have been taught to a child, there is no guarantee that he or she will be able to utilize this skill functionally within the complex dynamics of conversation. In many cases, the mand repertoire of the child with autism is quite inflexible, in that they are extremely limited in the generality and spontaneity of mands. While some success may be seen in the child's generalization of question-asking across settings and listeners, there remains considerable difficulty in his or her ability to generate novel questions or to alter the question asked following a change in the conversation. This problem suggests that all possible mands would need to be taught individually to the child in order for him/her to converse functionally. If this is the case, this would present a rather daunting task for anyone endeavoring to teach conversational skills to young children with autism.

A solution to this dilemma emerged in the early 1970's with Murray Sidman's work on stimulus equivalence and equivalence relations. Through a series of experiments, Sidman (1971) demonstrated the phenomenon of equivalence relations, which suggests that relations between stimuli can be established without direct training. His earliest study involved teaching the matching of spoken words to pictures, and spoken words to printed words. The subject of the study was a 17-year old boy with severe mental retardation, who then proceeded to spontaneously match the printed words to the pictures – a task that had not been specifically trained during the experiment.

The implications of stimulus equivalence within early intensive behavioral intervention (EIBI) programs, particularly in the teaching of language are significant. Rather than limiting instruction to rote responses that are directly taught, establishing equivalence relations can yield generative (untrained) verbal responses resulting in more natural language development in children with autism (Gulick & Kitchen, 2007). So, with establishing novel or alternate mands, stimulus equivalence may provide a means of arriving at a more flexible mand repertoire without explicit instruction.

Taking this a step further, the account of human language and cognition described by Hayes, Barnes-Holmes, & Roche (2001), known as relational frame theory (RFT), extends this notion of equivalence relations to what Hayes refers to as derived relational responding. "Derived relational responding involves the ability to relate stimuli in a variety of ways even though one has never been reinforced (i.e., directly trained) for relating those stimuli in those specific ways" (Blackledge, 2003, p 425). RFT not only suggests that stimuli can be related in this manner, but that the function of one of those stimuli can transfer to other stimuli – again without explicit training. For example, if a young child says "water" to request a drink of water, then "water" functions as a mand. If the child subsequently learns that "acqua" is the Italian word for water, "water" and "acqua" then would participate in an equivalence class. Should the child begin to mand for water using the word "acqua," she would be demonstrating the derived transfer of function – with both words functioning as a mand. In this case "water" was an explicitly trained mand whereas "acqua" would be considered a derived mand (Murphy, Barnes-Holmes, & Barnes-Holmes, 2005).

Recent research in the area of derived mands has supported this theoretical basis for the derived transfer of function between verbal stimuli. Rehfeldt & Root (2005) first taught three adults with severe mental retardation to mand for preferred items using pictures. They then utilized conditional discrimination training to teach them to match those same pictures to spoken words and then spoken words to text. Follow up probes revealed that all three participants demonstrated derived manding skills – i.e., they requested the preferred items using text.

In 2007, Rosales & Rehfeldt conducted a similar study with 2 adults with severe developmental disabilities and language deficits. A contrived transitive motivating operation was utilized to evoke derived mands in the completion of chained tasks. Both participants were taught to use the Picture Exchange Communication System (PECS) to mand for an item needed to complete a chained task. Conditional discrimination training was then used to set up an equivalence class between the PECS picture icons and the corresponding printed words. Posttest probes revealed that both participants demonstrated the emergence of derived mands (requesting needed items via printed words).

While both of these studies demonstrated that equivalence relations could be used to foster derived transfer of mand function, they limited their investigation to adults with severe disabilities. Murphy et al. (2005) extended this line of inquiry to include young children with autism in a series of three experiments. Again, contriving a transitive motivating operation, they first taught three children diagnosed with autism to mand for two different types of tokens (X1 and X2) using cards depicting two specific nonsense syllables (A1 and A2). They then established equivalence between the first set of cards (A1 and A2) and a new set of cards (B1 and B2) through conditional discrimination match-to-sample training. Further equivalence was then established between the B1 and B2 cards and a new set of cards (C1 and C2). Tests for derived transfer of mand function from the A1 and A2 cards to the C1 and C2 cards were conducted. In other words, they wanted to determine if the children would now use the C1 and C2 cards to mand for X1 and X2 tokens respectively. The results from this, the first experiment, indicated that two of the three participants demonstrated derived transfer of mand function following the conditional discrimination training. The third subject initially failed to display derived manding. Following transfer training using multiple exemplars, he too began to demonstrate derived transfer of mand function.

Both the Murphy et al. (2005) and the Rehfeldt & Root (2005) studies advanced the idea that relational frame theory could be synthesized with Skinner's analysis of verbal behavior as suggested by Barnes-Holmes, Barnes-Holmes, & Cullinan (2000). They also provided direction as to the development of instructional technology for fostering relational responding in children diagnosed with autism.

Traditional EIBI programs are often criticized for fostering a rather rigid use of language. Learners who have participated in EIBI are often seen to demonstrate highly formal or robotic conversational skills. While these children respond very well to the tight stimulus control that characterizes many behaviorally-based language programs and can benefit from its ability to teach rote skills such as tacting, echoic responding, and intraverbal usage, they often display great difficulty in generating novel responses. To date, discrete trial programs have had little success in consistently establishing the flexible use of language. The following study investigated the possibility of children with autism acquiring and demonstrating novel mands without direct teaching. In doing so, the researchers sought to address this critical need of EIBI programs by incorporating the findings of derived manding research into EIBI curricula.

The benefits of teaching a child with autism to have a more flexible mand repertoire are far-reaching. First and foremost, it would allow the child to ask varied questions when circumstances require him to do so rather than asking the same question over and over again. An example of this might involve a child who is requesting puzzle pieces to complete a puzzle. At a certain point in the process, the child may no longer need another puzzle piece but rather is in need of assistance in placing a specific piece in the puzzle frame. Faced with this predicament, the child with autism may likely continue requesting puzzle pieces and not ask for help. If such a child possessed a more flexible mand repertoire, he/she would have been able to ask for help and avoid the obvious frustration.

Additionally, a child's ability to ask questions and effectively make his or her needs known in a more flexible and fluent manner will have a significant positive impact on the child's reliance on problem behavior. As is commonly accepted, most problematic behaviors demonstrated by children with autism are, in fact, a means by which they make their basic wants and needs known to those involved in their care and education. Simply ignoring a problem behavior (as is often prescribed in a behavior plan) does not fully address this issue as it leaves the child without an appropriate alternative for making his or her requests. Having a more extensive range of verbal requesting skills to choose from will fill this gap – allowing the child to function more independently in a wide variety of environments.

The following study also served to extend the work begun in the Murphy et al. (2005) study to a more naturalistic teaching situation that is often encountered with our young children with autism. One such typical instructional scenario involves a "guessing game" that requires the child to systematically guess the hidden object on a card held by the teacher. Guessing in this sense involves a series of varied mands – i.e., asking questions to obtain information. This program is designed to foster turn-taking, question-asking, and systematic problem solving.

What is commonly seen during this game is the child with autism once again asking the same questions repeatedly – even when told that their initial guess was incorrect. This study utilized equivalence training as employed in the Murphy et al. (2005) study to establish novel question-asking during the guessing game.

METHODOLOGY

Participants

Three children ages 7 to 9 years old with autism spectrum diagnoses participated in the study. Participant #1 (Oscar) was 9 years old and had diagnoses of Asperger's Disorder, Attention Deficit Hyperactivity Disorder (ADHD), and mild mental retardation. Participant #2 (Jack) was 7 years old and carried diagnoses of Autism Spectrum Disorder and ADHD. Participant #3 (Kate) was 8 years old and diagnosed with ASD and ADHD. Selection criteria required that the participants used vocal speech at the sentence level, demonstrated the ability to mand at the Wh-question level, possessed receptive and tact skills for identifying function/feature/class (FFC), and displayed simple rule-following behavior – i.e., the prerequisites for the "guessing game" program. Finally, participants could not have had any previous instructional contact with the "guessing game" program.

Setting

All sessions were conducted in the individual participants' homes. Sessions were conducted either in designated therapy rooms or in semi-isolated areas of the homes, such as family rooms, dining rooms, or recreational rooms. Participants and investigators were either seated at tables or on the floor for all sessions. Sessions were conducted daily in accordance with the families' schedules and averaged four per week. Session duration varied with the phase of the study. Baseline sessions involved blocks of 10 trials and were limited to either 30 minutes or 100 trials – with 5-minute breaks between blocks of trials. Direct Mand Training (DMT) sessions also involved blocks of 10 trials and were limited to either 60 minutes or 100 trials – with 5-minute breaks after every fifth block. Conditional Discrimination Training (CDT) sessions involved blocks of 10 trials and were limited to 15 minutes or 50 trials – with 2-minute breaks between blocks.

Materials

All phases of the study utilized 2"x 2" color picture cards representing individual examples of members of the following categories (animals, vehicles, foods, toys, furniture, and clothing). The token economy system employed in the DMT and CDT phases incorporated a 4"x12" token board constructed of laminated cardstock and 2"x2" neutral token cards (printed with blue 5-pointed stars), and 2"x2" color picture cards depicting valued reinforcers for the individual participants as well as the corresponding tangible reinforcing items.

Research Design

A multiple probe design (Horner & Baer, 1978) was employed whereby Participant #1 (Oscar) began with baseline trials (no instruction) until stability in data was achieved. He then began DMT and moved to CDT once the specified criterion was met. Once Oscar began CDT, probes for derived transfer of mand function were conducted intermittently.

Participants #2 (Jack) and #3 (Kate) remained in the baseline phase while Oscar received DMT. Once Oscar proceeded to CDT, Jack (having stable baseline responding) began DMT. Jack continued with DMT until he met criterion. He then moved through CDT during which, probes for derived transfer of mand function were conducted.

Likewise, Kate did not begin direct mand training until she had achieved stable baseline responding and until Jack had begun his DMT. Once Kate met the DMT criterion she began CDT. Kate then proceeded through CDT and derived mand testing according to the same criterion as Oscar and Jack.

Procedure

Baseline

A deck of picture cards was placed on the table between the participant and the investigator. The picture cards in the deck included items that represented six categories (vehicles, animals, foods, toys, furniture, and clothing). Investigator #1, seated across the table from the participant, selected one card from the deck and held it up so that the participant was unable to see the picture on the card. The investigator then said:

"I want you to guess what I have by asking a question."

Regardless of the participant's response (correct or incorrect guesses), the investigator provided no verbal affirmation or praise. The investigator would, without saying anything, simply show the card to the participant. A 3-second inter-trial interval (ITI) was then observed and the subsequent trial commenced with the drawing of the next card.

The following two types of responses were scored as incorrect (-) on the data sheet: (1) tacting the specific item; or (2) asking questions pertaining to the function or attributes of the item. When the participant responded incorrectly, the investigator said:

"No. Try again"

The investigator continued using the same card until the participant guessed correctly. Responses using the mand form of "Is it (a) [category label]?" or "Do you have a [category label]?" (even if the child guessed the wrong category) were scored as correct (+) on the data sheet. Progression to DMT would begin once baseline data demonstrated stability over three consecutive blocks of trials (30 trials).

Direct mand training (DMT). Prior to the mand training session, Investigator #1 showed the token board to the participant and explained to him/her that when the board was filled with six picture cards, he/she would earn a preferred tangible. As the DMT session commenced, a deck of picture cards was placed on the table between the participant and the investigator. All of the cards in the deck were examples of items from one category (e.g., all vehicles). Investigator #1, seated across from the participant, selected one card from the deck and held it up so that the participant could not see the picture on the card. Investigator #1 then said

"To get your (reinforcer), you will need to fill up this card with 6 pictures. I will give you a picture each time you can guess what I have. To guess, you will need to ask a question."

Investigator #1 then started the first trial by saying:

"Guess what I have by asking a question."

For the initial few trials, the investigator prompted the correct mand response "Is it a (category label)?" by using an echoic prompt ("Say 'Is it a vehicle?'"). Reinforcement for responding with the correct mand was verbal affirmation ("That's right. It's a [category label]!"). The investigator then handed the picture card to the participant who was prompted to place the card on the token board. When the token board was filled (six picture cards), the participant was provided with his/her pre-selected tangible reinforcer.

The echoic prompt was faded over subsequent trials (using the standard time delay procedure – i.e., gradually increasing the time between S^D and prompt until the participant responds solely to the S^D) until the participant responded with the correct mand with no prompts.

When the participant made an incorrect mand response (e.g., "Is it a car?") or failed to make any response within 3 seconds, the investigator said "No, you need to ask 'Is it a [category label]?" Following a 3-second ITI, a new trial commenced with the investigator saying "Ok, let's try again."

Correct responses were recorded on the data sheet as a (+) and incorrect responses were recorded as a (-). Prompted responses were recorded as (p). Both investigator #1 and #2 collected data simultaneously for all trials in this phase.

The initial mand ("Is it a [category label]?") was considered mastered when the participant filled three consecutive token boards without error – or 18 consecutive trials.

Conditional discrimination training (CDT). A 10-token reinforcement board was utilized during this phase of training. The tokens were not the pictures used in the DMT phase because the stimuli that the participants were expected to match were spoken words and not the visual representation of the categories. Rather, neutral non-specific tokens were used (colored stars of the same size as the picture-tokens used during DMT). Prior to the training session, investigator #1 told the participant:

> To get your (reinforcer) you will need to fill this card with 10 stars. When I say "Is it a (sample category)?" you say "Is it a (comparison category)". I will give you a star each time you say "Is it a (comparison category)?"

The modified block trial procedure developed by Smeets and Striefel (1994) and also used in the Murphy et al. (2005) study was employed during this phase of training. At the start of each block of 10 trials, Investigator #1 spoke the sample category question aloud. Investigator #1 then prompted the participant to say the comparison category name aloud. Verbal praise was provided (e.g., "nice work", "good job") as well as a token for his/her token card. A 3-second ITI followed the trial. Three trials were conducted with this first set of stimuli.

The next three trials involved a different sample category question and a different comparison category question. Before conducting these trials, investigator #1 told the participant:

> Now, we're going to change the words. When I say "Is it a (sample category), you say "Is it a (comparison category)."

The final four trials involved random presentations of both sample category questions. Prior to conducting these final trials, Investigator #1 said:

> Now we're going to do both questions.

For each trial, if the participant said the correct category question, he/she would be provided with verbal praise and a token. Cash-in tangibles were provided when ten tokens had been earned (approximately every 10 trials).

If the participant said the incorrect category question, Investigator #1 said "You should say 'Is it a [category label]'." The 3-second ITI then occurred with the next trial immediately following.

Correct responses (saying the correct comparison category question) were scored as a (+) on the data sheet. Incorrect responses (saying anything other than the correct comparison category question or failing to respond within 3 seconds) were scored as a (-) on the data sheet. Both Investigators #1 and #2 collected data simultaneously for all trials within this phase. A training mastery criterion was set at 10 consecutive correct responses.

When the participant met mastery criterion on the first two sample stimuli, then the training commenced for the next level of equivalence training – where the comparison stimuli from the first set of trials became the sample stimuli for the second set of trials. Two new category labels were selected as comparison stimuli. The training was designed to continue until all 6 categories had been used as the sample stimuli twice (6 levels – each involving 2 sample stimuli as described above). Mastery criterion was required to be met at each level before moving on. The table in Figure 2 represents how this was arranged.

Levels	Stimuli	
	Sample	Comparison
Level 1	1. Vehicles	Toys
	2. Animals	Foods
Level 2	3. Toys	Furniture
	4. Foods	Clothing
Level 3	5. Furniture	Animals
	6. Clothing	Vehicles
Level 4	7. Animals	Furniture
	8. Vehicles	Clothing
Level 5	9. Furniture	Toys
	10. Clothing	Foods
Level 6	11. Toys	Animals
	12. Foods	Vehicles

Figure 2.

Probes for the Derived Transfer of Mand Function

When participants were engaged in equivalence training for the six categories (vehicles, animals, toys, food, furniture, and clothing), they were intermittently exposed to probes to determine if the untrained category questions would now function as mands during the guessing game. During the test, Investigator #2 served as the trainer while Investigator #1 served as the secondary data collector.

The procedure for the probe was similar to that described for DMT, except for the following details. The deck of picture cards placed on the table was a mixture of pictures from all six categories (vehicles, animals, toys, food, furniture, and clothing).

Trials progressed as outlined in DMT. However, no verbal praise was provided for correct responding. Additionally, incorrect responding received neither prompting nor error correction. The picture card was simply given to the participant following an appropriate accurate mand (he or she guessed one of the 6 categories and was correct) or following an appropriate but inaccurate mand (he or she guessed one of the 6 categories but was incorrect). No investigator response was provided for inappropriate mands – i.e., perseverative asking of the same category question or the asking of specific category member questions such as "Is it a hamburger?"). Following an incorrect mand response, the 3-second ITI was observed and then the investigator began a new trial by saying "Ok, let's try again."

Interobserver Agreement (IOA)

Investigators included three graduate students, as well as the participants' parents. Sessions were conducted by two investigators, one parent and one graduate student. During all sessions the second investigator acted as an additional data collector. The first investigator, who provided training, also collected data. For each trial, correct responses were scored with a plus (+), while incorrect responses were scored with a minus (-). IOA was calculated by dividing the total number of agreements by the number of agreements plus disagreements and multiplying by 100%. IOA data was calculated for 25% of all trials. Agreement between the two investigators averaged 98%.

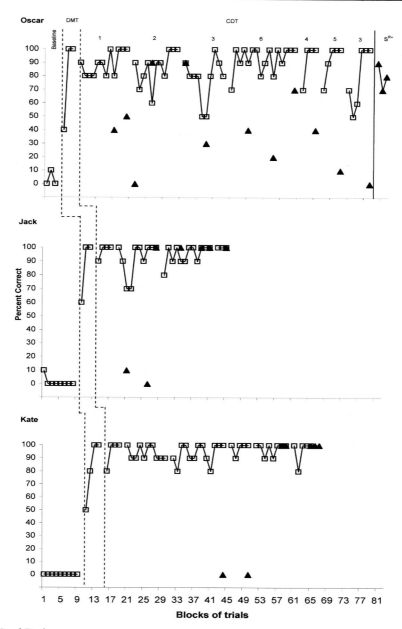

▲ = Derived Mand Probe.

Figure 3. The above graphs depict the performance of all three subjects. Jack and Kate remained in the baseline phase until Oscar commenced Direct Mand Training (DMT). Conditional Discrimination Training (CDT) then followed DMT. The CDT was designed to introduce up to 12 combinations of sample and comparison stimuli. These combinations were divided into 6 levels which are denoted by the numerals 1- 6 within the CDT phase of the graph. In Oscar's graph, S^{R+} refers to a procedural revision involving an enhanced schedule of reinforcement that he required for success. The derived mand probes (denoted by the filled triangle symbol) replicated the directive ("Guess what I have by asking a question.") that was presented to the subjects during baseline sessions.

RESULTS

The graph in Figure 3 illustrates the performance of all three participants at baseline and across the three phases of training. [Note: Due to collateral compliance issues experienced with Oscar and the procedural modifications made during his sessions, we will begin the review of our findings with Jack and Kate.]

Jack. There were eight blocks of baseline trials conducted with Jack. He made one correct response (i.e., asked an appropriate category question) during the first block of baseline trials. During the remaining seven blocks of baseline trials, Jack did not ask any further category questions – yielding a stable baseline at zero. Jack required three blocks of trials to learn to ask "Is it a vehicle?" during direct mand training.

Conditional discrimination training was then initiated to establish an equivalence class that included the initially-trained category question of *Is it a vehicle?* and the remaining five category questions. Jack moved quickly through Level 1 of CDT in four blocks of trials. Level 2 proved to be more difficult with Jack requiring 10 blocks (100 trials) to meet criterion. His first two derived mand probes were conducted during this level of CDT, with Jack scoring 0% on both. A follow-up probe coinciding with the final block of Level 2 resulted in a score of 100% - indicating the emergence of derived mands.

Levels 3 and 4 of CDT then proceeded with ongoing derived mand probes at Blocks 30, 35, 37, and 40. Jack scored 100% accuracy on all four of these derived mand probes indicating that the derived transfer of mand function had successfully occurred following 14 blocks of CDT – in approximately five days of training. This being the case, it was determined that further CDT to the completion of Levels 5 and 6 was unnecessary.

Kate. Kate's nine-day baseline yielded an extremely stable rate of zero accuracy. She then moved immediately into DMT where, like Jack, she required three blocks of DMT trials to meet the 100% mastery criterion in manding when using one category question.

Conditional discrimination training sessions were then begun to establish the equivalence class. Kate's performance during Levels 1, 4, 5, and 6 enabled her to successfully complete those levels within relatively few blocks (eight or less). Levels 2 and 3 required ten and thirteen blocks respectively before Kate met mastery criterion.

Derived mand probes were initiated on the final block of Level 3 with Kate scoring 0% accuracy on that and the subsequent probe on the final block of Level 4. Derived mand probes conducted in both Levels 5 and 6 yielded scores of 100% on all five probes. Her performance on these final probes suggested that the derived transfer of mand function occurred sometime during these last two levels of CDT – after approximately eight days of training.

Oscar. Three 10-block trials were conducted during Oscar's baseline with one appropriate category question being asked out of the thirty baseline trials conducted. This near-zero accuracy percentage at baseline prompted movement to DMT after three blocks of baseline trials. As with the other participants, Oscar was able to master the single category question mand within three blocks of direct mand training trials.

Conditional discrimination training for Oscar proved lengthy and problematic. Considerable compliance problems were observed following the completion of Level 2 and continued over the next 41 blocks (or 410 trials). Level 3 in particular saw poor performance and therefore prompted its temporary suspension. In its place Oscar was presented with a random sequence of the remaining levels (6, 4, 5, and then returning to level 3).

Oscar's initial derived mand probes indicated emergence of the derived transfer of mand function. His first probe conducted at Block 9 indicated a 40% accuracy and his second probe three blocks later yielded a 50% accuracy. The subsequent two probes both indicated 90% accuracy – again suggesting that Oscar was beginning to derive the transfer of mand function. It was at this point in the CDT sessions that Oscar began displaying non-compliance and problematic behavior. His performance data in both the conditional discrimination trials and the next seven derived mand probes demonstrated a decided downward trend. During these next seven probes, Oscar averaged 30% accuracy.

In response to Oscar's inconsistent performance, a procedural change was made following the successful completion of Level 3 – at Block 64. As a means of increasing Oscar's motivation to participate in the sessions, the token economy system was supplemented by intermittent reinforcement with a tangible item (candy). This change did not result in the direct reinforcement of novel category questions. The tangible reinforcer was provided intermittently during probe sessions to encourage participation only. The delivery of candy never immediately followed Oscar asking a novel category question. Following this adjustment, Oscar's performance improved to the point where the next three probes averaged 80% accuracy.

CONCLUSION

The results of this study replicated the Murphy et al. (2005) findings that the establishment of an equivalence class through conditional discrimination training is a viable means to facilitate the derived transfer of mand function. All three participants demonstrated at least the emergence of derived mands within eight days of implementation. Training of the CDT procedure was relatively straightforward, with both graduate students and parents demonstrating proficiency within one training session.

By addressing the conversational use of complex mands, the study extended the Murphy, Barnes-Holmes, & Barnes-Holmes (2005) findings beyond basic manding for tangible reinforcers to more advanced applications, such as manding for information. This required the investigators to modify CDT slightly to include a match-to-sample procedure that involved spoken words instead of visual stimuli. While this resulted in some rather awkward phrasing being required of the implementors (e.g., "When I say 'Is it a vehicle?' you say 'Is it a food?'"), it did not seem to affect the participants' performance in establishing an equivalence class.

Additionally, this work can be seen as a positive step toward improving the capability of EIBI programs to foster more natural, flexible language repertoires for young children with autism. As noted earlier, EIBI has been routinely criticized for poor outcomes in regard to developing generative language amongst its recipients. The CDT procedure, if incorporated into EIBI practice, could help ameliorate this limitation by providing an effective means for facilitating relational responding in this population.

One possible drawback might be that the CDT procedure is slightly awkward and unfamiliar to most EIBI practitioners. Specific training of therapists and educators would obviously be required prior to any implementation. However, as noted previously, the graduate students and parents involved in this study were able to become proficient in this process within one training session. This was evidenced in participants' significant improvement in performance following the first few levels of CDT. This might suggest a positive correlation between implementer proficiency and child performance.

A possible limitation in the research design was the inconsistent application of derived mand probes across the three participants. Probes were not initiated during DMT but rather were begun at varying times for each participant during their CDT phase. Conducting probes throughout all three training phases would have been more consistent with the traditional multiple probe design, and thus would have established a more definite relation between the independent and dependent variable.

Another inconsistency within the study, as described earlier, was the alteration in the sequence of CDT levels for Oscar. Poor compliance on level 3 prompted this modification as well as the addition of a supplemental tangible reinforcer (candy). This alteration in the levels would appear to be inconsequential as the order in which the levels were presented was selected arbitrarily by the authors and had no functional significance.

On the other hand, the introduction of the edible reinforcer (which was intended to only reinforce compliant participation in the sessions) could have compromised the derivation of Oscar's mands – in that some of his mand responses during probes may have been directly reinforced with the candy.

Further exploration into the derivation of complex mands could be accomplished most simply by extending this study to include the subsequent steps in the guessing game. These typically involve requiring the players to guess not only the categories, but other dimensions of the stimuli, such as their functions and features. It would be interesting to observe to what level of complexity our young children with autism could take the derivation of novel mands within a multi-level problem-solving task.

While this study extended the procedure into a more typical instructional activity than was used in the Murphy et al. (2005) study, it might be more socially valid to inquire directly as to how this process of establishing novel mands could assist children who choose to engage in serious problem behavior. As discussed, a flexible mand repertoire may provide such a child with not just one replacement response but a variety of appropriate mands with which to react to the ever-changing environments that they encounter at home, school, or in their community.

Extended Applications of RFT to EIBI Programs

Relational Frame Theory posits that *derived relational responding* is an operant – that is, derived relational responding is a generalized learned behavior which, like other operant behavior, is sensitive to the effects of reinforcement, extinction, and punishment (Hayes, 2001). Typically developing children learn this *skill of relating* at a very young age via the multiple exemplars with which they come in contact in their verbal community. Non-human animals do not demonstrate this skill.

Unlike lower animals, humans are capable of responding to arbitrary relations – i.e., relationships between stimuli that are not based on the physical properties of the stimuli For example, all English-speaking adults of normal intelligence would acknowledge a relationship between the spoken word "cow" and a cow. However, the auditory stimulus "cow" has no physical properties that one could reasonably say are similar to the visual properties of an actual cow, we still make the connection between the two.

This skill of derived relational responding differs from the direct contingency-shaped behavior that typically is taught via standard EIBI programming in that it involves learning how to discriminate relationships *between* stimuli, rather than on discriminating individual stimuli. Children with ASD demonstrate an extremely limited ability to engage in relational responding. This may account for their notable reliance on concrete, formal relations during conversation, their difficulties in picking up on subtleties of language such as idiom and metaphor, and their struggles with even basic language usage such as comparisons and personal pronouns. A core failure to respond relationally (and our subsequent failure to address it) might be the missing piece in our EIBI programs that prevents children with ASD and other developmental disabilities from acquiring more flexible and natural language repertoires.

Before moving on to specific applications of relational frame theory to EIBI curricula, let's first clarify what we mean by a relational frame. As defined earlier within the derived mand study, derived relational responding involves "the ability to relate stimuli in a variety of ways even though one has never been reinforced (i.e., directly trained) for relating those stimuli in those specific ways." To elaborate further on this definition, it should be noted that derived relational responding has three contextually controlled characteristics – *mutual entailment, combinatorial entailment, and the transformation of stimulus function.*

Mutual entailment simply involves the symmetrical relationship between the related stimuli. For example, if we establish that stimulus A is related to stimulus B in a certain context, then we can safely say that stimulus B is related to stimulus A in that same context. While this may seem straightforward, it should be noted that the relations between stimuli need not always be identical or equivalent. So, if A is *better* than B, then B is *worse* than A. It is said that the second relation (B to A) is *entailed* by the first – i.e., it is not possible to have a *better* relation without having a *worse* relation (Hayes, 2001).

The second characteristic of derived relational responding, combinatorial entailment, takes mutual entailment a step further by considering entailment between sets of relationships. When, in a given context, A is related to B and B is related to C, then, in that same context, a relation is entailed between A and C and another between C and A. For example, if A is bigger than B, and B is bigger than C, than a *bigger-than* relation is entailed between A and C and a *smaller-than* relation is entailed between C and A. (Hayes, 2001)

Within a child's verbal community, instances of both mutual and combinatorial entailment are regulated by contextual cues. Consider a child who is told that "This is a ball" in the presence of a ball. It is the context that has been described in the previous sentence that determines what type of relation will be brought to bear on these two stimuli (the word "ball" and the object). The form of the sentence "This is a ball", the tone of voice in which it is delivered, the words involved (particularly the word "is"), and the specification of the particular object (such as pointing toward the ball) all are contextual cues which indicate a relation of *sameness* or *equivalence* (Hayes, 2001).

The final defining characteristic of derived relational responding is the transformation of stimulus function. Environmental stimuli that we come in contact with every day have a variety of functions. At a very basic level, stimuli possess perceptual functions – they can be seen, heard, tasted, smelled, and felt. From a motivational standpoint, stimuli can have conditioned reinforcing functions – they possess value for us and can play an important role in evoking behavior via motivational operations. Stimuli can also have conditioned emotional functions – they can carry with them feelings of fear, sadness, or happiness due to stimulus-stimulus pairing.

This last type of stimulus function suggests the psychological importance of derived relational responding. If a particular event, A, has a psychological function and that event is placed in relation with another event, B, under certain conditions B may acquire a new psychological function. The nature of B's function will depend on its relation to A. If A and B are opposites and A has positive attributes, then B may now have negative attributes. Conversely, if A and B are placed in an equivalence relation, and A has positive attributes then B may now have positive attributes.

To illustrate the transformation of simple perceptual functions, consider your response after being told to "picture a lemon." Even with no lemon present, most of us would visualize a lemon. We "see" the color, shape, and texture of a lemon. We may even go so far as to "imagine" the smell or taste of the lemon – all without it being present. A derived relational responding explanation of this phenomenon would begin by noting that actual lemons have visual/perceptual functions such as color, shape, and texture. Secondly, actual lemons and the word "lemon" are in a relational class of coordination. As such, we view the two stimuli (the word and the object) as equivalent. Finally, the words "picture a" serve as a context in which visual/perceptual functions are actualized in terms of the underlying relation of coordination (Hayes, 2001)

So to summarize, this type of behavior that we have been describing as derived relational responding is manifested in different forms called *relational frames* (Hayes, 2001) which:

- involve mutual and combinatorial entailment
- involve the transformation of stimulus function
- are due to a history of relational responding relevant to contextual cues
- are derived from the arbitrary characteristics of the stimuli

Hayes (2001) suggests that there exist various types of relational frames. This variation in relational framing accounts for the many ways in which a human being, responding to different contextual variables, relates things, actions, thoughts, ideas, and emotions in very different ways. It is beyond the scope of this chapter to conduct an exhaustive review of the types of relational frames. We will however discuss a few that have a particularly obvious application to EIBI curriculum.

The most straightforward relational frame is the *frame of coordination*. Simply put, a frame of coordination involves relations of identity, sameness, or similarity. With identity relations, an object and its name come to be identified with one another. The tact "This is a ball" made by an adult to a child in the presence of a ball might be an example of how, with direct reinforcement, a young child is taught the name of one common object in his environment. Over time, many other object/name pairings are introduced in the presence of these same contextual variables – a specific tone of voice, the presence of an object, and the words "this is." This exposure via multiple exemplar training in the child's natural language environment causes the child to eventually begin deriving identity relations without having to be directly taught subsequent examples– i.e. derived relational responding begins to be demonstrated. The child learns that a relation of sameness should be brought to bear on situations when these contextual variables are present (Hayes, 2001).

The demonstration of mutual entailment by frames of coordination would play a critical role in teaching children with ASD or other developmental disabilities listener-selection and tacting skills. Whereas traditional EIBI curricula stress the importance of teaching a child to select objects given the spoken label (traditionally - *receptive labels*) before teaching the child to tact the objects (traditionally – *expressive labels*), an approach grounded in RFT might suggest teaching both the receptive and expressive modes simultaneously. The child would be taught to select the ball when she is asked "Which one *is* a ball?" – in effect learning the relation that the object (ball) is identical to spoken word ("ball"). Conversely, the child would be taught to say the word "ball" when asked "What *is* it?" in the presence of the ball. In both situations, the contextual variables of having a ball present and the use of the word *is* included in the verbal instruction inform the child that she is dealing with a relation of identity. The first relation (ball = "ball") would necessarily entail that "ball" = ball.

Mutual entailment may be expedited by this process and derived identity relations may be established earlier for the child. In doing so, we may be able to significantly decrease the number of object labels (both receptive and tact) that will need to be individually taught in discrete trial instructional sessions and have the child more prepared to expand her repertoire of both operants (listener-selection skills and tacting) in a manner more similar to that of the typically developing young child.

Consideration of another relational frame, the *frame of comparison*, might also enhance the current teaching technology of EIBI programs. A frame of comparison is concerned with relations such as bigger/smaller, faster/slower, and better/worse (Hayes, p36). The contextual variable most readily identifiable in a frame of comparison would be the use of the word *than* in the description of the relation. "This ball is bigger *than* that ball" would be an example of how a child might describe such a relation.

Mutual entailment within frames of comparison typically involves opposition. So if ball A is bigger than ball B, then ball B is *smaller* than ball A.

If A>B, then B<A

Combinatorial entailment would set up more complex relations between three different stimuli. So if ball A is bigger than ball B and ball B is bigger than ball C, we can then derive that ball A is also bigger than ball C.

If A>B and B>C, then A>C

The issues surrounding the teaching of comparatives to our children with ASD and developmental disabilities can be quite daunting. The tight stimulus control that is established during discrete trial instruction, while critical to early teaching of rote language skills such as receptive discrimination of objects, tacting, and echoics, can actually be detrimental when introducing comparatives, opposites, and other attributes.

Our children tend to have difficulty with even simple stimulus generalization – i.e., responding to even slightly different versions of the same discriminative stimulus. Having once learned to select a specific picture of a dog when instructed to "Point to the dog," a child with ASD might have to be directly taught to respond in like manner to a dozen more variations of dogs before generalized selection of dogs emerges for the child.

So when faced with tasks that require the discrimination of comparative relationships, previously established stimulus control can hinder the child's performance. Instructions such as "Point to the big dog" when presented with photographs of a Chihuahua and a Beagle can usually be taught relatively easily via mass trials. Unfortunately, in most cases the child's selection of *big dog* is largely controlled by the photograph of the Beagle. When a new array of photographs are presented that juxtapose the Beagle with a Great Dane, the child will likely continue to select the Beagle as the *big dog*. The concept of relative size has not been successfully taught.

The traditional EIBI method of teaching relative size is to train a multitude of examples of big vs. small stimuli and then hope for generalization to novel pairings of the same stimuli and to pairs of altogether novel stimuli. This can be a protracted and exhausting process for the child and really does not teach the comparative relation. It teaches the discrimination between individual stimuli rather than discriminating the relationship between stimuli.

An alternate more efficient approach might initially involve the teaching of *bigger than* and *smaller than* relations with a variety of stimuli. To extend our example with dogs noted above, we might present the child with an array of dogs of varying sizes. A comparison stimulus - a dog that is bigger than all but one dog in the array, is presented to the child as he is asked "Which dog is bigger than this one?" The mutually entailed relation of *smaller than* would likewise be trained on the very next trial using the same comparison stimulus and array. The instructional cue would simply be switched to "Which dogs are smaller than this one?" Novel combinations of stimuli could subsequently be presented randomly over time until the child is able to make accurate selections based on size without direct teaching. Once the relation has been solidly established, then the instructor could return to tasks that involve the selection of *the big dog* or *the small dog*. Although the authors are unaware of any applied research that has tested this process[1] a derivation between the two tasks would seem likely.

This alternate process involves training the *relation* of comparative size rather than teaching the rote assignment of the adjective *big* to a multitude of nouns. By not using the latter, traditional EIBI approach, the instructor can avoid falling into the trap that often results from the overly stringent stimulus control created when we try to teach relational attributes via standard discrimination procedures.

The final type of relational frame that we will discuss in regard to EIBI curricula is the *deictic frame*. Whereas the frame of comparison example was based on the formal properties of the stimuli (size), deictic frames are based on the relationship between the individual and other events (Hayes, 2001). Deictic frames specify a relation in terms of the speaker – relations such as right/left, I/you, here/there, and now/then. In conversation we might ask "What are *you* doing *now*?" or "What did *you* do *then*?" or perhaps "What were *you* doing over *there*?" With each of these questions, the formal, physical environment will likely be different. On the other hand, the relational properties of *I* vs. *you, here* vs. *there,* and *now* vs. *then* remain constant and thus remain the basis for the deictic relation (Hayes, 2001). Deictic framing is at the core of perspective-taking – a singularly difficult task for our more verbally adept individuals with ASD.

---

[1] A formal study to test this hypothesis is being developed by the first author.

The groundbreaking basic research into deictic framing was conducted in 2004 by McHugh, Barnes-Holmes, & Barnes-Holmes at the University of Ireland, Maynooth. What has been since termed the Barnes-Homes Protocol was developed within this initial study and will be discussed briefly here.

The Barnes-Holmes Protocol begins by teaching a child the basic I/you relation. The child is presented with two colored blocks and asked the following questions – "If I have a green block and you have a red block, which block do I have? Which block do you have?" A reversal of the deictic relation is then trained where the perspective of the speaker and the listener changes. The questions are then rephrased to "If *I* was *you*, and *you* were *me*, which block would *you* have? (green block) Which block would *I* have?" (red block)

Here/there and *now/then* relations can be trained in the same fashion – both with simple relations and with reversals. Examples of simple relations might be:

"I am sitting *here* on the black chair and you are sitting *there* on the blue chair. Where are you sitting? Where am I sitting?"

"Yesterday I watched TV, today I am reading. What am I doing *now*? What was I doing *then*?"

Examples of reversals of these same relations would be:

"I am sitting *here* in the black chair and you are sitting *there* in the blue chair. If *here* was *there* and *there* was *here*, where would you be sitting? (In the blue chair.) Where would I be sitting? (In the black chair.)"

"Yesterday I watched TV, today I am reading. If *now* was *then* and *then* was *now*, what would I be doing *now*? (Watching TV.) What would I be doing *then*? (Reading.)"

The protocol goes a step further and trains the child on double-reversals where two relations are reversed. An example of a double reversal between I/you and here/there might be:

"*I* am sitting *here* on the black chair and *you* are sitting *there* on the blue chair. If *I* was *you* and *you* were *me*, and *here* was *there* and *there* was *here*, where would you be sitting? (In the blue chair.) Where would I be sitting? (In the black chair.)"

As can be seen from these deictic framing exercises, the child is required to perform some rather complicated perspective-taking "gymnastics" - shifting her viewpoint back and forth between herself and the other person. There has been some preliminary applied research that has shown that engagement in deictic frame training can improve generalized perspective-taking skills in the ASD population. A study by Weil & Hayes (2007) involved pre and post-testing with standard Theory of Mind (ToM) evaluations that specifically measure perspective-taking abilities. Following exposure to deictic frame exercises, the subjects in the study performed significantly better on the ToM testing than those in the control group who did not partake in the deictic frame training. These results would suggest that engagement in this ostensibly non-functional wordplay might have far-reaching positive effects on how our children interact with their peers.

Application of deictic frames to more complex, psychological functions can also be explored. Presenting I/you frames that are imbued with emotional or other psychological functions can be an effective means of training our children to become more attuned to the thoughts, feelings, and motives of others. An example of a deictic frame exercise with emotional variables might be:

"I am at home eating ice cream and you are on the playground being teased by some other kids. If I were you and you were me, how would you feel? How would I feel?"

Again, these exercises encourage the child with ASD or other developmental disabilities to see the world through the eyes of another - a skill which, particularly with autism, does not come easy. The potential for the application of deictic framing to these more advanced social/language issues appears to be great. Further applied research in this area is needed if we are to move the teaching technology forward.

SUMMARY

The excellent work that has been completed to date by behavior analysts, parents, teachers, and therapists working in effective EIBI programs speaks for itself. Children previously viewed as un-teachable have been taught to speak, to play, to socialize with their friends, and to become more independent with the basic life skills of dressing, feeding, and toileting. The role of Applied Behavior Analysis in this journey has been central. Its scientific and data-based approach has proven time and again to be the most effective means of treating children with ASD and other developmental disabilities. The addition of Skinner's analysis of verbal behavior to the general science of human behavior has further enhanced the effectiveness of EIBI programs in teaching these children to functionally communicate.

With the advent of RFT, new avenues to these same objectives are opening that may allow for more complete and natural language outcomes for our children. The derived manding study is just one example of new research initiatives that are bridging the basic and applied fields to provide tested methodologies for establishing derived relational responding as a skill among our children diagnosed with ASD and other developmental disabilities. Improving our children's ability to discriminate relationships between people, events, thoughts, and feelings rather than limiting their learning to the discrimination of a finite number of stimuli that must be directly taught can only serve to enhance existing EIBI curricula. Having such a goal – establishing a flexible, fluent, and natural language repertoire for our children, is nothing new. We all want our children to develop the skills to, as Steven Hayes so succinctly puts it - "speak with meaning and listen with understanding." The path to that goal has now been made clearer.

REFERENCES

American Psychiatric Association. (1994). *Diagnostic and statistical manual of mental disorders* (4th ed.). Washington, DC: Author.

Barnes-Holmes, D., Barnes-Holmes, Y., & Cullinan, V. (2000). Relational frame theory and Skinner's *Verbal Behavior*: A possible synthesis. *The Behavior Analyst, 23,* 69-84.

Blackledge, T. (2003). An introduction to relational frame theory: basics and applications. *The Behavior Analyst Today, 3,* 421-433.

Green, G. (1996). Early Behavioral Intervention for Autism: What Does the Research Tell Us? In C. Maurice, G. Green, & S.C. Luce (eds.). *Behavioral Intervention for Young Children with Autism.* Austin, TX: Pro-Ed.

Gulick, R.F. & Kitchen, T.P. (2007). *Effective instruction for children with autism.* Erie, PA: The Gertrude A. Barber National Institute.

Hayes, S. C., Barnes-Holmes, D., & Roche, B. (2001). *Relational Frame Theory: A Post-Skinnerian Account of Human Language and Cognition.* New York: Plenum.

Lovaas, O. I. (1987). Behavioral treatment and normal educational and intellectual functioning in young children with autism. *Journal of Consulting and Clinical Psychology, 55,* 3-9.

Maurice, C. (1993). *Let Me Hear Your Voice: A Family's Triumph Over Autism.* NY: Fawcett Columbine.

McHugh, L., Barnes-Holmes, Y., & Barnes-Holmes, D. (2004). Perspective-taking as relational responding: A developmental profile. *The Psychological Record, 54,* 115-144.

Murphy, C., Barnes-Holmes, D., Barnes-Holmes, Y. (2005). Derived manding in children with autism: synthesizing Skinner's verbal behavior with relational frame theory. *Journal of Applied Behavior Analysis, 38,* 445-462.

Partington, J.W., & Sundberg, M.L., (1998). *The Assessment of Basic Language and Learning Skills: Scoring Instructions and IEP Development Guide.* Pleasant Hill, CA: Behavior Analysts, Inc.

Rehfeldt, R.A., Root, S.L. (2005). Establishing derived requesting skills in adults with severe developmental disabilities. *Journal of Applied Behavior Analysis, 38,*101-105.

Rosales, R., Rehfeldt, R.A. (2007). Contriving transitive conditioned establishing operations to establish derived manding skills in adults with severe developmental disabilities. *Journal of Applied Behavior Analysis, 40,* 105-121.

Sidman, M. (1971). Reading and auditory – visual equivalences. *Journal of Speech and Hearing Research, 14,* 5-13.

Skinner, B.F. (1957). *Verbal Behavior.* Englewood Cliffs, NJ: Prentice Hall.

Smeets, P. M., & Striefel, S. (1994). A revised block-trial procedure for establishing arbitrary matching in children. *Quarterly Journal of Experimental Psychology, 47,* 241-261.

Sundberg, M.L., & Partington, J.W. (1998). *Teaching Language to Children with Autism or Other Developmental Disabilities.* Pleasant Hill, CA: Behavior Analysts, Inc.

Sundberg, M. L., & Michael, J. (2001). The benefits of Skinner's analysis of verbal behavior for children autism. *Behavior Modification, 5,* 698-724.

Weil, T. & Hayes, S.C., (2007). *The Impact of Training Deictic Frames on Perspective Taking in Young Children: A Relational Frame Approach to Theory of Mind.* Paper presented at The 33rd Annual Convention - Association for Behavior Analysis International. San Diego, CA.

Reviewed by Tom Kitchen, M.S., and BCBA. Mercyhurst College, Erie PA, 6-26-08.

In: Multimedia in Education and Special Education
Editors: O. Demir and C. Celik

ISBN 978-1-60741-073-7
© 2009 Nova Science Publishers, Inc.

Chapter 5

THE USE OF A RACETRACKS PROCEDURES TO IMPROVE THE ACADEMIC BEHAVIORS OF STUDENTS IN SPECIAL AND REMEDIAL EDUCATION: SUGGESTIONS FOR SCHOOL PERSONNEL

T. F. McLaughlin[*]*, Kimberly P. Weber, K. Mark Derby,*
Carrie Hyde, Amy Violette, Christina Barton, Brigetta Petersen,
Cassie Green, Shelby Verduin, Kathleen Printz,
Ramona Gonzales, and Maighain Arkoosh
Department of Special Education, Gonzaga University, WA USA

ABSTRACT

The history and development of racetrack procedures in special education were outlined. The outcomes of employing a game like procedure called racetracks were reviewed and discussed. The basic tenants of racetrack procedures were presented. The various formats of racetracks were provided. Data for various action research projects completed at Gonzaga University were presented. The use of these procedures has been effective in both resource and self-contained classroom settings. In addition, racetracks were found to be effective with a wide range of student populations ranging from those at-risk for school failure to students with autism. Racetracks have been effective in reading (reading racetracks), math (math racetracks, and spelling (spelling racetracks). Directions for future research and possible uses of racetrack procedures were made.

[*] Requests for reprints should be send to: T. F. McLaughlin, Department of Special Education, School of Education, Gonzaga University, Spokane, WA 99258-0025 or via email at mclaughlin@gonzaga.edu

Educators as well as policy makers have become very concerned about teaching students with and without disabilities academic skills (Heward, 2005; National Institute of Child Health and Human Development, 2000; National Reading Panel, 2002; Osborne, 1994). Students who have low academic skills are more likely to drop out of school (Chambers, Dunn, & Rabren, 2004; Lloyd, 1978, have difficulty with the law (Gersten & Keating, 1987; Howard, McLaughlin & Vacha, 1996), and experience chronic unemployment or underemployment (Livingstone, 1998; Rivera-Batiz, 1992).

With the recent advent to evidence-based procedures, a wide range of teacher implemented interventions are now available to those who work with children with and without disabilities (Alberto & Troutman, 2008; Heward, 2005). Several research studies (Greenwood, 1998; Marchand-Martella, Slocum, & Martella, 2004; Slavin et al., 1994) have found that providing students with excellent instruction in the basic skills has social as well as economic benefits. A common set of characteristics employed in many of these studies include (a) teaching appropriate pre skills (Greenwood, 1996; Marchand et al., 2004; Johnson, Luiten, Derby, McLaughlin, Weber, & Johnson, 2002) (b) frequent evaluation of student performance (Marchand-Martella et al., 2004; Rinaldi, Sells & McLaughlin 1996; Slavin, 1996; Slavin, Karweit, & Wasik, 1994); (c) error correction procedures (Greenwood et al., 1998; Marchand-Martella et al., 2004; (d) use of students or other school personnel to provide additional instruction or review (Greenwood, 1996, 1996, Greenwood, Delquadri, & Carta, 1988; Slavin, 1996; Slavin, Madden, Dolan, & Wasik, 1996; Wasik & Slavin, 1993); (e) additional time in instruction (Greenwood et al., 1998; Kameenui, 1993; 1998; Slavin, 1996; Slavin, R. E., et al., 1996).); (f) use of well planned lessons or clear concise teaching procedures (Marchand-Martella et al., 2004; Greenwood et al., 1998; Slavin, Madden, Dolan, Wasik, Ross, S. & Smith, 1994; Slavin et al., 1996); and (g) increased the opportunity for students to respond in the curricula (Heward, 1994; Greenwood, 1996; Greenwood, Hart, Walker & Risley, 1994; Kameenui, 1998; Rinaldi et al., 1996; McLaughlin & Skinner, 1996; Skinner, McLaughlin, & Logan, 1997; Slavin, 1996; Slavin et al., 1994, 1996). Racetrack procedures contain many of these evidence-based instructional components.

A BRIEF HISTORY OF RACETRACK PROCEDURES

In 1994, a graduate student (Carol Hern) in the department of special education at Gonzaga University and a special education teacher in the local school district, developed the idea of employing racetracks with her students. She felt the racetrack could provide daily feedback to students and motive them to improve their performance. At that time she was a resource room teacher providing in class as well as pullout services to students with mild disabilities (C. Hern, personal communication). The first data-based evaluation of these procedures appeared 1996 and 1997 with the publication of articles in the peer reviewed literature in the *Journal of Precision Teaching* and the *Journal of Behavioral Education*. Since that time, we have expanded the use of racetrack procedures to include a more diverse population students and in different curricular areas such as math and spelling. Replications of racetrack procedures have appeared in *the International Journal of Special Education*, the *Open Rehabilitation Journal*, and the *Journal of Precision Teaching and Celeration*. Finally, undergraduate and graduate students have presented research dealing with racetracks at both regional and international conferences.

GENERAL CHARACTERISTICS AND COMPONENTS OF RACETRACK PROCEDURES

The various racetracks that have been developed typically contain 28 boxes or cells drawn in a racetrack format (see examples). These cells may contain sight words (Rinaldi & McLaughlin, 1996; Rinaldi et al. 1997), district word lists (Falk, Band, & McLaughlin, 2000), basic math facts (Beveridge, Weber, McLaughlin, & Derby 2002), or spelling words (Arkoosh, Weber, & McLaughlin, 2008; Verduin, McLaughlin, Derby, & Dhillon, 2008). Each track typically contains a picture of a car (we have usually employed Ford Mustangs) where the teacher or instructional assistant can place which word list, problem or word set that the student is working. The student practices these materials and is typically timed on the words, problems, etc. using the track itself. We have employed the tracks themselves as well as flashcards to enhance student practice. The students plot their performance on either standard celeration charts (Lindsley, 1994; Caletti et al., 2008; Green et al., 2008) or on traditional graph paper (Anthony, Rinaldi, Hern, & McLaughlin, 1997; Beveridge et al., 2005; Falk et al., 2003; Printz, Band, & McLaughlin, 2006; Rinaldi et al., 1997).

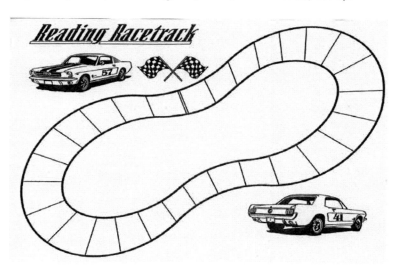

We have also had our undergraduate and graduate students design some very interesting racetracks depending on the subject matter areas taught or covered or the special interests of the student. A few examples of unique tracks follow.

Insect Racetrack Format for Teaching Letter Names.

Dinosaur Racetrack Format for Teaching Letter Names.

Two Ocean Themed Racetracks for Teaching Letter Names and Sounds.

It appears that a wide variety of items can be employed as part of a racetrack procedure. It has been our experience that school personnel can develop some very interesting and unique racetracks out of a wide range of materials (cloth to Velcro). We have also employed a wide range of items to provide student feedback or progress on a particular racetrack.

Reading Racetracks

Reading fluency is gaining new recognition as an essential element of every reading program, especially for students who struggle in reading (Hudson, Lane, & Pullen, 2005.) Quick and effortless word identification in a fluent reader is important because when one can read words automatically, one's limited cognitive resources can be used for comprehension (NICHD, 2000). For example, in 2000, the National Reading Panel stated," Fluency is one of the critical factors necessary for reading comprehension, and is often a component neglected in classrooms today."

Reading racetracks (Rinaldi & McLaughlin, 1996) are an instructional and review strategy that focuses on improving fluency. Studies with reading racetracks have shown to be effective with students who have various ability levels (Rinaldi et al., 1997.) Reading racetracks have been shown effective when being paired with flashcards to improve sight word recognition (Anthony, Hern, Rinaldi, & McLaughlin, 1997; Falk, et al., 2002; Printz et al., 2004).

We have placed various items (sight words, irregular words, high use words, error words, etc.) on reading racetracks. We also require a review track. A review track is used after four different tracks have been completed by the student. For sight words, materials, the criteria to change tracks, as well as which type of data to collect, the forms to use to record data, and finally, how to display or graph student performance follow.

Materials

A wide variety of reading materials can be placed on a reading racetrack. These can include. but or not limited to, lists of Dolch sight words, words from passages of a basal readers, sight word lists, vocabulary lists, etc. The teacher will need a timing device (stopwatch, kitchen timer, etc.), scratch paper, red and blue ink pens or pencils, and a data collection sheet (Rinaldi et al., 1997; Peterson et al., 2008). A sample data collection sheet follows.

Student Name: _Brooklyn_____

Primary Observer: _____

Date	Session	B/I	Correct	Incorrect	% Correct	Reliability
Pretest	Pretest	Pretest	28	28	50	100
March 2	1	B	6	6	50	100
March 3	2	B	6	6	50	100
March 4	3	B	12	0	100	100
March 5	Weekend					
March 6	Weekend					
March 7	4	Racetrack				
March 8	5	I	7	5	58	100
March 9	6	I	12	0	100	100
March 10	No Data					
March 11	7	I	12	0	100	100
March 12	Weekend					
March 13	Weekend					
March 14	8	Racetrack				
March 15	9	I	8	0	100	100
March 16	10	I	8	0	100	100
March 17	11	I	8	0	100	100
March 18	12	I	8	0	100	100
March 19	Weekend					
March 20	Weekend					
March 21	13	Give List				
March 22	14	B	11	1	92	100
March 23	No Data					
March 24	15	B	11	1	92	100
March 25	16	B	11	1	92	100
March 26	Weekend					
March 27	Weekend					

Words put and read from the racetracks can be taken from the lists of Dolch Sight Words. We like to employ words in sets of four. The fifth set should be a review set. The words placed on a reading racetrack should be carefully selected to avoid having any two words on a particular racetrack that were either auditorily or visually similar (Rinaldi et al., 1997).

For reading there are two different types of racetracks, each containing 28 cells. The first type of racetrack consists of seven target words that are repeated in random order. The random order is used to avoid the occurrence of patterns which may interfere with the students learning the words instead of focusing on and learning the pattern in which the sight words appear Every fifth racetrack is a review racetrack. This track contains the accumulation of the 28 different error words that were introduced in the four previous racetracks.

What to Score and Measure on Reading Racetracks

Two measures should be taken. The first is the number of words read correctly from the reading racetrack during a 1-min timing. The second is the number of errors noted in the same 1-min timed reading. An error is typically defined as a word being pronounced incorrectly, an omission or addition of the word, or reading any words out of order. An error is scored if the student self corrects before going on to the next word. Fluency measures have been shown to be quire accurate in assessing student performance or depicting changes in academic output (Johnson & Layng, 1994, 1996). At other times, we have converted student scores to a percent correct. However, correct and error rate are a superior measure (Lindsley, 1994).

Criteria for Changing Reading Racetracks

Students are required to remain on a given racetrack until they had reached the criterion of 90 words read correctly per minute with zero errors, or until they had completed five sessions on that particular racetrack. We have also employed other performance standards when something other than sight words are being taught. Students may change to a new track they have perfect performance with no errors on three consecutive data days.

General Procedures for Using Reading Racetracks

At the beginning of each reading session, the student is given the particular racetrack that he or she is working. The student is then instructed to inform the teacher or instructional assistant when he or she was ready to begin. This is followed by the teacher or instructional assistant giving the cue, "On your mark, get set, go!" The teacher keeps track of the number of words read by placing a mark each time the participant completed a full circle around the track. At the end of the 1-min timing, the teacher must say, "Stop!" The participant and the researcher then place a mark the word that was just read. Upon completion of each 1-min timing, the student and teacher count the number of words that he or she read and self-record the data. The teacher tallies the number of errors, give this number along with specific feedback to the participant, who would then records these data below the number correct. These data are then collected and placed on a data sheet by the teacher and or student. A sample data collection sheets appear next.

Error Correction with Reading Racetracks

At this point, the teacher or aide must use the "model, lead, test and retest" Direct Instruction procedure (Marchand Martella et al., 2004) to teach or review the words that were missed by the participant. This procedure consists of first modeling the correct pronunciation of the word, then saying the word with the participant, the participant would reads the word independently, and finally, the participant is required to reread the word correctly several more times. This procedure should take only about one minute, depending on the number of errors. We have found this procedure effective and it can be even more effective if flashcards are employed for additional drill on errors (Alexander et al., 2008; Falk et al., 2004; Green et al., 2008; Petersen et al., 2008; Printz et al., 2006).

Some data dealing with reading racetracks follows. These data were taken across a wide range of students and disability designations.

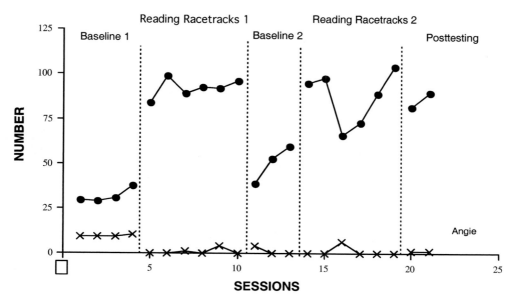

Filled circles are corrects and x's represent errors for our participant Angie.

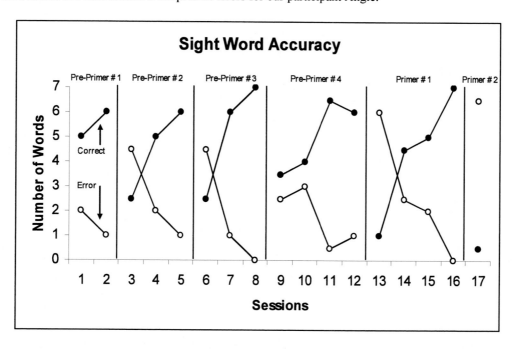

Sight word vocabulary for a student with autism using reading racetracks.

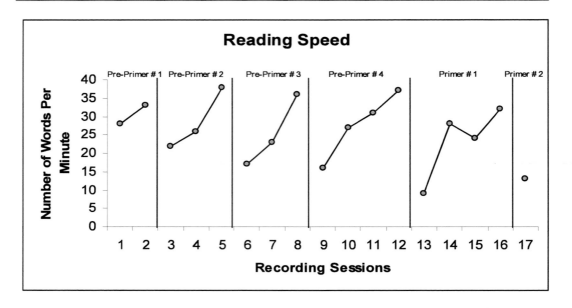

The number of correct words per minute with reading racetracks for pre-primer and primer word lists for a student with autism.

Math Racetracks

Math racetracks employ many of the same characteristics and components of racetracks. The only change that is required is the type of curricular materials. These have been basic math facts. These math facts can be written in either a vertical or horizontal format. Beveridge et al., (2005) published the first peer-reviewed article with math racetracks. Each math track employs from 4 to 7 problems that her students had missed during baseline. The remainder of the math racetrack consisted of problems her students did not miss. Each participant had three different racetracks. Each contained 21 problems they knew and seven different problems they did not know in baseline. The problems were arranged in an order that presented two to four problems they already had mastered with one they had not This interspersing technique (Cates, Skinner, Watson, Meadows, Weaver, & Jackson, 2003) is very similar to what we have done with sight word vocabulary reading racetracks (Falk et al., 2003; Printz et al., 2005; Rinaldi et al., 1997).

During the racetrack phase, the participants were timed while completing the racetrack, a maximum of five seconds was given to the participants to complete each problem. If a problem was answered incorrectly, or the participant was unable to answer in the five-second allotment, then the correct answer was provided by the teacher. After the racetrack was completed, the participant reviewed their answers to all problems. This specific racetrack was required until the participant showed an increase in the number of problems they answered correctly. In the Beveridge study a token economy (McLaughlin, & Williams, 1988) was also put in effect. Each student was shown the record sheet used to keep track of their points, and adding their points at the end of each session. Each of the students were required to say rather than write they answers to the problems found on the tracks. Interspersing incorrect with correct problems have been shown to improve student outcomes (Cates et al. 2005; McLaughlin & Skinner, 1996; Skinner et al., 1997).

Beveridge et al. (2005) found an increase corrects with the use of math racetracks. Likewise, a decrease in errors was also found for each of their participants. Each of the students found the procedures very enjoyable and repeatedly asked for additional work.

The differences between this research to that reported using reading racetracks are several. First, no criteria for changing tracks was employed other than each student had to show improvement was required. Second, the students were allowed more than one-minute for their timings. Third, no review tracks were employed due to high stakes testing that took place in the spring. Finally, a token reinforcement program was also employed with the math racetrack procedures. The role of each should be examined in future research.

Spelling Racetracks

We have just begun to gather data on the efficacy of employing spelling racetracks. Our first pilot research indicated that the use of spelling racetracks improved the inclass performance of three intermediate grade school special education students with mild disabilities. What follows is a brief description of those procedures and outcomes.

We have used a wide variety of spelling materials. These have ranged from school district grade-level core word lists to the words found in more basal spelling texts. Spelling racetracks for each grade-level core word list have been constructed. In addition such materials as a timer, pencils, and notebook paper for taking the spelling tests have been employed.

Our spelling racetracks were created based upon the grade-level core word lists. The tracks were designed to resemble an automotive reading racetrack. (Rinaldi et al., 1997). These words were taken at random form the various grade level core lists. We examined these words carefully to prevent placing words that were visually or auditorily similar on the same racetrack. This is something that is also required for reading racetracks. The students were tested in baseline with three sets of words. To obtain a baseline measurement, we assessed the three participants on 25 words from three different grade level core word lists (kindergarten, first grade, and second grade). The words were selected at random from each of these lists. Since there were only 12 words on the kindergarten core word list, all 12 were used. The students were told the word and then given the word orally in a sentence. They then had to write the word on a numbered piece of paper. This baseline testing lasted for one to two school days.

Our participants were introduced to spelling racetracks by their student teacher. Each racetrack contained 15 cells, each employing 15 error words. The racetracks were then copied on the front and backside of a piece of paper. They were leveled using the grade level core word lists. Because two core word lists had more than 15 words, these grade levels had multiple racetracks (1st – A, 1st – B, etc.). Each cell contained the error word, and a space below it to copy the word.

Initially, the students were given one minute to make their way around the track. As they were going around the track, the participants were required to say the word aloud, then spell the word aloud, and then write the word in the given space. For example, if the first word was 'mom,' the student would say the word "mom," and then spell the word aloud, "m-o-m," and then they would write the word in the given space.

After this practice procedure, the students were paired with another student for a partner practice. During partner practice, one participant would go around the track saying the word aloud and spelling the word aloud. The partner followed along to make sure the other student was saying and spelling the word correctly. Once the track was completed, the other partner would follow the same procedure.

After completing the partner practice, the participants turned the papers over and prepared for a second one-minute timing. The students followed the same procedure as they did for the first timing (say the word aloud, spell the word aloud, write the word). This second timing was scored and used for data collection.

If the students completed the track before the one-minute timing had stopped, they were instructed to continue going around the track as many times as possible. Data were taken daily on the number of words accurately completed during the second one-minute timing.

The participants were required to obtain at least an 80% on the end of the week spelling test in order to move to the next racetrack. If the participants did not meet the 80% requirement, they continued on the same track during the next week. The participants were automatically moved to the next track after three week regardless of their performance.

When the classroom staff observed that the weekly spelling test scores were declining for all three children, the spelling racetrack procedures were altered. First a motivational system was added. The students created sticker charts, and based on daily performance (effort, handwriting, and correctly following the procedure), the participants were allowed to place a sticker on their individual charts. Effort was determined by the student teacher. When the students earned a minimum of 12 stickers each, a party was given for the whole classroom. In addition, two of the students were given an additional 30 seconds to complete their daily racetrack, thus increasing the timings to one minute and thirty seconds. Student outcome data indicated these were positive changes to the spelling racetracks procedure. Increases in percent correct ranged from 20 to 25% with the modified spelling racetracks procedure. Also, the number of words spelled correctly during the timings increased over time. These findings were replicated with all three students.

Spelling racetracks, aside from being effective, were easy to implement. Little or no costs were incurred by the teacher or school. The process took the first five minutes of class to complete each day. The grading of the racetracks and weekly tests was minimal. We also felt spelling racetracks could be implemented effectively with a large group of students, with similar or different skills in spelling. The development of the materials was initially somewhat time intensive. However, the spelling racetracks were shown to be an effective and efficient way to teach spelling. Another benefit for using spelling racetracks in the classroom was that the participants truly enjoyed doing them every day.

There are some considerations to remember when using spelling racetracks as an intervention procedure in spelling. First, a review, at least monthly, should be completed to ensure that retention is occurring over the words that are being taught. The tracks themselves do not necessarily promote retention, as systematic review was not built-in as part of this pilot research. An additional procedure would be to employ review tracks as we have done in reading and math (Beveridge et al., 2005; Rinaldi et al., 1997) or something that many spelling curricula contain (McLaughlin, 1991).

The use of spelling racetracks were found to be effective with a small sample of students enrolled in a resource room setting. I would suggest that additional studies be carried out to determine what role a racetrack procedure could be in spelling.

Recently, we just completed a controlled case study with a general education student enrolled in the fourth grade. We employed a spelling racetrack procedure using the spelling words from in the general education curriculum. We also employed an interspersal procedure (e. g. where know and unknown words were placed on the track). Using an ABAB single case design (Kazdin, 1980) we found a significant difference between baseline and the spelling racetrack conditions. As in the resource room study in spelling, this participant enjoyed the procedure and his outcomes.

FUTURE DIRECTIONS FOR RACETRACK PROCEDURES AND RECOMMENDATIONS FOR SCHOOL PERSONNEL

From the available evidence, racetrack procedures appear to be effective three skill areas (reading, arithmetic, and spelling). Additional replications could take place in language arts where a discrete response is required. For example, a student could learn the various article adjectives, proper nouns, or other parts of speech. Another area of interest would be to employ racetracks at the middle and high school levels. Such subject matter areas as chemistry or history appear appropriate this type of format. Racetracks could be designed for important dates or specific individuals during the revolutionary war. In chemistry, the symbols found on the periodic table could be taught. Also, certain compounds such a water or rust could be presented. Vocabulary in Spanish or French appears to have some applicability for this type of racetrack format.

Different researchers need to present or publish research dealing with racetrack procedures. At this writing, all the research dealing with reading, spelling, or math racetracks has been published by a single group of researchers. Have other independent researchers publish in the area would add greatly to the validity (Kazdin, 1982; Sidman, 1960) of these procedures.

Another important issue would be to begin to see these procedures implemented in general education settings. We have only one case report where spelling racetracks were implemented in general education. I would add a great deal to the applicability of racetracks if they could be employed by a single teacher in a general education setting. This is something we have examined using single case designs and behavioral measurement procedures (McLaughlin, 1993). Such an extension should add a great deal to the acceptance of such a procedure in both general or special education personnel. Such academic interventions such as the various formats of peer tutoring as well as copy, cover, and compare, have had such replications in the literature.

ACKNOWLEDGEMENTS

A special note of thanks to all our former and current students and their classroom master teachers. These professionals have carried out and continue to complete action research to assess student outcomes, but also to provide evidence as to the efficacy of these racetrack procedures.

REFERENCES

Alberto, P., & Troutman, A. (2008). *Applied behavior analysis for teachers* (8th ed.). Upper Saddle River, NJ: Prentice-Hall/Pearson.

Alexander, C., McLaughlin, T. F., K. M. Derby, & Cartmell, H. (2008). The effects of reading racetracks on sight words across four elementary students with differing disabilities. *The Open Rehabilitation Journal, 1,* 47-52

Anthony, C., Rinaldi, L., Hern, C., & McLaughlin, T. F. (1997). Reading racetracks: A direct replication and analysis with three elementary students. *Journal of Precision Teaching and Celeration, 14*(2), 31-36.

Arkoosh, M., Weber, K. P., & McLaughlin, T. F. (2007). *The effects of a motivational/reward system and a spelling racetrack on spelling performance in general education: A case report.* Manuscript submitted for publication.

Beveridge, B., Weber, K. P., Derby, K. M., & McLaughlin, T. F. (2005). The effects of a math racetrack with two elementary students with learning disabilities. *International Journal of Special Education, 20*(2), 58-65.

Cates, G. L., Skinner, C. H., Watson, T. S., Meadows, T. J., Weaver, A., & Jackson, B. (2003). Instructional effectiveness and instructional efficiency as considerations for data-based decision making: An evaluation of interspersing procedures. *School* Psychology Review, 32, 601–616.

Chambers, D., Dunn, C., & Rabren, K. (2004). Variables affecting students' decisions to drop out of school. *Remedial & Special Education.25,* 314-325.

Cooper, J. O., Heron, T. E., & Heward, W. L. (2007). *Applied behavior analysis* (2nd ed.). Upper Saddle River, NJ: Pearson Prentice Hall.

Falk, M., Band, M., & McLaughlin, T. F. (2003). The effects of reading racetracks and flashcards on sight word vocabulary of three third grade students with a specific learning disability: a further replication and analysis. *International Journal of Special Education.* 18(2). 57-61

Gersten R., & Keating, T. (1987). Long term benefits from direct instruction. *Educational Leadership, 44*(6), 28-31.

Green, C., McLaughlin, T. F., Derby, K. M., & Lee, K. (2008, April). *The effects of reading racetracks and flashcards on the teaching of sight words to two sixth grade students with moderate disabilities.* Paper presented at the Intercollegiate Research Conference, Spokane, WA.

Greenwood, C. R. (1996). Research on the practices and behaviors of effective teachers the Juniper Gardens Children's Project: Implications for education of diverse learners. In D. L. Speece & B. K. Keogh (Eds.), *Research on classroom ecologies: Implications for inclusion of children with learning disabilities* (pp. 39-67). Hillsdale, NJ: Lawrence Erlbaum and Associates Publishers.

Greenwood, C. R., Delquadri, J. C. Carta, J. J. (1988). *Classwide peer tutoring (CWPT)*. Seattle, WA: Educational Achievement Systems.

Greenwood, C. A., Hart, B., Walker, D., & Risley, T. R. (1994). The opportunity to respond and academic performance revisited: A behavioral theory of developmental retardation and its prevention. In R. Gardner III, D. M. Sainato, J. O. Cooper, T.E. Heron, W.L. Heward, J. W. Eshelman, & T. A. Grassi (Eds.), *Behavior analysis in education: Focus on measurably superior instruction* (pp. 213-223). Pacific Grove, CA: Brooks/Cole.

Heward, W. L. (1994). Three "low-tech" strategies for increasing the frequency of active student response during group instruction. In R. Gardner III, D. M. Sainato, J. O. Cooper, T. E. Heron, W. L. Heward, J. Eshleman, & T. A. Grossi (Eds.), Behavior analysis in education: Focus on measurably superior instruction (pp. 283-320). Monterey, CA: Brooks/Cole.

Heward, W. L. (2005). Reasons applied behavior analysis is good for education and why those reasons have been insufficient. In W. L. Heward, T. E. Heron, N. A. Neef, S. M. Peterson, D. M. Sainato, G. Cartledge, R. Gardner III, L. D. Peterson, S. B. Hersh, & J. C. Dardig (Eds.), *Focus on behavior analysis in education: Achievements, challenges, and opportunities* (pp. 316-348). Upper Saddle River, NJ: Merrill/Prentice Hall.

Howard, V. F., McLaughlin, T. F., & Vacha, E. F. (1996). Educational capital: A proposed model and its relationship to academic and social behavior of children at risk. *Journal of Behavioral Education, 6,* 135-152.

Hudson, R., Lane, H., & Pullen, P. (2005). Reading fluency assessment and instruction: What, why, and how? *The Reading Teacher, 58,* 702-714.

Johnson, K. R., & Layng, T. V. J. (1994). The Morning Side Model of generative instruction. In R. Gardner III, D. M. Sainato, J. O. Cooper, T. E. Heron, W. L. Heward, J. W. Eshelman, & T. A. Grossi (Eds*.). Behavior analysis in education: Focus on measurably superior instruction* (pp. 173-197). Pacific Grove, CA: Brooks/Cole.

Johnson, K. R., & Layng, T. V. J. (1996). Fluency. *The Behavior Analyst, 19,* 281-288.

Johnson, J. J., Luiten, L. M., K. M Derby, T. F. McLaughlin, K. P. Weber, & Johnson, M. (2001). Evaluating the effectiveness of Teach Your Child to Read in 100 Easy Lessons using graded word lists. *Proven Practice: Prevention and Remediation Solutions for Schools, 3,* 68-74.

Kameenui, E. J. (1993). Diverse learners and the tyranny of time: Don't fix blame; fix the leaky roof. *The Reading Teacher, 46,* 376-383.

Kameenui, E. J. (1998). The rhetoric of all, the reality of some, and the unmistakable smell of mortality. In J. Osborn & F. Lehr (Eds.), *Literacy for all* (pp. 319-338). New York: Guilford.

Kazdin, A. E. (1982). *Single case research designs: Methods for clinical and applies settings.* New York: Oxford University Press.

Lindsley, O. R. (1991). Precision teaching's unique legacy from B. F. Skinner. *Journal of Behavioral Education, 1,* 253-266.

Livingstone, D. W. (1998). *The education-jobs gap: Underemployment or economic democracy.* Boulder, Co: Westview.

Lloyd, D. N. (1978). Prediction of school failure from third grade data. *Educational and Psychological Measurement, 38,* 1193-1200.

Marchand-Martella, N. E., Slocum, T. A., & R. C. Martella, R. (2004) (Eds.), *Introduction to Direct Instruction*. Boston, MA: Pearson Education, Inc.

McLaughlin, T. F. (1991). Use of personalized system of instruction with a without a same-day retake contingency on spelling performance of behaviorally disordered children. *Behavioral Disorders, 16*, 127-132.

McLaughlin, T. F. (1993). An analysis and evaluation of educator selected data collection procedures in actual school settings: A brief report. *Child & Family Behavior Therapy, 15*(2), 61-64.

McLaughlin, T. F., & Skinner, C. H. (1996). Improving academic performance through self-management: Cover, copy, and compare. *Intervention in School and Clinic, 32*, 113-118.

McLaughlin, T. F., & Williams, R. L. (1988). The token economy in the classroom. In J. C. Witt, S. N. Elliott, & F. M. Gresham (Eds.). *Handbook of behavior therapy in education* (pp. 469-487). New York: Plenum.

National Institute of Child Health and Human Development. (2000). Teaching children to read: An evidence-based assessment of the scientific research literature on reading and its implications for reading instruction. *Report of the National Reading Panel.*

National Reading Panel. (2000). Teaching children to read: An evidence-based assessment of the scientific research literature on reading and its implications for reading instruction. Available on-line: http://www.nichd.nih.gov/publications/ nrp.findings.cfm

Petersen, B., McLaughlin, T. F., Derby, K. P., & Higgins, S. (2008, April). *The effects of reading racetracks on the acquisition and fluency of sight word recognition for a student diagnosed with autism*. Paper presented at the Student Intercollegiate Research Conference, Spokane, WA.

Printz, K., McLaughlin, T. F., & Band, M. (2006). The effects of reading racetracks and flashcards on sight word vocabulary: A case report and replication. *International Journal of Special Education, 21*(1), 103-108.

Rinaldi, L., & McLaughlin, T. F. (1996). The effects of reading racetracks on the fluency of see-to-say words in isolation by a student with learning disabilities. *Journal of Precision Teaching and Celeration, 13*(2), 44-52.

Rinaldi, L., Sells, D., & McLaughlin T. F. (1997). The effects of reading racetracks on sight word acquisition of elementary students. *Journal of Behavioral Education*, 7(2), 219-234.

Rivera-Batiz, F. L. (1992). Quantitative literacy and the likelihood of employment among young adults in the United States. *Journal of Human Resources, 27*, 313-328.

Sidman, M. (1960). Tactics of scientific research. New York: Basic Books.

Skinner, C. H., McLaughlin, T. F., & Logan, P. (1997). Cover, copy, and compare: A self-managed academic intervention across skills, students, and settings. *Journal of Behavioral Education, 7*, 295-306.

Slavin, R. E. (1996). *Education for all: Contexts for learning styles*. London: Taylor & Francis.

Slavin, R. E., Karweit, N. L., & Madden, N. A. (1989). *Effective programs for students at risk*. Boston: Allyn & Bacon.

Slavin, R. E., Karweit, L., & Wasik, B.A. (1994). *Preventing early school failure: Research on effective strategies,* Boston: Allyn & Bacon.

Slavin, R. E., Madden, N. A., Dolan, L. J., & Wasik, B. A. (1996). *Every child, every school: Success for all*. Thousand Oaks, CA: Corwin Press.

Slavin, R. E., Madden, N. A., Dolan, L. J., Wasik, B. A., Ross, S. M., & Smith, L. J. (1994). Whenever and where ever we choose: Replication of success for all. *Phi Delta Kappa, 75,* 639-647.

Verduin, S., McLaughlin, T. F., Derby, K. M., & Dhillon, A. (2008). *The effects of spelling racetracks on the spelling of grade level core words with fourth-grade students with disabilities.* Manuscript in preparation.

Wasik, B., & Slavin, R. E. (1993). Preventing early reading failure with one-to-one tutoring: A review of five programs. *Reading Research Quarterly, 28,* 178-200.

In: Multimedia in Education and Special Education
Editors: O. Demir and C. Celik

Chapter 6

ANALYSIS OF SOCIAL STORIES INTERVENTIONS TO TEACH SOCIAL SKILLS TO STUDENTS WITH ASD

Sir Balázs Tarnai[1,], Pamela S. Wolfe[2], Frank R. Rusch[2], David L. Lee[2]*

[1]Seton Hill University, Division of Education, Greensburg, PA, USA
[2]The Pennsylvania State University, Department of Educational and School Psychology and Special Education, State College, PA, USA

ABSTRACT

Literature on Social Stories refers to the method as a "popular trend" in the instruction of students with ASD and describes potential benefits but also cautions that there is little empirical evidence to demonstrate their effectiveness. A recent review of the literature reports highly variable effects, primarily due to inconsistencies in Social Story structure, research design, and variation across participants and behaviors. Because of a conflict between recommendations for story construction and actual results with conformist or non-conformist stories, researchers have called for further investigations to determine the components of Social Stories that contribute to their efficacy. The present study included two phases. In Phase 1, a review of the literature was conducted to identify the core characteristics of documented procedures. This resulted in a 10-step approach to constructing and evaluating Social Stories for students with ASD. In Phase 2, the 10-step model, as a new method to guide and monitor a controlled implementation of Social Stories, was implemented with six students with ASD. Procedural fidelity could be established, and the implementation resulted in behavioral goals being attained by all participants.

[*] M.Phil., M.Ed., Ph.D.-candidate, Assistant Professor of Special Education. Contact: G9 St. Joseph Hall, Seton Hill University, 1 Seton Hill Drive, Greensburg, PA-15601. E-mail: tarnai@setonhill.edu

A Social Story is a short story defined by specific characteristics that describes a situation, concept, or social skill using a format that is meaningful for people with autism spectrum disorders (ASD) (Reynhout & Carter, 2006). Originally, Social Stories[TM] were developed by Gray to teach children with autism how to play games while increasing their ability to interact socially with others (Gray, 1995). Social Stories have been used to teach children with varying degrees of severity of autism or Asperger syndrome the cues and behaviors they need to know to interact with others in a socially appropriate manner. Behavioral targets included aims to decrease disruptive or challenging behaviors, and to increase social interaction, communicative behaviors, or on-task behavior (Barry & Burlew, 2004; Reynhout & Carter, 2006).

Literature indicates that Social Stories often are used in the instruction of students with ASD (Barry & Burlew, 2004). Potential benefits have been reported but authors also caution that there is little empirical evidence demonstrated about their effectiveness (Yarnall, 2000; Elder, 2002; Reynhout & Carter, 2006). A recent review of the literature (Reynhout & Carter, 2006) reported highly variable effects, mainly due to inconsistencies in Social Story structure, research design, and a broad variation across participants and behaviors. Because of a conflict between recommendations for story construction and actual results with conformist or non-conformist stories, Reynhout and Carter (2006) have called for further research to determine the exact components of Social Stories that are central to their efficacy.

Typically, Social Stories are constructed with six basic sentence types (Reynhout & Carter, 2006) that are presented in Table 1. Gray (2003) recommended a ratio of two to five descriptive, perspective, and/or affirmative sentences for every directive and/or control sentence in a Social Story[TM]. However, as Reynhout and Carter (2006) point out, these recommendations for story construction are not based on empirical evidence; and in some cases, their own review of the literature yielded higher percentages of non-overlapping data (PND) for "inappropriately modified" stories (p. 462) that violated Gray's ratio by using less descriptive and more directive sentences, or using a higher proportion of consequence sentences.

Besides the ratio of basic sentence types, practitioner-oriented literature (e.g., Scott et al., 2000; Gray, 2003) also describes, and suggests the use of, additional research-based instructional strategies to make Social Stories more effective for students with ASD. According to these authors, the perspective of the child for whom the story is written should always be adopted and maintained. Adherently, stories are typically written in the first (or sometimes in the third) person singular. Further, behavioral responses should be stated in positive terms (e.g., 'I am going to use my low voice' vs. 'I am not going to yell out'). Words and/or images may be used to supply the student with a permanent product to which he or she can refer back when practicing the target social skill. The student's comprehension of the story should be checked before proceeding to skill practice with the story. This is typically done either in a written or spoken questions-and-answers format, with a comprehension checklist, or by letting the student fill in a version of the story that has blanks. Gray (2003) suggested that the Social Story first be read in close proximity to a situation where the student is likely to need to use the target skill, which can then be practiced in relevant real-life contexts and situations. Depending on progress made, the reading of the story can become less frequent, parts of it may be faded out, leaving the student with an increasingly simpler procedural facilitator until the target behavior becomes a routine part of the student's repertoire.

Table 1. Basic Sentence Types Used in Social Stories

Sentence Type	Definition[a]	Example
Descriptive	Describes the social situation in terms of relevant social cues.	In the morning, when it is time for me to get up and get dressed, Mom or Dad lays out clothes for me onto the bench at the end of my bed.
Directive	Describes an appropriate behavioral response.	When I get up and out of bed, I have to take off my pajamas and put on the clothes that my Mom or Dad laid out for me.
Perspective	Describes the feelings and/or responses of the student OR others in the situation.	If I get dressed properly and in time, my parents will not be nervous and worried that I may be late for catching the school bus.
Affirmative	Expresses a commonly shared value or opinion within a given culture.	Because parents are busy in the morning with preparing breakfast for the family and getting ready for going to work, it is nice to help them by getting dressed independently and save time for them to finish their jobs.
Control	Written by a person with ASD to identify personal strategies to recall and use.	When I see Mom or Dad in the morning laying out clothes on the bench at the end of my bed for me to wear, I will get out of bed, take off my pajamas and put on those clothes.
Cooperative	Describes what others will do to assist the student.	If I need help with buttons or zippers, I can tell Mom or Dad "please help me", show what I could not do on my own and they will help me do it.

Note. [a]Definitions are based on the literature review by Reynhout and Carter (2006).

Reynhout and Carter (2006) concluded that because of a high degree of procedural variation among reviewed studies, and issues of treatment fidelity, no sufficient experimental control was available to ascertain solid empirically based findings on the efficacy of Social Stories. The present investigation reviewed and analyzed Social Stories interventions in the instruction of students with ASD to identify central elements of implemented intervention packages, in order to establish an empirical basis for comparison. The rationale was that in order to determine if a particular variation of Social Story implementation yields more effective outcomes than others, a validated and uniform procedure for the intervention has to be isolated and defined, so that systematic experimental manipulations can be introduced while leaving other components uniformly constant.

The present study included two phases. Phase 1 identified typical Social Story intervention components by reviewing literature that reported utilizing Social Stories. The objective was to isolate the core characteristics of documented procedures of Social Stories interventions, as opposed to elements found in theoretical (and not empirically validated) descriptions and suggestions for implementing these interventions. Phase 2 sought to implement a model Social Story intervention as defined by the literature base. Because several recent reviews of the literature (e.g., Barry and Burlew [2004]; Reynhout & Carter [2006]) pointed out issues of treatment fidelity as compromising the validation of findings, the purpose of Phase 2 was to achieve procedural fidelity implementing the pilot Social Story model from Phase 1.

PHASE 1: IDENTIFYING PROCEDURAL COMPONENTS AS REPORTED BY INVESTIGATORS WHO HAVE IMPLEMENTED SOCIAL STORIES, AND DEFINING A MODEL SOCIAL STORY INTERVENTION PACKAGE

Method

The objective of the Phase 1 study was to identify agreed-upon components of Social Story interventions as defined by existing empirical studies. In order to identify appropriate empirical studies on Social Stories with participants having ASD, two recent literature reviews (Sanosti et al., 2004; Reynhout & Carter, 2006) were used that have established a consensus on what elements compose an acceptable empirical implementation of Social Stories. Specifically, Sanosti et al. (2004) reviewed the PsycINFO and ERIC databases for empirical studies relating to the effectiveness of Social Stories interventions for children with ASD. Specific behavioral outcomes had to be reported in the studies for inclusion in their review. Ten studies were selected. Reynhout and Carter (2006) searched ABI/INFORM Global, Academic Research Library, Current Contents Connect, ERIC, Expanded Academic ASAP, First Search, Ingenta, Inspec, Kluwer Online, Proquest Education Complete, PsyARTICLES, PsycINFO, Science Direct, and ISI Web of Science. They also conducted a manual search and ancestral search for articles in the 1990-2005 issues of the *Journal of Autism and Developmental Disorders*. The authors included 11 peer-reviewed journal articles and 5 dissertations that used Social Stories and reported on learner performance.

For the current review, peer-reviewed studies were selected from those agreed-upon (i.e., rated by expert reviewers as appropriate Social Stories) procedures included by Sanosti et al. (2004) and/or Reynhout and Carter (2006), as follows. (a) For studies dated 2002 or earlier (inclusion deadline by Sanosti et al., 2004), studies had to be agreed-upon as appropriate Social Stories procedures and as such, included in both of these literature reviews: six studies were identified (Brownell et al., 2002; Hagiwara & Myles, 1999; Kuttler et al., 1998; Lorimer et al., 2002; Scattone et al., 2002; Swaggart et al., 1995). (b) Reynhout and Carter's (2006) review contained two more peer-reviewed studies, evaluated as appropriate Social Stories procedures, conducted after the search of the review by Sanosti et al. (2004); these (Bledose et al., 2003; Kuoch & Mirenda, 2003) were also included. (c) One additional empirical and peer-reviewed study (Scattone et al., 2006) was identified and included in the present study that was published after Reynhout and Carter's (2006) review but matched their inclusion criteria. Altogether, the search procedures yielded nine empirical and peer-reviewed studies, containing 21 cases, on the use of Social Stories with participants having ASD that were included in the present analysis.

Results and Discussion

The present review examined and categorized Social Stories implementation studies by variables such as (a) demographics (participants); (b) dependent variables (target behaviors); (c) independent variables (setting, study duration, research design [see these in Table 2], method of story presentation, comprehension checks, additional strategies used [reinforcers, prompts or other], sentence ratio; and finally (d) as a measure of treatment effectiveness, PND [percentage of non-overlapping data points] between baseline and treatment phases [see these in Table 3]).

The analysis revealed some commonalities in implementation procedures, but also some variations primarily in story construction (sentence ratios) and/or research designs. In spite of expected differences, only a few basic implementation variations repeated across studies (see Tables 2 and 3). Unfortunately, even these common variations do not lend themselves to clear interpretation because variables were not systematically manipulated across replicated interventions, and the studies usually differed along more than just one single implementation variable with no common set of characteristics systematically held constant.

Table 2. Overview of Participants, Target Behaviors, Settings, Duration and Research Design of Social Story Implementation Studies

Study	Participants[a]	Target Behaviors	Setting	Duration	Research Design
Bledose et al. (2003)	1 boy, 13y, with Asperger's syndrome & ADHD (IQ=82)	Food/drink spill, napkin use	School dining area at lunchtime	7 days baseline, 5 days treatment, 5 days return to baseline, 4 days return to treatment	ABAB
Brownell (2002)	4 boys, 6-9y, with autism, verbal, at least pre-reading skills	Follow directions, using quiet voice, delayed echolalia	Classroom	5 days baseline, 5 days Social Story read, 5 days return to baseline, 5 days Social Story sung	ABAC (interventions counterbalanced across participants)
Hagiwara & Myles (1999)	3 boys, 7-9y, with autism, basic listening or written language skills	Hand washing (2 participants), on-task (1 participant)	Dining area, resource room, classroom at school	4-19 days baseline, 4-19 days treatment (depending on each behavior/participant)	Multiple baseline across settings
Kuoch & Mirenda (2003)	3 boys, 3-6y, with autism	Playing games, sharing toys, eating	Home / preschool / school; depending on each participant	7-13 days baseline(s), 5-8 days treatment(s), depending on each behavior/participant	ABA for 2 participants, ACABA for 1 participant (C = book & reminder

Table 2. Continued

Study	Participants[a]	Target Behaviors	Setting	Duration	Research Design
Kuttler et al. (1998)	1 boy, 12y, with autism & fragile-X, vocalizations enhanced by communication book & manual signs	Inappropriate vocalizations and dropping to floor (as precursors to tantrum)	Self-contained classroom for children with autism	5 days baseline, 5 days treatment, 3 days return to baseline, 6 days return to treatment	ABAB
Lorimer et al. (2002)	1 boy, 5y, with mild to moderate autism, language skills commensurate with chronological age	Talking, waiting (interrupting vocalizations as precursors to tantrum)	Home	7 days baseline(s), 7 days Treatment(s)	ABAB
Scattone et al. (2002)	3 boys, 7-15y, with autism, capable of communicating using speech	Shouting, looking at girls, sitting on chair (no tipping)	School	4-13 days baseline, 7-16 days treatment (depending on each behavior/participant)	Multiple baseline across participants
Scattone et al. (2006)	3 boys aged 8-13y, diagnosed with ASD, intelligible speech in complete sentences	Talking to peers at playtime/lunchtime	School, natural settings of playtime or snack time (10 minutes 3X a week)	11 weeks of data collection (baseline & intervention)	Multiple baseline across participants
Swaggart et al. (1995)	1 boy with PDD, 1 boy & 1 girl with autism, 7-11y, limited expressive language	Appropriate social interactions (greeting, touching, grabbing, sharing, aggression)	School	9-51 days baseline, 9-18 days treatment (depending on each behavior/participant)	AB

Note. [a]y = years; dash indicates range, not year/months.
ADHD = attention deficit hyperactivity disorder.
ASD = autism spectrum disorders.
PDD = pervasive developmental disorders.

Table 3. Overview of Story Construction, Implementation Strategies, and Effectiveness (PND) of Social Story Implementation Studies

Study	Case	Implementation	Comprehension check	Additional Strategie				Gray's	
				None	Reinforcers	Prompts	Other	Ratio[a]	PND
Bledose et al. (2003)	Spilling / napkin use	Social Story read by researcher. Social Story accessible to student following intervention. Photos.	None	X				Yes	16
Brownell (2002)	Brian	Social Story read or sung by researcher (Story presented in traditional and in musical format).	None	X				+DIR	88
	Justin			X				Yes	90
	Nathan			X				+DIR	80
	Peter			X				+DIR	90
Hagiwara & Myles (1999)	Hand washing	Social Story presented in computer based format, operated by participants. Use of visual symbols.	None			X Verbal and/or physical		+DIR (89%) & only PER (11%)	38
Kuoch & Mirenda (2003)	Neil	Social Story read by parent (who was a teacher) in the home; and by early interventionist in the preschool/school. Use of visual symbols.	None	X				Yes	75
	Andrew			X				Yes	66
	Henry			X				Yes	100
Kuttler et al. (1998)	Lunchtime	Social Story read by researcher. Social Story accessible to student following intervention. Use of visual symbols.	None		X Stickers / prize bag			+DIR (50%)	90
	Schoolwork							Yes	100

Table 3. Continued

Study	Case	Implementation	Comprehension check	None	Reinforcers	Prompts	Other	Ratio[a]	PND
				Additional Strategie				**Gray's**	
Lorimer et al. (2002)	Talking	Social Story read by parents and therapists. Social Story accessible to student following intervention. Use of visual symbols.	None	X				Yes	43
	Waiting			X				Yes	43
Scattone et al. (2002)	Howard	Social Story read by teacher, teacher's aid, or student. Social Story accessible to student following intervention.	Yes			X Verbal		Yes	57
	John					X Verbal		Yes	92
	Kenny					X Verbal		Yes	100
Scattone et al. (2006)	Steven	During first session, teacher read Social Story (and re-read Social Story until comprehension OK). Then, student read Social Story to teacher once a day just prior to the free-time activity.	Yes: set of predetermined questions	X				Yes	10
	Drew			X				Yes	89
	Billy			X				Yes	69
Swaggart et al. (1995)	Greeting	Social Story read by teacher or paraprofessional. Use of visual symbols.	None			X Verbal and/or physical (for both)	X	+DIR (60%)	88
	Social play interactions				X Edibles		X Response cost sys.	Yes	0

Note. [a]Gray's Ratio: 2-5 descriptive/perspective/affirmative sentences for each directive/control sentence. [+]=more of a sentence type than by Gray. DIR=directive sentences. PER=perspective sentences. PND=percentage of non-overlapping data points. Sys=system.

Demographics and Dependent Variables

There was consistency in demographic variables. Participants (N = 1 – 4 per study) were mostly boys (only one girl among 21 cases) with ASD between 3 – 13 years of age, with relatively good language/literacy skills that enabled them to read their personalized Social Stories. Both decreasing inappropriate (e.g., using loud voice, dropping to floor for tantrum, spilling food/drink) and increasing appropriate (e.g., napkin use, sharing toys, greeting) social-interaction behaviors were targeted across Social Stories interventions (refer to Tables 2 and 3 for exact characteristics of each reviewed case study).

Independent Variables: Commonalities

Most settings were in the schools of the participants; fewer studies were conducted in home settings, but all interventions were set around naturally occurring routine activities (e.g., lunch, class, playtime; refer to Tables 2 and 3 for exact characteristics of each reviewed case study). Usually, a teacher or teacher's aid (or the literate student him/herself) read the Social Story prior to the upcoming natural routine in which the target skill should be applied (variations: non-disabled peers read along; multimedia story on computer). This routine was adherent to suggestions from the theoretical literature (e.g., Scott et al., 2000; Gray, 2003) for the implementation of Social Stories.

Most Social Stories implementations used no additional strategies (e.g., added contrived reinforcers or prompts) except reading the Social Story itself; relying on naturally available reinforcers in routine social-interaction situations where the interventions were set. The implementations typically were relatively short, spanning over 4-19 days of treatment.

Another common, but rather unfortunate, characteristic of Social Stories implementation studies proved to be the omission of comprehension checks before proceeding to skill practice with the story, as suggested by Gray (1995, 2003). Only one group of researchers (Scattone et al., 2002; 2006) consistently assessed the participants' understanding of the stories with a set of questions, prior to the skill practice phase.

Independent Variables: Dissonances

There remains some variability across Social Stories implementations. For example, although each study referenced Gray's guidelines (1995, 2003) for Social Stories construction, her recommended sentence ratio (i.e., two to five descriptive, perspective and/or affirmative sentences for every directive and/or control sentence in a Social Story[TM]) was not adhered to in all cases. Fifteen of the 21 cases in the reviewed nine studies adhered to Gray's ratio (see Table 3), and those that did not, typically violated the ratio by adding more directive sentences to the formula; in one case (Hagiwara & Myles, 1999) using perspective sentences only (11%) besides the overwhelming majority of directive ones (89%). However, Gray's (1995, 2003) original intention was to describe more than to direct with a Social Story[TM], thus, differentiating it from a mere task analysis chain.

In 6 of the 9 studies, some visual aids other than printed words (e.g., photos or images) were used within the Social Story, supplying the participants with an enhanced permanent product. Gray first discouraged (1995) then allowed, but did not require (2003), the use of graphical visual aids for supporting the Social Story[TM], so that students could refer back to them when practicing a target skill.

Additional differences existed across studies with respect to the research designs applied (see Table 2). Three of the nine reviewed studies used multiple baseline designs with their cases, three studies used a pure ABAB design and three used variations thereof (ABAC; ABA; ACABA; AB).

Treatment Effectiveness

Scruggs and Mastropieri (1994) advocated for the utility of PND scores when judging the outcomes of single-subject research, as opposed to other (statistical) methods of quantifying graphed results. The PND score represents the proportion of observations that exceeds the measures of a target behavior observed during baseline. In many cases, there are not sufficient data points in single-subject graphs for standard effect size computation, but PND can easily be obtained. Scruggs and Mastropieri (1994) maintain that in their analyses, PND scores were strongly related to qualitative expert ratings of graphs. In their seminal research on the utility of the PND, they "did not conclude a treatment was effective unless the PND score was in excess of 70" (p. 881). Empirical literature on Social Stories often reports PND scores, as evident from the review conducted for Phase 1 (see Table 3).

Regardless of procedural variation, existing studies reported some positive outcomes; 14 of the 21 examined cases (that is, 67%) reported a PND at or above the criterion level of 70 (see Table 3). Positive outcomes are likely linked to the fact that certain component variables were not systematically manipulated across replicated interventions, and some (not isolated; thus, not identifiable) effective components may be randomly included in them.

Table 4. Tarnai's 10-Step Approach to Constructing and Evaluating Social Stories

Task Steps	Strategies	Outcomes	Evaluation[a]
1) Identify behavior in need of change	Improvements in this behavior should likely lead to increased functional/adaptive behaviors, social functioning, or safety.	Behavior pinpointed and defined	....
2) Identify target social skill for instruction	The social skill (alternative behavior) chosen for instruction should increase social competence (i.e., skill is functional for the student).	Target skill (alternative behavior) defined	....
3) Collect baseline data	Observe and record the occurrence of targeted non-desirable behavior(s) and/or desired (alternative) behavior(s).	Recorded and graphed baseline data	....
4) Create Social Story	The teacher[b] writes the Social Story: a) in the first ("I") and/or third person ("he/she/they"); b) in present or future tense; c) at the comprehension level of the student – use as much student input as possible (check comprehension after initial reading); d) label the	Personalized and formatted (a–g) Social Story ready for implementation with the student (comprehension demonstrated)	....

	Social Story with a title that quickly relates to the topic; e) give the story an introduction, body, and conclusion; f) state behaviors positively ("do" vs. "don't"); and g) use Gray's sentence ratio.		
5) Select additional visual cues and materials	a) Select visual cues (e.g., photos, drawings, icons, graphic/bulleted schedules); b) set the fading schedule and use cues accordingly.	Visual cues / schedule of use identified	....
6) Rehearse Social Story linked to practice of the target social skill	The Social Story should be read prior to the actual situation in which the target social skill will be used. Skill practice scenarios (settings and contingencies) should be linked to the Social Story.	Accurate story readings and skill rehearsal contingencies	....
7) Collect performance data	Observe and record/graph performance of the desired target behavior, after the introduction of the Social Story.	Recorded and graphed intervention data	....
8) Adapt Social Story implementation procedures, if necessary	According to changes in the targeted behavior shown by the performance data, changes in the Social Story implementation procedure (e.g., story structure or rehearsal format; skill practice scenarios) may be necessary to ensure ideal performance.	Reviewed and adapted procedures (story/ routines) in place; skill is demonstrated	....
9) Promote generalization	If stable social skill performance reaches the expected criteria in the trained practice situation, establish at least two new settings (general case programming) where the same target skill would be helpful. Adapt procedures and monitor performance.	Reviewed and adapted procedures in place; generalized target skill performance	....
10) Fade Social Story	Gradually and systematically fade out the Social Story (e.g., less frequent readings, gradual reduction of the story length, switching to visual cues like graphic/bulleted schedules as reminders, etc.).	Reviewed and adapted procedures in place; skill is maintained	....

[a] This 10-Step overview form may be used to check out steps and to add comments for the evaluation of the implementation of a particular Social Story program.

[b] Or another professional who will be working with the student (e.g., a teacher's aid, or a parent).

Three studies (Brownell, 2002; Kuttler et al., 1998; Swaggart et al., 1995) used both adherent and non-adherent sentence ratios (to Gray's recommendations) for different included case studies, with inconsistent corresponding outcomes (PND). It holds for all reviewed studies, that because of additional variables were unequal, no clear correlation can be established between the sentence ratio used to construct the Social Stories and the respective outcomes.

Model Intervention Package for Social Stories

For the purpose of creating a clearly defined intervention package, a model guide for Social Story implementations was developed, based on the literature review of empirical studies and of recommendations of researchers for the evaluation of Social Stories. Some model components were agreed-upon in most reviewed case studies; and some were not generally agreed-upon but needed to be included in the model to ensure empirical rigor for this research:

(1) Adhering to the agreed-upon components in existing empirical literature, a pilot Social Story would be used (a) in isolation with no additional contrived strategies such as prompt hierarchies or added reinforcement. (b) The researcher would construct a personalized Social Story in collaboration with those who know the participant well (e.g., teacher, assistants, parents, peers). (c) Initially the teacher or parent, then the participant would read the Social Story aloud just prior to the upcoming natural routine of the day in which the target skill should be applied. (d) Participant(s) would be selected from school-age children diagnosed with ASD, having sufficient language/literacy skills to meaningfully read their personalized Social Story. (e) Settings would adhere to naturally occurring routine activities in which the target skills are desirable and useful.

(2) Regarding intervention components that were not generally agreed-upon in the reviewed literature, the following selections were made for the purposes of a pilot study. (f) Following Gray's (1995, 2003) original, defining recommendations, a sentence ratio of two to five descriptive, perspective and/or affirmative sentences for every directive and/or control sentence would be used in the story construction. (g) Also in Gray's legacy, a comprehension check would be conducted after initial reading of the Social Story and prior to proceeding to skill practice. In order to judge the effectiveness of a Social story intervention, it is important to know if the story is actually meaningful to the participant. This step confirms the match between the participant's and the story's reading level. A mismatch could misleadingly fault the general intervention procedures for unsuccessful outcomes. The readability level of a Social Story is not pre-defined, but rather adjusted to the needs of each participant; if the initial comprehension check fails, the story can still be re-adjusted (and comprehension re-checked). (h) In order to keep the model Social Story isolated, no images would be used to enhance the Social Story. (j) An individual pilot study would take the simple AB form as for a single tier in a multiple baseline design.

The identified components for a model intervention were organized in 10 steps to ease practical implementation. Table 4 presents the resulting 10-step approach to constructing and evaluating Social Stories. This structured model was developed not only to summarize the model Social Story components that emerged from the literature review (thus, guiding practitioners through the process of reliably constructing a model Social Story intervention) but also to keep Social Story interventions uniform and replicable, ensuring procedural fidelity. In addition, the 10-step model establishes a basis of comparison for future research on the efficacy of Social Stories, by enabling researchers to select isolated variables for systematic manipulation while leaving other components uniformly constant. Sample procedures for using the model 10-step approach are presented in Phase 2 of the current study.

PHASE 2: IMPLEMENTATION OF THE 10-STEP APPROACH TO CONSTRUCTING AND EVALUATING SOCIAL STORIES

The purpose of Phase 2 was to achieve procedural fidelity with a pilot Social Story model intervention package, identified from the literature. Procedures adhered to the resulting 10-step approach to constructing and evaluating Social Stories (Table 4) that was developed in Phase 1.

Method

Participants

Phase 2 of this study was carried out in collaboration with the 'Agency Program' (name altered) of a human service agency in Pennsylvania. The Agency Program is a social skills training program serving approximately 12-15 school-age children (age range: 9-13 years) diagnosed with ASD. The program meets twice a week for two hours in the afternoon. The program includes diverse structured and guided activities under the supervision of certified staff. Participants were selected from the pool of students with ASD attending the Agency Program who had sufficient language/literacy skills (as judged by Agency Program staff) to meaningfully read a personalized Social Story. Because the readability level of a Social Story is adjusted to the needs of each participant, and comprehension checks confirm the match between participants' and their story's reading level, no formal criteria of language skills were established beyond staff recommendations. Informed consent was obtained from parents/guardians of prospective participants.

Six of the regularly attending twelve students (one girl and five boys) were selected to participate in the study (see Table 5 for an overview of age, diagnosis, and school programming of participants). All participants were literate and used verbal speech for communication. Johnny was the only one participant who did not often use his expressive language spontaneously, but he was able to adequately answer questions directed to him. Two participants (Kevin and Brandon) only attended one of the two weekly sessions of the Agency Program; their regularly alternating absence resulted in either Kevin (Mondays only) or Brandon (Wednesdays only) being present at the observation/intervention sessions. Thus, five students were observed at each session.

Identification and Training of Project Staff

Three staff members of the Agency Program were identified by the program coordinator to participate in the study. The program coordinator served as co-observer (20% of sessions) for reliability checks of the observations (the principal investigator served as the primary observer). The program coordinator and two additional staff members, all of them familiar to the children in the Agency Program, read the personalized Social Stories with the six participating students. The principal investigator provided the necessary staff training and continuous performance feedback to the project staff before and during the study. Criteria consisted of adherence to the 10-step approach (Table 4) for procedures, and a minimum of 85% agreement on observations.

Table 5. Overview of Participants, Schooling Types, Target and Replacement Behaviors of Social Story Implementations in Phase 2

Student	Age[a]	Diagnosis	School Type	Target Behavior	Replacement Behavior
Johnny	13y	Autism	Home schooled, partially attends a specialized private school for students with ASD	Leaving the Agency Program room (to go to the bathroom) without asking a teacher, or when asking but being denied permission. Includes reaching door area by time staff realizes he is about to leave the Agency Program room.	Student asks a teacher when he wants to leave the Agency Program room, and does not leave without asking or when denied permission. (As agreed on with staff, Johnny is only allowed to go to the bathroom once during every Agency Program session.)
Susan	9y	PDD-NOS	Life skills class at a public elementary school	Touching underwear in public with a scratching motion over pelvis.	Student will not touch/scratch underwear area in public.
Henry	10y	PDD-NOS	Life skills class at a public elementary school	Touching (hitting) another person's body in order to get the person's attention. Includes occurrences accompanied by vocalization.	Student will use his words and not touch another person to get his/her attention.
Peter	13y	PDD-NOS	Partially attends inclusive classes at a public middle school	Touching his hand to or very close to his nose and/or picking nose with a rubbing motion; without apparent function to remove	Student will not touch/rub his nose area with his hands in public; this does not include occurrences with an apparent meaningful/valid

				dirtiness or scratching an itch.	function to remove dirtiness or scratching an itch.
Kevin	10y	PDD-NOS	Attends general education classes at a public elementary school	Laughing out in a loud voice; judged by staff as inappropriate / disturbing in social environment.	Student will not laugh out in a loud voice disturbingly; this does not include low volume occurrences of same behavior.
Brandon	11y	Autism	Attends general education classes at a public elementary school	Spontaneously (no prompts) asking another person to play/work with him or if he can join in the game/ project others are playing. Specific topography does not matter.	Student will spontaneously (without external prompts) ask another person to play/work with him or if he can join in the game/project others are playing.

[a]y=years. PDD-NOS=pervasive developmental disorder, not otherwise specified. ASD=autism spectrum disorders.

Dependent Measures

The principal investigator consulted Agency Program staff who knew the identified participants well, about their general perceptions on social behaviors of the participants that represented a management problem, and thus, presented a need for improvement or for teaching a new social skill. The pinpointed behaviors were preliminarily defined, and the principal investigator conducted observations to determine which of these behaviors were overtly observable and exhibited at a rate that justified a socially valid need and opportunity to intervene. A repeated consultation with staff finalized and operationalized a target behavior for each participant. In Brandon's case, the selected target behavior needed to be increased; in all other cases, a decrease of the target behavior (and redirecting to an appropriate alternative response) was the objective.

Agency Program staff pinpointed the following problem behaviors that were selected for intervention: (1) Johnny was "obsessed" with bathrooms, especially water faucets, and he tended to "disappear" from activities, going to the bathroom. At home, his bathroom visits were time-limited. Johnny was only allowed to go to the bathroom once during every Agency Program session. (2) Susan often publicly and overtly touched her underwear with a scratching motion over the pelvis (often when sitting with inappropriately wide-spread legs). Staff or students looking at her sometimes seemed to trigger the behavior. (3) Henry often touched (and sometimes rudely hit) another person's arm or shoulder in order to get the person's attention. (4) Peter tended to touch and scratch his nose and/or his hands when excited or when bored; staff decided that the nose-scratching was less socially appropriate and a more urgent target. (5) Kevin's laughing out in a loud voice (often suddenly and to himself) was judged by staff to be inappropriate/disturbing in the given social environment. Baer et al. (1968) define successfulness of a behavioral intervention as producing large enough effects for practical value. Thus, the question of how much a behavior needs to be changed is best answered by those who must deal with the behavior. Consequently, the target level for Kevin was defined as any time an Agency Program staff member had to tell him to use his quiet inside voice, or told him "shh". (6) Brandon tended to walk around his peers and talk to himself aloud without engaging in real, mutual conversation. The researchers decided to target spontaneously (without external prompts) asking another person to play/work (on a project) with him; or asking if he can join in the game/project others are playing. The specific topography would not matter in this case, solely the function of the behavior did.

Adhering to steps 1 and 2 of the 10-step approach (Table 4), all selected target and desirable replacement behaviors were operationally defined for observation and data collection. Table 5 presents an overview of the operational definitions of both target and replacement behaviors (corresponding to steps 1 and 2 in the 10-step approach; Table 4) for each participant.

Independent Measures – The Application of the Model 10-Step Approach

The procedures described in the following sections (Materials/Setting/Procedures) adhere to the 10-step approach to constructing and evaluating Social Stories (Table 4) that was developed in Phase 1. The principal investigator and Agency Program staff constructed six personalized Social Stories, according to student skill levels and selected target behaviors. The Social Stories interventions consisted of Agency Program staff reading aloud the participants' personalized Social Stories with them (in individual staff-student pairs) one time at the beginning of each Agency Program session, with as much active student reading input as possible.

Materials

The Appendix lists the Social Stories and comprehension questions used in the current Phase 2 study. The stories were printed on white paper with a 16-point font, one paragraph per page. The pages were mounted on mixed-color letter size construction paper sheets, the white paper trimmed so that each page was framed by a strip of color showing from the construction paper background. The colorful pages were stapled together to form a personal story book for each participant. The outside cover had the participant's name on it, and the inside cover page displayed a summative title in a question-format, to which each story represented an answer. The story books were hole-punched and mounted on a metal ring and hung up on hooks in a designated area on the Agency Program room's wall, so the participants had access to, and could freely revisit, their stories any time.

Setting/Procedures

The Social Stories were read with the participants, sitting at a table, in a small, quiet, non-distractive room of the Agency Program area, where the routine activities of the Agency Program sessions occurred in which the target behaviors were naturally displayed. Participants were asked to come sit with a staff member who then read the participants' personalized Social Story with them. The Social Stories were read aloud one time at the beginning of each Agency Program session, before activities started, with as much active student reading input as possible (depending on literacy skills of each participant). For example, if a participant struggled with a word or phrase, staff would read the word to ensure a fluent and meaningful reading of the stories. Eventually, a fading schedule was introduced by gradually shortening each story (see Results for individual student input and fading schedule information). The reading of a Social Story quickly became a comfortable routine for the participants, and usually took about 2-3 minutes. The students picked their story books off the hooks on the wall, and put them back themselves after the reading.

A comprehension check was conducted after the initial reading of the Social Story and prior to proceeding to skill practice. Three pre-formulated comprehension questions were printed on the inside back cover of the individual story books, which were read immediately after the Social Story at each session until the participant was able to answer them, thus demonstrating an understanding of the concepts in his/her story. In case of apparent difficulties, the given Social Story formulation would need to be altered for clearer understanding (however, in the presented case studies, there was no need for that – all participants answered all of their comprehension questions correctly, and without additional prompting, after the initial reading).

Experimental Design

Because participants were selected from an intact cohort of students with ASD served by the Agency Program, it would have been an unrealistic expectation to find very similar target behaviors in need of intervention; thus, a variety of existing problem behaviors was addressed simultaneously. A multiple baseline design across participants and behaviors was used to evaluate the effectiveness of the intervention. The design was selected to strengthen the internal validity of the simple AB phase change design of each participant's single tier (Kazdin, 1982) within the multiple baseline design. The intervention was introduced adjutant to each baseline after stability had been demonstrated, with only a minimal delay for each tier after the preceding one. Because of the great variety of individual target behaviors, no substantial carry-over effects were anticipated.

Data Collection Procedures

Baseline and treatment data were collected using an identical observation format. A sequential partial-interval recording system was developed by the principal investigator to periodically observe each participant for a 10-sec. interval then move on to the next participant; after rotating through all participants, the sequential cycle began again. Thomson, Holmberg, and Baer (1974) compared a similar periodic observation system with the continuous recording of behavior of four participants. Sequential observation for 10-sec. intervals, rotating through the participants, resulted in a much smaller discrepancy relative to individual continuous observation than did observing one of the four participants for the first quarter of the full period and then moving on to the next participant for a next quarter period.

In the present study, both Kevin (Mondays only) and Brandon (Wednesdays only) attended just one of the two weekly sessions of the Agency Program, thus, five students were observed during each daily session. Consequently, each participant was observed for 10 sec., then not observed for 40 sec., within each 50-sec. time slot of a full rotation. Six such full rotations (6X50=300 sec.) added up to a five-minute observation block. Twelve five-minute observation blocks were distributed across the routine activities of a typical Agency Program session, according to the length of each activity period. Thus, the initial free time period contained two five-minute observation blocks; the following circle time three such blocks; the group activity four such blocks; snack time two such blocks; and closing story time one such block. Transition times were exempt of observations because of their less structured and controllable nature. Altogether, the 12 five-minute observation blocks covered one full hour of total observation time; and each participant was observed for a total of twelve minutes during each Agency Program session.

Partial-interval recording was selected because the majority of the target behaviors needed to be decreased, and partial-interval recording tends to overestimate behavior, hence represents a more conservative system when judging decrease (Bailey & Burch, 2002). Powell et al. (1975) compared the accuracy of continuous observation with momentary time sampling, whole-interval recording, and partial-interval recording of the same behavior. Partial-interval recording gave slightly increased scores; and both whole- and partial-interval methods were within 5% accurate, compared to continuous observation, when the length of observation intervals remained in the 10-20 second range. Harrop and Daniels (1986) concluded from a similar contrasting of behavior recording systems that partial-interval recording was more sensitive in detecting relative changes in behavior than momentary time sampling was.

Data Analysis

Data collected during baseline and treatment observations were graphed and visually inspected, as typical for single-subject research designs (Kazdin, 1982). For representing observation data, the total number of scored intervals per participant per full observation unit (one Agency Program session; 72X10-sec. intervals) was graphed. In addition, percentages of non-overlapping data (PND) were calculated, as this was a common feature in the Social Stories implementation studies reviewed for Phase 1 of this current study (see Table 3).

Treatment Integrity and Reliability of Observations

As described in earlier research (Barry & Burlew, 2004; Reynhout & Carter, 2006), treatment integrity was problematic, and a threat to the validity of findings in previous studies. The current study intended to put a strong emphasis on controlling variables for treatment integrity. The model 10-step approach to constructing Social Stories for students with ASD, outlined in Table 4, did not only guide the construction and implementation of Social Stories according to the analysis of Phase 1, but also served as a reference to facilitate the evaluation of treatment integrity. For the purposes of this pilot study, steps 1 through 4, 6 through 8, and step 10 of the general framework represented the valid procedures for the implementation of the model Social Story intervention (as of step 5, additional visual cues were purposefully avoided in order to adhere to the model intervention as defined in Phase 1; and step 9 concerning generalization, although carrying clinical importance, was not part of this pilot intervention package, because that phase is not necessary for judging the effectiveness of the basic intervention itself).

The principal investigator and the program coordinator of the Agency Program independently monitored the eight applicable steps defined in Table 4 and tallied the steps that were appropriately carried out during the implementation process. Eventually, some steps became redundant (e.g., behaviors were only defined once, and stories became finalized; either baseline or intervention data were collected, etc.), and those no longer applicable steps were not re-checked at each session. Inter-rater agreement was calculated by dividing the smaller number of tallied steps by the larger number of agreed-upon steps, multiplied by 100 (Salvia & Ysseldyke, 2004). Total inter-rater agreement for following the procedures to construct and implement Social Stories, as defined in Table 4, was 100%; with all eight applicable steps tallied (i.e., rated as carried-out).

Table 6. Social Validity Rating of Social Story Implementations by the Human Service Agency Program Staff[a]

Student	Target Behavio	Expected Outcome	Is Goal Acceptable?[b]	Is Intervention Unobtrusive and Easy to Implement?[b;c]
Johnny	Leaving the Agency Program room (to go to the bathroom) without asking a teacher, or when asking but being denied permission.	Student asks a teacher when he wants to leave the Agency Program room, and does not leave without asking or when denied permission.	5.00	4.66
Susan	Touching underwear in public with a scratching motion over pelvis.	Student will not touch/scratch underwear area in public.	5.00	4.33
Henry	Touching another person's body to get the person's attention.	Student will use his words and not touch another person to get his/her attention.	4.66	4.33
Peter	Touching his hand to or very close to his nose and/or picking nose with a rubbing motion; without apparent function to remove dirtiness or scratching an itch.	Student will not touch/rub his nose area with his hands in public; this does not include occurrences with an apparent meaningful/valid function to remove dirtiness or scratching an itch.	5.00	4.33
Kevin	Laughing out in a loud voice; judged by staff as inappropriate / disturbing in social environment.	Student will not laugh out in a loud voice disturbingly; this does not include low volume occurrences of same behavior.	4.66	4.66
Brandon	Spontaneously asking another person to play/work with him OR asking if he can join in the game/project others are playing.	Student will spontaneously (no prompts) ask another person to play/work with him OR ask if he can join in the game/project others are playing.	4.66	4.00
Total average			4.83	4.39

[a] Average values per student/behavior calculated with ratings obtained from five Agency Program staff members.

[b] 1-5 scale: 1=strongly disagree; 2=disagree somewhat; 3=indifferent; 4=agree somewhat; 5=strongly agree. [c]Implementation: reading Social Story with student, with as much active student participation as possible, once at the beginning of each Agency Program session.

The Social Stories constructed for Phase 2 were supposed to maintain Gray's sentence ratio of two to five descriptive, perspective and/or affirmative sentences for every directive and/or control sentence (see Table 1). The principal investigator and an expert in communication sciences and disorders independently coded the sentences of the constructed stories (see Appendix) to identify them as either type 1 (descriptive, perspective and/or affirmative sentences) or type 2 (directive and/or control sentence). The ratio of type 1 to type 2 sentences was calculated for each Social Story by each rater. For an agreement, the ratio had to be between 2.00 and 5.00 as judged by both raters. Inter-rater agreement was calculated by dividing the number of agreements by the sum of agreements plus disagreements, multiplied by 100 (paralleling agreement-per-occurrence; Salvia & Ysseldyke, 2004). Inter-rater agreement for adhering to Gray's sentence ratio was 100%; obtained sentence ratios ranged from 2.00 to 4.44.

The principal investigator served as the primary observer and data collector for this study. The program coordinator of the Agency Program conducted reliability checks of the observations; 20% of all sessions were co-observed (adhering to recommendations by Kazdin, 1982). For reporting observation data, the total number of scored intervals per participant per full observation unit (one Agency Program session; 72X10-second intervals) was obtained. Inter-rater agreement was calculated by dividing the smaller number of scores by the larger number of scores, multiplied by 100 (Salvia & Ysseldyke, 2004). Mean inter-rater agreement for the reliability of observations was 92.82% with a range from 87.5% – 100%.

Social Validity

Bernstein (1989) defines as one standard of good professional practice in ABA the ability to provide interventions that are both effective and socially acceptable. Social validity may be mapped out by examining the acceptability of the goals, procedures, and effects of an intervention to the consumer, the therapist, and society in large (Bernstein, 1989). For the scope and realities of the current study, it was possible to interview Agency Program staff, while witnessing the pilot Social Story implementations, about their perceptions of the acceptability of the goals (presented here: targeted behaviors plus expected outcomes) and of the procedures (asked here: unobtrusiveness and ease of implementation). Table 6 presents the instrument.

Five Agency Program staff members independently rated two questions on a 1-5 Likert-type scale; separately for each of the six participants. Not all of these staff members assisted directly in the research, only three of them were actively involved (see Method); but all five were in the settings and working with the students during the social skills program itself – so they all knew the participants, and they had a good impression about the acceptability of the goals and the obtrusiveness of the intervention itself. Table 6 shows the actual questions to rate, the rating code, and the obtained average scores per question per participant plus total average scores per question. Total average inter-rater score for the acceptability of the goals was 4.83 with an individual range from 4.66 – 5.00.Total average inter-rater score for the unobtrusiveness and ease of implementation was 4.39 with an individual range from 4.00 – 4.66.

Results and Discussion

Because Social Stories intuitively draw on a strength of many individuals with ASD (i.e., a reliance on routines), Social Stories may represent an effective technique to establish a routine or a rule that the individual can apply to targeted social situations (Scattone et al., 2002). However, reviews of the literature by Sanosti et al. (2004) and by Reynhout and Carter (2006) concluded that poor treatment fidelity compromised the validation of findings from Social Studies implementation studies. The purpose of Phase 2 of the current study was to achieve procedural fidelity with a pilot Social Story model intervention package as defined from a review of the literature in Phase 1; as a basis for future research on the efficiency of Social Stories interventions. The rationale was that in order to determine if a particular variation of Social Story implementation yields more effective outcomes than others, a validated and uniform core intervention had to be isolated and defined, so that systematic experimental manipulations could be introduced while leaving other components uniformly constant. A 10-step approach to constructing and evaluating Social Stories for students with ASD was theoretically developed, and empirically introduced, in this study as a new method to guide and monitor a controlled implementation of Social stories.

Settings and Context

The 10-step model social story intervention, as defined in Phase 1, was implemented in Phase 2 with six participants diagnosed with autism/PDD. The intervention proved to be non-intrusive, as collected social validity data reveal (Table 6). A routine was quickly established, as outlined in the procedures, and the children at the Agency Program were used to observers around them with note pads collecting data (Agency Program staff regularly collects their own behavioral data). Three of the six participants have asked multiple times when they could take home their story books because they liked them and wanted to keep them. We agreed that they could keep them after our 'story time' program was over.

The principal investigator was concerned about Susan's participation when cold weather came in and she started to wear long pants instead of her usual short skirts. The observers expected that this would strongly influence her behavior under observation (i.e., the public touching of her private areas); but in fact, there was no noticeable difference and her behavior stayed at a plateau level by the end of the intervention (see Figure 1). Her occasional return to wearing skirts or to wearing long pants again did not alter the rate of the target behavior.

Procedures

Johnny, Peter, Kevin, and Brandon read their stories independently after the initial reading by a staff member and the successful answering of their comprehension questions (all participants succeeded on the comprehension questions after the initial reading). Susan and Henry preferred the stand-by assistance of staff and asked them to read difficult words or longer passages for them. Continuing help was offered throughout the intervention, so that the reading would maintain a meaningful fluency.

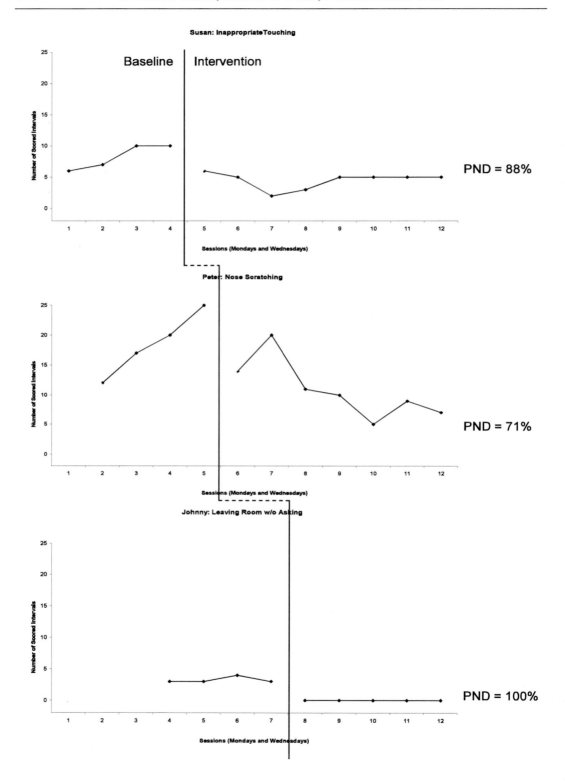

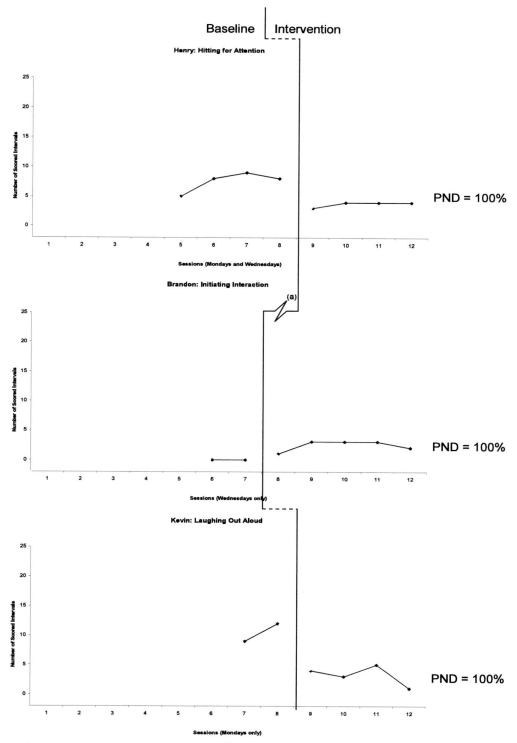

Note. [a] Brandon and Kevin came, in an alternating way, to every other Agency Program session.

Figure 1. Performance Graphs of the Phase 2 Model Social Story Interventions.

Johnny and Brandon have spontaneously, and independently, asked if they could read their stories alternating with their paired staff; so first the child would read one paragraph then the staff member would read the next one and so on. The principal investigator agreed to this routine for these participants because this individual variation did not conflict with intervention steps under fidelity control, it was initiated by the participants (sense of ownership), it made the reading more enjoyable for them, and it did not jeopardize the accomplishment of the objective of having their stories read through fluently.

Because all participants read and knew their stories well after about four readings, and a change in the rate of their target behaviors could be observed; the intervention was put on a fading schedule by gradually shortening each story, beginning at the fourth or fifth reading. Specifically, the stories were gradually shortened by leaving out one, then sequentially more paragraphs from the beginning of the stories. The starting paragraphs described more the general settings of the Agency Program and gave a larger context to the targeted behaviors, whereas the second halves of the stories focused more directly on the target and replacement behaviors (see Appendix). These latter paragraphs remained constant, while some general introductory paragraphs were gradually faded out.

Participants

Figure 1 shows the performance graphs of each participant in a multiple baseline design. Susan displayed the target behavior of inappropriate touching in 6 to 10 observation intervals during baseline. The rate decreased during intervention and then plateaud firmly at five intervals. PND is 88% with only one intervention data point overlapping with baseline.

Peter started out with a high baseline rate of 12-25 intervals in which nose scratching was observed. His target behavior showed a gradual decreasing trend during intervention and did not end in a plateau. PND is 71% with two intervention data points overlapping with baseline.

Johnny had the most success among the participants. He started with a stable baseline of going to the bathroom without asking about three times each session. The rate of the target behavior decreased to zero right after the initial reading of his social story and remained at that level throughout the intervention period (PND is 100%).

Henry's hitting behavior to get others' attention decreased from a baseline rate of five to nine scored intervals to a stable plateau of four. Even though some undesirable behavior still remained, the PND is 100%.

Brandon's active initiating social interaction was targeted for increase from an observed baseline of zero. During intervention, he displayed the desirable target behavior stably in about three observed intervals, where it reached a plateau (PND is 100%).

Kevin's laughing out aloud was observed in nine to twelve intervals during baseline and it gradually decreased with a marked change both in level and trend. The observed rate did not end in a plateau, PND is 100%.

All participants were successful in decreasing or increasing, respectively, the rate of displaying their target behaviors during intervention. Some reached a plateau from where further improvement would still be possible; but overall, the results are supportive of the identified model social story intervention. Treatment fidelity was maintained, and the reliability of observations was high (see Method section of Phase 2).

Limitations

A limitation to the generalizability of the results of this study is posed by the fact that a single-subject multiple baseline design was implemented with some select individuals having autism/PDD and with their particular behaviors and histories; that is, both across participants and across behaviors, within an intact group. On the other hand, the wide range of target behaviors and the good general success give reason to support an individualized, but carefully engineered intervention, carried out with fidelity. The fact that the intervention was successful within an intact group, and addressing diverse, spontaneously occurring target behaviors, supports the practical utility of the model for practitioners in real-life implementations.

For the explicit purposes of this study, no additional strategies were used to address the target behaviors beyond the isolated model social story intervention. Perhaps, in situations where clinical utility were more important than research rigor, some of these target behaviors (especially where a plateau was reached) could have been addressed even more effectively with added strategies/materials known as good practices (and reported as being used jointly with Social Stories in some empirical studies; see Table 3), such as contrived reinforcement schedules, functional communication training, additional pictures or graphic organizers, etc.

The reporting of the percentage of non-overlapping data points (PND) between baseline and treatment phases is common in the literature (see Table 3). In some cases, PND reflects well on the performance of the participants; however, it is possible that a calculated PND score is lower but the performance of a participant is still encouraging. For example, in Peter's case the PND is 71% (barely above the effectiveness criterion score of 70; Scruggs & Mastorpieri, 1994) but the intervention data path reveals a consistently decreasing trend with a marked reversal compared to baseline. Thus, individual results should not be judged on PND alone.

Future Research

Social Stories incorporate instructional tools that are empirically based practices in special education, and specifically in the treatment of autism (Barry & Burlew, 2004); with characteristics such as being visual, permanent, written in simple language, focused and factual (Tarnai & Wolfe, 2008). The literature on effective teaching emphasizes the importance of explicit teaching (Ellis et al., 1994; Elbaum et al., 1999; Vaughn et al., 2000), clear demonstrations (Ellis, 2001), explicit instruction paired with drill-practice of basic skills (Ellis, 2001), small steps and practice of each step (Rosenshine, 1997; Swanson & Hoskyn, 1998; Vaughn et al., 2000), extensive active practice (Rosenshine, 1997; Swanson & Hoskyn, 1998), numerous opportunities to learn and to practice (Brophy & Good, 1986), systematic feedback (Rosenshine, 1997), guided practice with feedback (Ellis, 2001), organizing questions for review (Elbaum et al., 1999), graphic organizers (Rosenshine, 1997), independently useable/accessible strategies (Elbaum et al., 1999) or a "plan of action" (procedural facilitators; Vaughn et al., 2000). All of these are tools that typically appear in the descriptions of how to practically implement Social Stories (Scott et al., 2000; Gray, 2003; Barry & Burlew, 2004; Reynhout & Carter, 2006), in the forms of task analysis, visual aids (line drawings or photographs), modeling, repetition/ review, opportunities to practice (for maintenance and generalization), and corrective feedback.

In the light of these methodological overlaps, Reynhout and Carter (2006) argue that there may be other elements, especially the reinforcement component itself, that has the most effect on the students, and that the effectiveness of Social Stories should be investigated in isolation from additional techniques. I would not question whether Social Stories could be useful in isolation, or should be used at all in addition to 'other good practices', but I would argue that Social Stories can be applied as good practice themselves, as a particular form and realization of evidence-based instruction. Just as Quill (1995) recommends, "reading a social story may be listed as a 'first step' of a positive behavioral plan or intervention, followed by a sequence of additional steps to assist the child in learning a new social skill" (p. 229). Tarnai's novel 10-step model offers a reliable method to guide and monitor controlled implementations of Social Stories.

The incongruences in implementation and effects of Social Stories discussed in the review by Reynhout and Carter (2006) should be understood as a call for a better analysis (and eventual perfection) of the actual components and the practical implementation of Social Stories. Further research is needed to determine if a particular variation of the identified model intervention (some common ones reported in reviewed studies include violations of Gray's sentence ratio, and/or modified formats with added materials/procedures) of Social Story implementation yields more effective outcomes than others. Such findings would support the work of practitioners with an empirical evidence base.

Conclusions

Social Stories draw on a visual strength that many individuals with ASD typically may have, and offer a structured, tangible organization of social concepts that many individuals with ASD typically may need. Social Stories incorporate instructional tools that are empirically based good practices in special education. The literature reports incongruences in implementation and respective effects of Social Stories; there was a need to clarify and define the model intervention package. In Phase 1 of this study, a 10-step approach to constructing and evaluating Social Stories for students with ASD was developed, based on theoretical and empirical literature. The purpose of Phase 2 was to achieve procedural fidelity with the model Social Stories intervention package.

The 10-step model intervention was implemented in Phase 2 with six participants diagnosed with autism/PDD. The intervention was non-intrusive as supported by social validity data; and all participants were successful in decreasing or increasing, respectively, the rate of displaying their target behaviors during intervention. The novel 10-step approach to constructing and evaluating Social Stories for students with ASD, introduced and empirically validated in this study, offers to practitioners a reliable method to guide and monitor controlled implementations of Social Stories.

Appendix : Social Stories and Comprehension Questions Used in Phase 2

Johnny's Story

Why should I not Leave the Agency Program room without Asking for Permission?

It is fun to be at the Agency Program! I can play games or read a book in free time. In circle time, we share interesting things that happened to us in school or at home. I will share something with my friends, too.

At the Agency Program, we also play group activities. Then I will work on a project together with the other kids. The Agency Program Bank is in the room, too. I can earn dollars for a job I do well. I will sign up for a job.

The teachers and helpers work with the children to make sure everybody is having fun. The teachers also have to make sure that all kids are safe. Nobody should get hurt, that is not fun. I would like to be safe and have fun!

To make sure that I am safe, my teachers always have to know where I am. I have to tell a teacher when I would like to leave the Agency Program room. I may want to leave the Agency Program room to go to the bathroom. If I need to go to the bathroom, I will go to a teacher and I will ask, "Can I go to the bathroom?"

I will always ask first before I leave the Agency Program room. This is smart. This way my teachers know where I am. I can be safe and I can have fun!

Comprehension Questions
1. To make sure that I am safe, do my teachers at the Agency Program always have to know where I am?
2. Whom do I have to tell if I want to leave the Agency Program room?
3. What will I ask a teacher if I need to go to the bathroom?

Susan's Story

How should I Sit in a Polite Way?

When we sit down at circle time, my teacher and the other children will tell us about interesting things that happened to them since we last met at the Agency Program. I will share something with them, too.

My friends will pay attention to what I would like to tell them, and they will try to listen quietly while I am talking. This is being polite, and this makes me feel they care about what I am saying. Me too, I will pay attention to others, and I will try to be quiet while they talk. This is being polite. This makes them feel I care about what they would like to share.

Being polite in circle time also means that first of all, I will pay attention to what everybody has to share with us, and not to other things in the room. If I talk out of my turn, it will be hard for the others to pay attention to the speaker. If I do something that the others find is not nice, that too, takes away their attention from the person talking. For example, making funny faces, or picking my nose, or spreading my legs wide open, or touching my underwear so others can see it, are all things that make it hard for the others to pay attention to the speaker.

I would like my friends to appreciate me and to listen to me when I talk in circle time. I would also like to make my friends feel that I appreciate them when they share things with me in circle time. I will try to listen quietly to the speaker, and I will try to avoid disturbing the others by things like talking out of my turn, or by making funny faces, by picking my nose, by sitting inappropriately with my legs wide open, or by touching my underwear. This would not be polite.

Sitting politely and paying attention in circle time makes everybody feel appreciated, and we can hear interesting things from each other.

Comprehension Questions
1. Is it polite to sit quietly in circle time so the speaker feels we care about what he or she would like to share with us?
2. Is it polite to do things in circle time that make it hard for the others to pay attention to the speaker?
3. What are things I will try to avoid to do in circle time so we all can pay attention to the speaker?

Henry's Story

How Can I Get Somebody's Attention in a Nice Way?

All of the kids at the Agency Program like to play at free time. Some kids like to play with jigsaw puzzles. We can play together and help each other finish the puzzle. Some kids like to play board games. We can laugh a lot when we play a board game together. Some kids like to draw a picture or do paper folds at the table. We can work together on the same project, or we can talk to each other about what each of us is making. We may also play a game together outside. I can help my team win the game!

Playing together is fun, because we can help each other, we can cheer each other on, we can give each other some good ideas, and we can enjoy showing each other what we have made. I will try to play with the other kids at free time. I will walk up to one of the kids and say, "Do you want to play with me?" or "Can I play with you guys?" It is nice to ask.

But touching, grabbing, or hitting people so they listen to me is not nice. It may scare them if I touch them by surprise. I will try to talk to my friends instead of touching them, when I want to play with them.

If I ask somebody to play a game with me and they say they don't like that game, that is OK. Then I will try to pick another game. Or I can find out what both of us would like. I can ask, "What else would you like to play with me?" It is nice to agree on a game.

It can also happen that the kid I ask to play with me would prefer to play alone at that time. That is OK. Then I will look around and find somebody else to ask to play with me.

The kids will like it if I ask them nicely to play with me. If we have fun playing together, my friends will want to play with me more often.

Comprehension Questions
1. Is touching a person or talking to a person the nice way to make them listen to me?
2. What can I say to ask a friend to play with me?
3. What can I do if the kid I ask to play with me doesn't like the game that I picked out?

Peter's Story

Why should I Try not to Pick my Nose in front of others, even when I am Excited?

It is fun to be at the Agency Program! I can play games or draw a picture in free time. In circle time, we share interesting things that happened to us in school or at home. I will share something with my friends, too.

At the Agency Program, we also play group activities. Then I will work on a project together with the other kids. We may also play a game together outside. I can help my team win the game. We can laugh a lot when we play together!

Sometimes when I really like what we are doing at the Agency Program, I am having so much fun and I may get really excited. It is hard to control what I do with my hands when I am excited. Sometimes when I am finished with a project and the other kids are busy yet, I may get bored. It is hard to control what I do with my hands when I am bored, too.

When I get excited or when I get bored, I may forget about what my hands are doing. Then it may happen that I start scratching and picking my nose. I may not even notice that. I will try to pay more attention to what my hands are doing.

If I scratch or pick my nose, my hands may get dirty. That is not good, because we use our hands a lot at the Agency Program. With dirty hands, I may spread around some dirty germs that can cause illness. I would like for me and my friends to stay clean and healthy. I will try to avoid scratching my nose.

If I scratch or pick my nose, my friends and teachers may see me do this. Picking my nose doesn't look good, and it is not polite. I would like to behave so I am nice and polite with my friends and teachers. My friends and teachers will appreciate me for being polite.

I will pay attention, and I will try to control what I do with my hands when I get happy and excited. I will try to control what I do with my hands when I am bored, too. I will try to avoid scratching or picking my nose, so I will stay clean and healthy, and so my friends will appreciate me for being polite.

Comprehension Questions
1. Is it easy to control what I do with my hands when I am having fun and I get really excited?
2. Is it easy to control what I do with my hands when I am bored?
3. What is it that I will try to avoid to do with my hands so I will stay clean and healthy, and so my friends will appreciate me for being polite?

Kevin's Story

Why should I Use my Quiet inside Voice, even when I am excited?

It is fun to be at the Agency Program! I can play games or read a book in free time. In circle time, we share interesting things that happened to us in school or at home. I will share something with my friends, too.

At the Agency Program, we also play group activities. Then I will work on a project together with the other kids. We can laugh a lot when we play together!

People laugh when they are having fun. It feels nice to laugh, HA-HA-HA! But it is not nice if I laugh in a loud voice. It may scare my friends if they hear me suddenly laugh aloud by surprise. Making a loud noise may disturb other kids or adults when they are playing quietly. Or when they are talking in circle time and they would like to pay attention to each other. I don't want to scare or to disturb my friends.

It is OK to feel like I want to laugh. But when I am excited, it can be hard to control my voice. When I feel like I want to laugh, I will try to be in control and I will try to laugh with my quiet inside voice. Like this, "HA-HA-HA".

My friends and teachers will appreciate it if I can laugh with my quiet inside voice. This is being nice. I would like my friends and teachers to appreciate me for being nice. I would also like to make my friends and teachers feel that I appreciate them by being nice.

Using a quiet inside voice instead of making sudden loud noises, even when we are excited, makes everybody feel good. This way, we won't scare or disturb each other. This way, we can all have fun at the Agency Program. Let's have fun! But let's show it with a quiet inside voice.

Comprehension Questions
1. Is it OK to feel like I want to laugh?
2. But is it nice to make sudden loud noises, like laughing in a loud voice?
3. When I feel like I want to laugh, I will try to be in control and I will try to laugh with my quiet inside voice. Let me show you, I will go like this: ... (Please show me how you will try to laugh nicely with a quiet inside voice.)

Brandon's Story

How can I Share the Fun of Playing with somebody Else?

All of the kids at the Agency Program like to play at free time. Some kids like to play with jigsaw puzzles. We can play together and help each other finish the puzzle. Some kids like to play board games. We can laugh a lot when we play a board game together. Some kids like to draw a picture or do paper folds at the table. We can work together on the same project, or we can talk to each other about what each of us is making. We may also play a game together outside, and then it is important that I pay attention to the other kids, and that we all follow the rules. I will try to pay attention, and I can help my team win the game!

Playing together is even more fun, because we can help each other, we can cheer each other on, we can give each other some good ideas, and we can enjoy showing each other what we have made. I will try to play with the other kids at free time. I will walk up to one of the kids and say, "Do you want to play with me?" Sometimes I could ask a friend to draw with me. Sometimes I could ask a friend to play a board game or a puzzle with me. If I ask somebody to play a game with me and they say they don't like that game, that is OK. Then I will try to pick another game. Or I can ask, "What else would you like to play with me?"

The kids will like it if I ask them to play with me. They will also like it if I talk to them when we play together. They will want to be my friend! If we have fun playing together, my friends will want to play with me more often.

Comprehension Questions

1. What are some games that kids at the Agency Program can play together?
2. How can I ask a friend to play with me at free time?
3. What can I do if the kid I ask to play with me doesn't like the game that I picked out?

REFERENCES

References marked with an asterisk indicate studies included in the review of interventions

American Psychiatric Association. (1994). Diagnostic and statistical manual of mental disorders (4th ed.). Washington, DC: APA.

Bailey, J. S., & Burch, M. R. (2002). *Research methods in applied behavior analysis.* Thousand Oaks, CA: Sage Publications.

Barry, L. M., & Burlew, S. B. (2004). Using social stories to teach choice and play skills to children with autism. *Focus on Autism and Other Developmental Disabilities, 19,* 45-51.

Bernstein, G. S. (1989). In response: Social validity and the report of the ABA task force on right to effective treatment. *The Behavior Analyst, 12*(1), 97.

*Bledose, R., Myles, B. S., & Simpson, R. L. (2003). Use of a Social Story[TM] intervention to improve mealtime skills of an adolescent with Asperger syndrome. *Autism, 7,* 289-295.

Brophy, J., & Good, T. L. (1986). Teacher behavior and student achievement. In M. C. Whittrock (Ed.), *Handbook of research on teaching* (3rd ed.) (pp. 328-375). Aera.

*Brownell, M. D. (2002). Musically adapted social stories to modify behaviors in students with autism: Four case studies. *Journal of Music Therapy, 39,* 117-144.

Elbaum, B., Vaughn, Sh., Hughes, M., & Moody, S. W. (1999). Grouping practices and reading outcomes for students with disabilities. *Exceptional Children, 65,* 399-415.

Elder, J. H. (2002). Current treatment in autism: Examining scientific evidence and clinical implications. *Journal of Neuroscience Nursing, 34(2),* 28-40.

Ellis, A. K. (2001). *Research on educational innovations* (3rd ed.). Larchmont, NY: Eye on Education.

Ellis, E. S., Worthington, L. A., & Larkin, M. J. (1994). *Effective teaching principles and the design of quality tools for educators: Executive summary.* A commission paper written for the NCITE, The University of Oregon.

Gray, C. A. (1995). Teaching children with autism to "read" social situations. In K. A. Quill (Ed.), *Teaching children with autism: Strategies to enhance communication and socialization* (pp. 219-241). Albany, NY: Delmar.

Gray, C. A. (2003). *Social Stories*. Retrieved April 13, 2003, from http://www.thegraycenter. org.

*Hagiwara, T., & Myles, B. S. (1999). A multimedia Social Story™ intervention: Teaching skills to children with autism. *Focus on Autism and Other Developmental Disabilities, 14*, 82-95.

Harrop, A., & Daniels, M. (1986). Methods of time sampling: A reappraisal of momentary time sampling and partial interval recording. *JABA, 19*, 73-77.

Kazdin, A. E. (1982). *Single-case research designs*. New York: Oxford University Press.

*Kuoch, H., & Mirenda, P. (2003). Social Story™ interventions for young children with autism spectrum disorders. *Focus on Autism and Other Developmental Disabilities, 18*, 219-227.

*Kuttler, L., Myles, B. S., & Carlson, J. K. (1998). The use of social stories to reduce precursors to tantrum behavior in a student with autism. *Focus on Autistic Behavior, 13*, 176-182.

*Lorimer, P. A., Simpson, R. L., Myles, B. S., & Ganz, J. B. (2002). The use of social stories as a preventative behavioral intervention in a home setting with a child with autism. *Journal of Positive Behavior Interventions, 4*(1), 53-60.

Quill, K. A. (1995). *Teaching children with autism: Strategies to enhance communication and socialization*. New York, NY: Delmar Publishers.

Powell, J., Martindale, A., & Kulp, S. (1975). An evaluation of time-sample measures of behavior. *JABA, 8*, 463-469.

Reynhout, G., & Carter, M. (2006). Social Stories™ for children with disabilities. *Journal of Autism and Developmental Disorders, 36*, 445-469.

Rosenshine, B. (1997). Advances in research on instruction. In: Lloyd, John Wills; Kameenui, Edward J.; and Chard, Kevin (Eds). *Issues in educating students with disabilities*. LEA's series on special education and disability (pp. 197-220). Mahwah, NJ: Lawrence Erlbaum Associates Publishers.

Salvia, J. & Ysseldyke, J.E. (2004). *Assessment in special and inclusive education* (9th ed.). Boston, MA: Houghton Mifflin Company.

Sanosti, F. J., Powell-Smith, K. A., & Kincaid, D. (2004). A research synthesis of social story interventions for children with autism spectrum disorders. *Focus on Autism and Other Developmental Disabilities, 19*, 194-204.

*Scattone, D., Wilczynski, S. M., Edwards, R. P., & Rabian, B. (2002). Decreasing disruptive behaviors of children with autism using social stories. *Journal of Autism and Developmental Disorders, 32*, 535-543.

*Scattone, D., Tingstrom, D. H., & Wilczynski, S. M. (2006). Increasing appropriate social interactions of children with autism spectrum disorders using Social Stories™. *Focus on Autism and Other Developmental Disabilities, 21*, 211-222.

Scott, J., Clark, C., & Brady, M. (2000). *Students with autism: Characteristics and instructional programming for special educators*. San Diego, CA: Singular.

Scruggs, T. E., & Mastropieri, M. A. (1994). The utility of the PND statistic: A reply to Allison and Gorman. *Behaviour Research and Therapy, 32*, 879-883.

*Swaggart, B. L., Gagnon, E., Bock, S. J., Earles, T. L., Quinn, C., Myles, B. S., & Simpson, R. L. (1995). Using social stories to teach social and behavioral skills to children with autism. *Focus on Autistic Behavior, 10,* 1-16.

Swanson, H. L., & Hoskyn, M. (1998). Experimental intervention research on students with learning disabilities: A meta-analysis of treatment outcomes. *Review of Educational Research, 68,* 277-321.

Tarnai, B., & Wolfe, P. S. (2008). Using social stories for sexuality education for persons having autism / pervasive developmental disorder. *Sexuality and Disability, 26*(1), 29-36.

Thompson, C., Holmberg, M., & Baer, D. M. (1974). A brief report on a comparison of time-sampling procedures. *JABA, 7,* 623-626.

Vaughn, Sh., Gersten, R., & Chard, D. J. (2000). The underlying message in LD intervention research: Findings from research syntheses. *Exceptional Children, 67,* 99-114.

Yarnall, P. A. (2000, November/December). Current interventions in autism: A brief analysis. *Autism Society of America, 27,* 26-27.

In: Multimedia in Education and Special Education
Editors: O. Demir and C. Celik

ISBN 978-1-60741-073-7
© 2009 Nova Science Publishers, Inc.

Chapter 7

VIRTUAL REALITY AS A TOOL TO IMPROVE THE QUALITY OF LIFE OF PEOPLE WITH AUTISM AND LEARNING DIFFICULTIES

Lucia Vera[*], *Gerardo Herrera*[2,†] *and Marcos Fernandez*[3,‡]

[1,3]Artec Group and [2]Autism and Learning Difficulties Group, Robotics Institute, University of Valencia, P.O. Box 2085, 46017 Valencia, Spain

ABSTRACT

In the last 10 years, the research in the area of Technology and Computer Science applied to specific treatment and training has increased. In the recent literature it is possible to find research in a wide variety of areas, from applications developed to treat phobias to systems for learning, training and improving the skills of people with special needs. Virtual Reality (VR) has been claimed as one of the most powerful environments to help in the learning and training process of people with special needs. This kind of application offers the possibilities of teaching in a controlled and structured environment, with opportunities for repetition and generalization to the real world, and facilitates the social participation and the representation of abstract concepts. These characteristics are suitable for helping people with autism and learning difficulties.

In this paper we focus our attention on the use of VR applications for improving the learning, training and quality of life of people with autism and learning difficulties. After revising the most recent developments in the area of computer graphics applied to people with learning difficulties, we will try to highlight the most relevant issues of this kind of application to better fit the necessities of the final user. As an example, we describe our two main applications developed for helping people with autism and learning difficulties in their learning process: a virtual supermarket and a virtual school. On one hand, the virtual supermarket was developed with the main objective of training people with autism

[*] E-mail: Lucia.Vera@uv.es
[†] Gerardo.Herrera@uv.es
[‡] Marcos.Fernandez@uv.es

in concept development and imagination. VR makes it possible to explicitly show imaginary/magic transformations in how an object can act as if it were a different one, which is useful for training both abstract concepts and imagination understanding. Additionally, this virtual environment allows the interaction with different virtual objects, making possible to learn more about their correct usage or how to play with them, both skills where people with autism has problems.

On the other hand, the virtual school is an application under development with the main purpose of training people with autism in social understanding and interaction, another problematic skill for this group. The integration of virtual characters who can interact with the user allows simulation of social situations in which users can participate and be involved, obtain affective engagement, and try to develop their social skills and communication. Also, it is possible to train them in emotion recognition and understanding and associate each emotion with specific situations.

This chapter concludes with a revision of the methodology used to test this type of application with people with autism, and with more relevant research outcomes obtained in this field.

INTRODUCTION

Nowadays, the area of computer graphics is widely used in a variety of applications for specific purposes. We can find information about 3D representations of future buildings or houses most of the time only with the objective of visualization; computer and console games with high-quality graphics, in which the player can live a different experience inside the virtual world; film scenes and characters that are generated using computer graphics; or virtual simulators for training in driving vehicles, such as cars, buses or trains. From entertainment to training, there is a wide variety of applications in which the use of computer graphics is very popular.

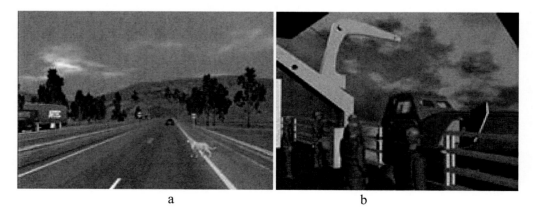

a   b

Figure 1. a) A virtual driving simulator developed at the Robotics Institute of the University of Valencia. b) A virtual simulator for training in collaborative sea rescue developed at the Robotics Institute of the University of Valencia.

In this context, it is possible to consider the use of computer graphics applications in education. In fact, there is an emergent research area that tries to analyze the results and improvements of the learning methodology by using interactive graphic systems for teaching specific concepts in an amusing environment. The technology is each day more accessible to children, not only at home but also at school. There are scholarly subjects only related to technology, and there is a common interest in all schools to introduce new computer-based programs and applications for teaching specific concepts included in the school curriculum.

In the area of people with special needs, the application of new technologies is starting to produce good results in the education and intervention process, which could help in the improvement of the quality of life of these people. In our context, the "intervention process" can be understood as daily work with people with learning difficulties, developed by professionals in psychology and special education, focusing on the specific skills in which these people have difficulties.

The idea of creating useful applications for teaching and training specific concepts (such as academic, social or communicative skills) seems to be of interest to all associations and special schools. There are efforts to describe the characteristics and possibilities of the use of new technologies in the education of students with special needs [WAT01]. These new technologies are defined in this context as 'technological instruments for the compensation and help in the intervention of students with special needs' [TD00].

This chapter is based on the idea of using new technologies—in our case, computer graphics—for people with learning difficulties. The projects described in this chapter try to promote the use of computer graphics to create helping tools for teachers and professionals in special education in their intervention and educational process for people with special needs.

In the following sections we describe the group of people to whom these graphic applications are addressed, the state of the art in computer graphics for education, the advantages of using computer graphics applications as educational tools, and a description of the two projects developed in this area. Finally, we present a methodology used to test these applications in people with autism, along with some conclusions and possible future work.

AUTISM AND LEARNING DIFFICULTIES

The area of special education is very wide and involves a large collective of people with different characteristics. We focus our attention on developing graphics applications for people with autism and learning difficulties. It is important to review these two concepts and clarify the main characteristics of the public to whom each of the applications is oriented.

First of all, Lorna Wing [APA94] defines autism spectrum disorders (hereafter referred to as 'autism') as the simultaneous presence of a triad of impairments in social interaction, communication and restrictive, repetitive and stereotypic patterns of behavior, interests and activities. This definition has been used by the American Psychiatric Association in its Manual for Diagnosis and Statistics [BOG03].

Approximately three out of every four people with autism also present learning difficulties. Within the context of educational interventions, we speak about 'learning difficulties' to make reference to those whose origin stems from a biological impairment rather than socio-environmental factors. Thus, learning difficulties are impairments that limit the development and putting into practice of communicative and/or academic and/or social abilities. The degree of development in this set of abilities is intimately related to the degree of autonomy and community integration (social, educational, labour) that the individual reaches, and it is also related to their quality of life.

Imagination is an ill-defined concept that involves conscious dissociation from reality and the mental manipulation of the environment. Behaviour that is said to entail imagination involves spontaneity and intention rather than response and creativity.

Another important characteristic of people with autism is the difficulty and delay in understanding symbolism, especially in relation to symbolic play. It is not clear whether such difficulties and delays represent a core deficit in imagination or whether they result from other aspects of autism [JOR03].

Those who suffer from both autism and learning difficulties especially tend to have problems in understanding imagination, which can be observed in a wide range of activities, including symbolic play activities.

The enormous attraction that people with autism and learning difficulties feels towards computers has motivated our group and other research groups to develop applications in this field.

BACKGROUND

Nowadays, the development of software oriented to help people with special needs in their learning process is a growing area of research. We can find applications with different characteristics, from web resources to virtual reality projects.

The most popular software and tools available for special and mainstream education are based on 2D graphics and web pages, with interactive content organised depending on the specific area of knowledge to work with. Most of these applications have interactive games to work in most of the areas included in the school curriculum. In most of them you can find contents in these four topics:

- *Tools to Work on Social Skills:* in this area it is possible to find games or interactive lessons to learn about personal cleanliness, products for personal cleanliness, external appearance, clothes, kitchen utensils and the rules and usage of kitchen utensils.
- *Tools to Work on Cognitive Skills:* in this area there are applications to learn about colours, shapes, basic concepts, objects classification, order, likenesses and differences.
- *Tools to Work on Written Language.*
- *Tools to Work on Numeric Skills:* where you can find concepts like decimal numeration, addition and subtraction.

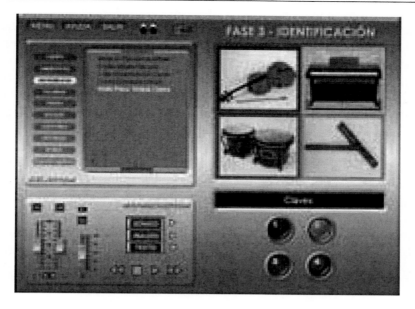

Figure 2. Snapshop of the interface used in the SEDEA program (copyright Onda Educa).

Some examples of these kinds of applications (used in Spain by a lot of schools and associations) are SEDEA Program, a computer application for the intervention process in the development of the hearing and language of children [OEP03] (see Figure 2); PEAPO, a web site with an easy to use resource that tries to promote the communication and autonomy capabilities in people with autism spectrum disorders (ASD) [PER00]; EDU356, a Web site with multimedia activities oriented to promoting and reinforcing the educative contents for children of different ages [DEC02]; Hola Amigo, an educational graphic interface for learning non-verbal communication using the language of SPC (or Pictographic Symbols System for non-verbal communication) [ASP99].

But if we pay attention to the state of the art of computer graphics applications and specifically 3D graphics, there are not many research projects developed in the area of education for people with learning difficulties. We can find a complete and more or less up to date review of virtual reality applications oriented to people with special needs in [LGK06]. In this review there is a classification of applications depending on the final user and the specific purpose of each system. They review the most important existing applications for blind children, people with physical disabilities, hearing and speech impaired children and people with some kind of phobias.

But our interest lies in virtual applications for people with autism and learning difficulties. In this field, they highlight some important projects:

- "Returning Home", a scenario for autistic children to help the educator to create a coherent organisation of certain important everyday activities [CKS00].
- The Aurora project, which develops an interactive robotic system for therapeutic purposes in teaching children with autism [AUR]. See Figure 3.
- Collaborative Virtual Environment to analyse the ability of children with autism to understand basic emotions represented by an avatar [MCM05].
- Some other projects and groups which use virtual reality for different purposes.

Additionally, we can highlight the developments done by two main groups, the VIRART Group at Nottingham University and the Autism and Learning Difficulties Group of the Robotics Institute at the University of Valencia, whose members are authors of this chapter.

The VIRART Group, using the author tool named Superscape (from Dimension International) has developed some software aimed both at people with learning difficulties and autism [BSL02]. Their software includes a set of virtual environments (see Figure 4) with the graphics quality and degree of adaptability to specific needs that this author tool allows (which are much lower than low-level real time graphics libraries, such as those that we mention further on). This software can be downloaded for free from the project Web site and is only available in English. Within those environments, it is possible to work on a wide variety of abilities. Whether or not individuals with autism adhere to particular social conventions in virtual environments was assessed. Different degrees of success were found [PML05], with results suggesting that some individuals with an ASD, low verbal IQ and weak executive ability require the most support to complete tasks successfully in the virtual environment (VE).

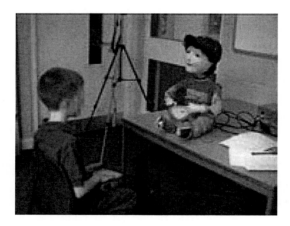

Figure 3. One of the robots used in the Aurora Project (copyright University of Hertfordshire)[RDB08].

Figure 4. Scene of the software developed by Virart Group (copyright University of Nottingham).

Figure 5. Virtual supermarket developed at the University of Valencia.

At the University of Valencia we have developed a virtual supermarket for teaching environmental understanding and for training in imagination (see Figure 5). This tool is freely distributed in Spanish, with the English version being under development [HLF01]. We are also developing another application, a virtual school oriented toward working on the social, cognitive and imagination skills for children with autism and Down syndrome [VHV05]. We will explain the main ideas of both applications in the following sections.

Even though these groups have done the largest amount of research into those aspects of learning difficulties related to this paper, other groups and studies also exist whose focus is slightly different from this subject. This is the case of the Virtual Environment Laboratory at the University of Southern California (USC), with an immersive virtual reality environment (a classroom) for the assessment (non educational) of attention deficits [RIZ00] or the University of Texas Medical branch, which developed a virtual reality meal preparation for the treatment of mental deficits due to traumatic brain injury [CAO98]. And other collaborative environments for people with Down syndrome and applications for teaching social skills for people with autism [LGK06].

All of these applications take into account the advantages of the use of VR to develop systems with specific purposes. In the next section we would like to highlight the main benefits of using this kind of technology for people with special needs.

ADVANTAGES OF VR TOOLS FOR PEOPLE WITH AUTISM AND LEARNING DIFFICULTIES

Information technologies (IT) have been claimed as effective, comfortable, facilitative and emotionally engaging contexts for learning in individual with autism [MUR97]. It is generally advanced that virtual reality offers new opportunities for the education of people with autism [SMM96]. As this and other later studies report, there is a great number of aspects of virtual reality that theoretically could benefit someone with learning difficulties and/or autism. In brief, we may say that virtual reality shares the advantages of computer-based learning, and has the additional advantage of making it more likely that the results will generalise to real-world settings in that it is a simulation of them. The possibility of customising the virtual environment to the specific profile and learning style of each individual is also an advantage for people with autism.

A virtual environment can be manipulated at will, which makes it possible to show how an object can be transformed into a different one (for helping them to understand imagination), and also to change in real-time the properties (size, shape, colour,...) of virtual objects (to foster understanding of those abstract concepts involved). This kind of applications provide a particularly facilitatory environment for people with learning difficulties in that it also offers structure, opportunities for repetition, affective (emotional) engagement and, additionally, control of the learning environment [HJV06].

Some clear characteristics provided by computer-based systems, which suit well the structured educational needs of autism and learning difficulties people are [MUR97]:

- clear boundaries
- controlled and step by step presentation of stimuli
- simple and obvious connection of information processed through one channel
- facilitating joint attention by selecting a compatible focus of interest
- restrictive context
- instilling feelings of safety, flexibility, adaptability and predictability of the learning environment or material
- enhancing development of autonomy, encouraging communication, boosting self-confidence and reinforcing optimism and respect

Additional analysis stands out the contribution of VR applications to improve the treatment, training and quality of life of children with disabilities [MJL98].

From a more accurate pedagogical point of view, VR offers advantages for the following areas [VCH07]:

Environment Understanding

Spatial concepts understanding: as it is possible to manipulate the height and the width of virtual objects at will, it is also possible to do it in order to illustrate the concept of size, including distinction between narrow and wide. The same advantage can be found when talking about concepts of relative position: in front/at the back, on top/below, first one/last one, put together/move apart, inside/out.

Quantity concepts understanding: it is possible to change in real time the number of objects that can be seen in a virtual environment, as well as being possible to change other variables for illustrating a lot/a few, everything/nothing, more/less, full/empty.

Visual concepts and adaptation to visual profiles: the sensory profile of people with learning difficulties may be very different to the typical one [BOG03]. As it is possible to change the colours, shapes, texture and luminance of any component at will, it is possible to adapt any virtual environment for the convenience of the sensory profile of a given individual with learning difficulties and/or autism. This possibility also allows teaching on recognising colours, lights and differences among a variety of things.

Virtual environments are also an ideal setting for working on those abilities that would be potentially hazardous when trained in reality, such as crossing the road, fire practice or how to face personal injuries. Another abstract concept is time, and it is also another thing that can be manipulated through programming. For example, it is possible to play with time in order to show the changes that occur between two different seasons, or to show the growing of a plant, or to teach concepts such as before/after or quick/ slow.

From Literality to Symbolism

Children's play evolves from simple manipulation of immediate reality to include more and more issues of a symbolic nature. As an example, at the beginning, the child starts playing functionally with realistic toys and later starts to make imaginary substitutions of some objects for others. Pretence itself offers a framework for the child to become familiarised with non literal language.

Within a virtual environment, it is possible to teach the preferred cultural use of each object (by showing virtual actors doing this use) and then teaching how an object can become or act as if it were a different thing (as in [HAJ04]).

The possibility of participating in first person in such processes is something that, a priori, would lead to a better learning (at least in those who have difficulties with imitation, as occurs with people with autism).

Social Abilities

People with learning difficulties often have problems in understanding people and themselves, what people think or feel and their expression of emotions.

It is hard to isolate and teach all these cognitive ideas in real-life situations due to competing and confusing stimulation from the social and environmental context. In reality, everything occurs very fast, with it being difficult to highlight subtle but relevant details that lead individuals to behave in a given way.

As another way of manipulating time, in virtual reality it is possible to "freeze" people's interactions and then carefully explain all the variables involved to those who find it difficult to understand or manage it socially.

Taking all these aspects into account, it is possible to create a complete tool which can help professionals in special education, to teach basic concepts and a variety of skills, most of them difficult to explain and show in the real world. Moreover, most of the concepts that can be integrated in the application are part of the school curriculum, thus being of special interest in the educational process of children, who can learn while they are playing (very important in making the system more appealing). All these ideas make this kind of application a potential tool to develop specific skills of people with autism and learning difficulties, improving in some sense, their quality of life.

DESCRIPTION OF VIRTUAL REALITY APPLICATIONS

With all of the previously described concepts and benefits in mind, we can review in more detail two of our computer graphics applications developed for people with learning difficulties.

As we mentioned before, the first case is a Virtual Supermarket and the second one is a Virtual School, this one still under development. Both environments were selected because of their familiarity to almost everybody. For that reason, entering in these places can be easier and more relaxed than in others, and the knowledge acquired in them can be generalized to the real world.

Virtual Supermarket

This application consists of a 3D supermarket with a variety of products, virtual actors representing different employees and different functionalities available. The basic task in this tool is to do the shopping. The user has to move inside the supermarket searching for the products specified in a shopping list (see Figure 6a and 6b). This shopping list is selected at the beginning and contains the objects to work with in each session. The teacher needs to organize each session to determine which lists they are going to use depending on the objects selected to work with.

Navigation inside the environment is done by using a joystick or the keyboard arrows. The use of a joystick facilitates the interaction for all users because it is more intuitive and easy to use than the keyboard. Location inside the supermarket is subjectively represented by a virtual trolley that moves with the user. This trolley also has the functionality of a real trolley in a supermarket, that is, it works as a container for the products that are necessary to buy to complete the list.

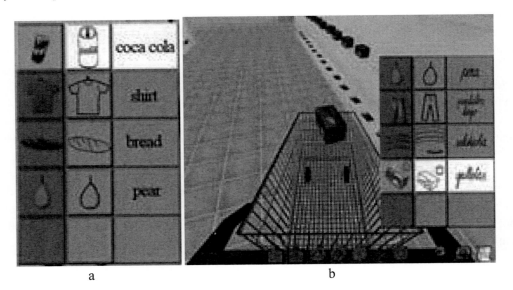

a   b

Figure 6. a) Shopping list. b) Picking an object from the shopping list.

Figure 7. Button panel.

For selecting objects or interactive elements in the virtual setting, it is possible to use the mouse or a tactile screen. Both interfaces are possible, depending on their availability in the school or centre where the software is used, but the tactile screen is easier to use for making selections inside the virtual world, because the individual only has to use his/her finger to touch the element to be selected.

Besides the traditional tasks inside a supermarket, we offer different functionalities to work in specific skills in people with learning difficulties, using the capabilities of the virtual reality applications to introduce educational contents. These functionalities are represented by pictograms in a toolbar (see Figure 7) and it is possible to change between them only by selecting the adequate button representing the mode to activate.

These modes are:

- *Functional Use and Play:* in this case it is possible to teach about the traditionally accepted usage of each object and how it is possible to play with miniatures of the object selected. In both cases the information is shown using pre-recorded videos integrated in the virtual world.

    These modes can be used to teach important concepts for daily life, associated with the work on cognitive skills and environment understanding. All the videos finish with a little social interaction to make it possible to also work on Social Skills.

- *Imaginary Play:* with this functionality it is possible to teach about imaginary play with *miniatures* of the objects. Again, the content is shown by videos integrated in the supermarket and can be associated with the work on cognitive skills. Although the imaginary play shown is individual, it is possible to arouse certain social skills with them, if the teacher tries to promote the same imaginary play but outside the computer and between him/her and the child.

- *Imaginary Transformations and Magic:* this is a more abstract concept and tries to take advantages of using Virtual Reality to show information difficult to explain and see in the real world. In this case, the user is shown an imaginary transformation of the *object* selected in the supermarket into another completely different one and with another functionality. This transformation consists of a 3D graphic animation integrated into the virtual scene (see Figure 8a).

    This attempts to promote the development of certain imagination abilities, considering them as a part of the cognitive skills. As was explained before, the task of the teacher is very important in all the functionalities, since it is possible to promote social skills from the information contained in these transformations.

- *Imaginary use:* in this case it is possible to learn about the imaginary usage of each object in a different context. Each product in the supermarket has a video associated with this information, trying to provide another tool to work on cognitive skills.

a   b

Figure 8. a) Imaginary sequence. b) Butcher's employee offering a product.

Another way used in the application to promote social skills in the user, was by integrating some virtual characters representing different employees inside the supermarket. The user can listen to how the avatar says hello or other expressions and offers some products. The individual has to interact with it and wait for the object that he wants to buy, making it possible to train in another important social skill which is the waiting ability (see Figures 8b and 9a).

Finally, the session finished when the user buys all the products indicated on the list. With all these objects in the trolley, it is necessary to go to the cash desk to pay for them. The user has to interact again with the virtual actor representing the cashier and give her the credit card to pay. After that, the user can exit and the session finishes (see Figure 9b).

The ideas behind this development are of double value as it is not only an educational game but also a tool for teaching symbolic play. The attraction that people with learning difficulties show towards computers increases the possibilities that this tool have in their educational process. They find it easy to use the hardware devices (tactile screen or mouse and joystick) and the graphical interface (with the help of the teacher in the first sessions), achieving high levels of interaction with the tool and, what it is more important, increasing their interest in educational contents.

a   b

Figure 9. a) Butcher's employee introducing himself. b) Cashier asking the user to pay for the products.

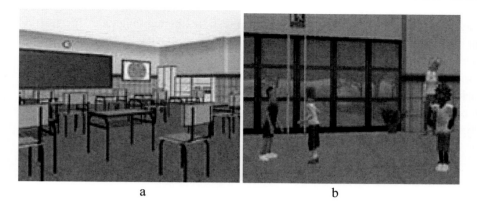

Figure 10. a) Classroom of the virtual school. b) Hall with different virtual characters.

This tool known with the name 'I am going to act as if...' ('Voy a hacer como si...' in Spain), has been distributed without any cost, to a wide variety of schools, special education centres, associations and parents, all over the Spanish country.

Virtual School

By its own nature, the school shapes in a bigger and more complex environment than the supermarket does -and also offers a wider range of pedagogical possibilities. It includes a whole set of sub-environments typically found in the most of real schools, with hall, classroom, dining room, playground and locker room, each of them including a variety of objects and virtual actors to work with (see Figures 10a and 10b).

Thanks to the large possibilities that this kind of environment offer, we try to develop an application with a wide variety of utilities to help in the development of different skills. The professional will have tools to work on different concepts understanding and imagination skills development, training specific skills and work in social skill development of people with learning difficulties. This application is under development and we would like to have a fist version as soon as possible, to evaluate and improve it to obtain a system to be distributed in special education centres, schools and associations. Let's describe the environment and the tools of this application [VHV05].

At the top level, the user is introduced with the role of a pupil in a school day. Activities taking part in the different sub-environments are arranged in a daily timetable, which serves as a task index and guides the user's evolution along the session. This timetable can be previously configured by the teacher, together with other session parameters, and selected at the beginning.

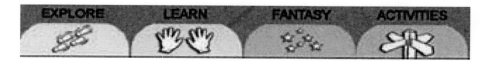

Figure 11. Virtual school button panel.

Navigation, object selection, and user-application interaction model in general, are all similar to those used in the supermarket. Subjective point-of-view is kept, too, but in this case the user has no visual representation inside the environment.

Inside each one of the sub-environments shaping the virtual school, the user can learn a big variety of concepts and train specific skills. At the moment, we are orienting our efforts in developing all these tools in three main areas of the school, the hall, the classroom and the playground. Available working modes can be grouped in the following four categories (see Figure 11):

- *Exploration:* a certain set of objects is highlighted while becoming selectable to the user. Selection of an object causes the object's name to be shown to the user through both visual and auditive channels. Explorable objects in a certain sub-environment are arranged in groups, in order to emphasize the closer relations between them, and in order to make easier the interaction by limiting the amount of information—explored objects—presented simultaneously to the user.

- *Learning:* this group is intended to teach the user the typical usage of objects, introduce him/her to ways of playing with them, and showing existing symbolic relations between objects. Between those inter-object relations taught here, there can be found generalization (different instances of a same object), alternative usage (different, non-trivial ways of using the same object) or substitution (other objects adopting the role and being used like the object selected). Typical usage and playing modes are presented through a pair of virtual hands, shown from a subjective perspective as if they were the user's own hands, which directly manipulate the object inside the virtual environment.

  On the other hand, inter-object relationships are better explained with real examples, and so are shown to the user using sets of photographs (see Figure 12).

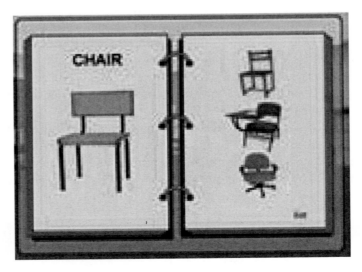

Figure 12. Example of generalization concepts shown in a notebook.

- *Fantasy:* here the imagination and fantasy features are emphasized. Virtual, three-dimensional objects are presented to the user and then transformed into other nonrelated, different ones. Morphing technology becomes the most suitable option here, because this allow for integrate imagination sequences in the virtual environment itself.

  The first stage begins by working with imagination/fantasy on single objects, showing the user individual transformations of the object selected (see Figure 13). The second, more advanced stage introduces more complex collective fantasy sequences, by transforming a whole group of school objects into a set of interrelated imaginary alter egos, all going around the same theme, to finally perform an imaginary animation including all of them.

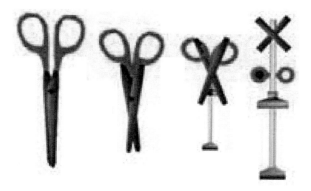

Figure 13. Imaginary transformation of scissors into a train sign.

- *Activities:* the last group presents different activities intended to work around spatial, timing or social relationships. A first group of generic activities lets the user learn basic spatial relationships and concepts described before, such as the size, quantity or relative position, as well as time-related concepts (such as slow/fast or before/after).

Figure 14. An interactive activity for playing with the size of the objects.

A second group of activities is intended to work with social relationships, by putting the user in the middle of specific situations where interaction with virtual actors is required in order to solve them.

Figure 15. Scene from the point of view of the user in the classroom. The teacher explains the emotion angry.

Among this kind of activities, we would like to work on emotion recognition, understanding and imitation. For that, we would like to use virtual characters which will describe certain emotions and reflect them in their face. All the basic emotions will be integrated and represented in the face of the avatar: neutral, happy, sad, angry, surprise and fear (see Figure 16).

Adaptability is a very important feature of this application, referring to the range of disorders it can be used to work with. From the very essentials of design, a requirement has been the ability to adapt sessions to the concrete user features, including in those features the kind of disorder involved.

In this way, the application is being developed to be used with individuals with Down syndrome, as well as with people with autism spectrum disorders, by simply changing the set of activities programmed for each specific session.

At the moment, the application is under development, with the collaboration of different professionals in the area. Most of the functions described above are completely developed, the 3D objects integrated in the environment have been test with children to know the level of understanding of these virtual representations of real objects and we are finishing the first prototype, for testing the interaction and environment understanding with people with learning difficulties.

Figure 16. Different emotions expressed by the face of a virtual character.

DEVELOPMENT

The characteristics of the applications presented before made it necessary to make a decision on the software to use for their development. We decided to use a real time graphic library (OpenGL Performer for the virtual supermarket and open scene graph (OSG), for the virtual school) integrated in an object-oriented language (C++), because of the potential of this kind of libraries for the creation of customized tools and the possibilities of achieving better quality and results than any other methodology. This library provides us with the basic scene graph and graphical control needed to structure and interact with the application in real time. The modularity of all the elements involved in the system allows the reusability for other new environments and the flexibility to integrate all the desired functions. The design and models creation as well as the animations integrated in the environments where developed using well-known graphic tools such as 3D Studio Max and Photoshop. All these components, integrated in a well defined and structured system, results in computer graphics applications used for a special group of people, trying to help them in their knowledge development and quality of life.

EXPERIMENTAL ASSESSMENT

For the experimental assessment, case studies are a good methodology for this kind of research. They differ from other methodologies as there are "intensive descriptions and analysis of a single unit or a closed system, which can be an individual, a group, an intervention or a community" [RM96]. Case studies are a very flexible method that can include as much qualitative as quantitative data, and be used from very different theoretical perspectives, basically in our case from IT and psychology. Together with this, technological development forces us into making an intervention with prototypes in a way where reflection on its results improves both the prototype and the intervention plan simultaneously.

Assessment is something that shall be done not only within scientific research, but also within any educational intervention. In every quality teaching process, it is necessary to objectively assess the impact of the intervention strategies that are applied to each individual.

In our case, only the virtual supermarket has been evaluate with people with autism, since the virtual school is still under development. In that application, the main important skill to be evaluate are the development of functional and symbolic play, abstract concept understanding and imagination. There are at least two standard tests for assessing functional and symbolic play: the SPT 'Symbolic Play Test' [LC76] that, despite its name, assesses functional play and the ToPP 'Test of Pretend Play' [LB97], which really assesses symbolic play. However, both tests incur a cost that sometimes is beyond the financial possibilities of many professionals in autism. In order to assess the progress in abstract concept understanding, it is possible to check the abilities involved with an ad hoc test prepared by teachers and also by using parts of a standard test (preferably non-verbal) such as the Leiter International Manipulative Scale [RM96].

For this reason, as occurs with the tool 'I am going to act as if...' [HJL04], it is appropriate that software tools come together with a method for assessing (at least informally) those abilities worked on with the tool. This assessment and recording must be done at least twice, before and after the intervention, in order to be able to objectively see if there was any advance or improvement.

The benefit of using a given tool itself is the backbone of major research in this field [SMM96] [PML05] [HAJ04], but it is also necessary to compare those new strategies with conventional ones, if it is aimed to justify new development and its funding in this field. For this aim, it is useful to follow a 'counterbalanced' design where some participants initially use a conventional version and then a VR version, while the rest are in reverse order.

Ideally, observers who analyse abilities at baseline (1, 2 or 3) should be blind to the order of giving tests (Figure 17). Results concerning the gain of 'play abilities' between the first and second assessment and between the second and third assessment will serve to compare both strategies when applied to a number of cases.

Another important aspect to measure is the satisfaction of the individual with autism while using any of the tools. This measure, together with effectiveness and efficiency, is part of the Usability of the tool [ALC00].

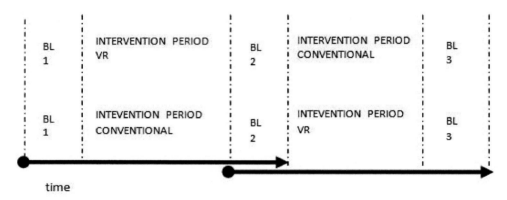

Figure 17. Assessment and intervention periods.

SOME RESULTS

Relevant results have been published in [HAJ04], and some case studies are described and analysed. The results obtained with some children after nearly three months of intervention, with sessions of about 20–30 minutes each, suggest a very high impact on play scores after using the tools measured with the Symbolic Play Test [LB97], and a very good level of generalisation of acquired knowledge to real settings in those who spontaneously initiate communication with others. The information provided by the tool to work on cognitive skills and environment understanding (such as the functional and imaginary use and play) helped them to better understand the usage and how to play with most of the objects included in the supermarket. Additionally, some of them improved their imagination skills and generalization to the real world.

In this table, it is possible to see the results of two of the participants in the study in the ToPP test, analysed by four different observers.

	Participant 1				Participant 2			
	Structured		Free		Structured		Free	
	Pre	Post	Pre	Post	Pre	Post	Pre	Post
First observer our team	10	21	8	12	15	18	0	6
Second observer our team	7	16	8	12	18	24	2	8
First independent observer	13	17	14	22	14	19	2	8
Second independent observer	11	13	12	16	15	20	2	6

Figure 18. Scores at ToPP by four observers.

In the following graphic it is possible to see the evolution of both participants along the three months of intervention.

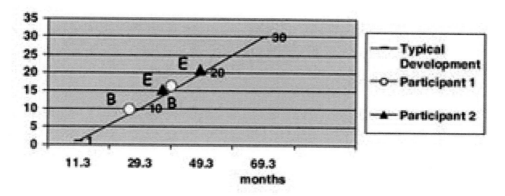

Figure 19. Evolution of two participant of the study.

CONCLUSION

The area of computer graphics and virtual reality for specific purposes is currently an increasing field of research owing to the advantages and flexibility provided by these types of applications. The development of graphic systems specially addressed to people with special needs constitutes a very important field of work applied to the education process of the individual.

Specifically, if we paid attention to the people with autism and learning difficulties, with special problems in social interaction and communication, and deficits in imagination and functional and symbolic play, it is possible to structure the content of graphic applications to try to help professionals in the area to provide training in these specific skills.

Thanks to these kinds of systems, it is possible to offer training in a wide variety of abilities without dangerous or hazardous situations, and with possibilities for structuring the information, repeating situations and explanations, representating abstract concepts (such as imagination and magical thoughts) and simulation of social situations using virtual characters, all within a completely controlled environment. All of this, together with the attraction that people with learning difficulties show towards computers, make these kinds of applications a potential tool for developing specific skills in which these individual have problems, providing positive experiences and the potential for improving their quality of life.

The tools presented in this chapter are good examples of these kind of systems whereby technology meets education to improve the learning experience and, in the end, the quality of life of the end users.

ACKNOWLEDGEMENTS

This work has been done thanks to the funding of the Spanish Ministry of Science and Technology (PROFIT), the Spanish Ministry of Social Affairs (IDI) and the Regional Government of Valencia, through the projects INMER, APRIL and AVISTA. We want to thank all members of the team from the Autism and Learning Difficulties Group and the Artec Group of the Robotics Institute at the University of Valencia, the collaboration of the Autism Association of Burgos, the Spanish Autism Confederation, COMUNICA Centre of Diagnosis and Intervention, the Down Syndrome Association at Huesca (Spain), the Down Syndrome Association at Burgos, and the knowledge received from Dr. Rita Jordan (University of Birmingham).

REFERENCES

[ALC00] Alcantud, F. Nuevas Tecnologías, Viejas Esperanzas. In *Las NNTT en el ámbito de la discapacidad y las Necesidades Educativas especiales. Murcia. Consejería de Educación y Universidades.* Spain 2000.

[APA94] A. P. Association. (1994). Diagnostic and Statistical Manual of Mental Disorders. Washington, DC: *American Psychiatric Press, Inc. 4th ed. Edition.*

[ASP99] Centro Obregon, Asprona, Valladolid. (1999). *User Manual of the Aplication Hola Amigo.*

[AUR] Aurora Project. Available in: http://www.aurora-project.com/

[BSL02] Brown, D.J., Shopland, N. & Lewis, J. (2002). Flexible and virtual travel training environments. In, *Proc. 4th Intl Conf. on Disability, Virtual Reality and Assoc. Technologies* (Sharkey, Sik Lányi and Standen, Eds),Veszprém, Hungary, 18-20 Sept. (2002), 181-188.

[BOG03] Bogdashina, O. (2003). Sensory Perceptual Issues in Austism and Asperger Syndrome. *Jessica Kigsley Publishers. ISBN 1 84310 1661.*

[CAO98] Christiansen, C., Abreu, B., Ottenbacher, K., Huffman, K., Masel, B. & Culpepper, R: Task performance in virtual environments used for cognitive rehabilitation after traumatic brain injuries. *Archives of Physical Medicine and Rehabilitation,* 79, (1998), 888–892.

[CKS00] Charitos, D., Karadanos, G., Sereti, E., Triantafillou, S., Koukouvinou, S. & Martakos, D. (2000). Employing Virtual Reality for Aiding the Organisation of autistic children behavior in everyday tasks. *Proc. 3rd Intl Conf. Disability, Virtual Reality & Assoc. Tech.,* Alghero, Italy 2000. ICDVRAT/University of Reading, UK; ISBN 0 7049 11 42 6

[DEC02] Education Department of the Cataluny Government (2002). Edu356, Catalunya, Spain. http://www.edu365.com/index.htm

[HAJ04] Herrera, G., Alcantud,F., Jordan, R., Blanquer, A., Labajo, G. & De Pablo, C. (2005). Development of symbolic play through the use of VR tools in children with autism. *In García Sanchez, J.N. (Ed) 'Aplicaciones para la intervención en los trastornos del desarrollo'*, Editorial Pirámide, (2005). And in *Autism: the International Journal of Research and Practice 2005*, to be published.

[HJL04] Herrera, G., Jorda, R., Labajo, J. & Arnáiz, J. (2004). Manual de Uso de la Herramiento 'Voy a hacer como si...' *Edited by the University of Valencia, (2004).*

[HJV06] Herrera, G., Jordan, R. & Vera, L. (2006). Abstract Concept and Imagination Teaching through Virtual Reality in People with Autism Spectrum Disorders. In *Technology and Disability* 18(4) (2006) 173–180. IOS Press.

[HLF01] Herrera, G., Labajo, G., Fernández, M., Lozano, M., Vera, L. & Carrasco, J. (2001). INMER-II. Una Nueva Herramienta Educativa en Autismo basada en Técnicas de Realidad Virtual. *Congreso Nacional de Informática de la Salud*, INFORSALUD, (March 2001).

[JOR03] Jordan, R. (2203). A review of the role of play in theory and practice in autistic spectrum disorders. *In Autism: the International Journal of Research and Practice (special edition, 2003), 7.*

[LB97] Lewis, V. & Boucher, J. (1997). Manual for the test of pretend play. *London: Psychological Corporation. (1997).*

[LC76] Loew, M. & Costello, A.J. (1976). Manual for the Symbolic Play Test. *Winsor, U.K:. NFER(1976).*

[LGK06] Lányi, C. S., Geist, Z., Károlyi, P., Tiliger, A. & Magyar, V. (2006). Virtual Reality in Special Needs Early Education. *The International Journal of Virtual Reality, 5(4): 55-68.*

[MCM05] Moore, D., Cheng, Y., McGrath, P, & Powell, N. (2005).Avatars and Austism, Assitive Technologies—From Virtuality to Reality. *A Pruski and H. Knops (Eds.) IOS Press, pp 442-448.*

[MJL98] McComas, J., Pivik, J. & Laflamme, M. (1998). Current uses of Virtual Reality for Children with Disabilities. Giuseppe Riva, Brenda K. Wiederhold, Enrico Molnari (Eds.). *Virtual Environments in Clinical Psychology and Neuroscience.* 1998 Ios Press: Amsterdam, Netherlands.

[MUR97] Murray, D. (1997). Autism and information technology: therapy with computers. In *S. Powell & R. Jordan (Eds) Autism and Learning: a guide to good London, David Fulton (1997).*

[OEP03] Onda Educa and The Rehabilitation Group of the School La Purisima of Zaragoza. (2003). Sedea Application. http://www.ondaeduca.com/index.php

[PML05] Parsons, S., Mitchell, P & Leonard, A. (2005). Do adolescents with autistic spectrum disorders adhere to social conventions in virtual environments?. In *Autism: an International Journal of Research and Practice. K2005, 9: 95-117.*

[PER00] Perez De La Maza, L. et all (2000). Peapo, Centro Pauta de Madrid. http://peapo.iespana.es

[PML05] Parsons, S., Mitchell, P., Leonard, A. (2005).Do adolescents with autistic spectrum disorders adhere to social conventions in virtual environments? *Autism: an International Journal of Research and Practise*, SAGE Publications, 9 (2005), 95–117.

[RDB08] Robins, B., Dautenhahn, K., te Boekhorst, R., Nehaniv, C. L. (2008). Behaviour Delay and Robot Expressiveness in Child-Robot Interactions: A User Study on Interaction Kinesics. Proc. ACM/IEEE 3rd International Conference on Human-Robot Interaction (HRI 2008).

[RIZ00] Rizzo, A.A. et al. (2000).The Virtual Classroom: A Virtual Reality Environment for the Assessment and Rehabilitation of Attention Deficits. *CyberPsychology and Behavior*, 3, (June 2000), 483–499.

[RM96] Roid, G. & Miller, L. (1996). Escala Manipulativa Internacional de Leitter-R. *Edición en Castellano Revisada y Ampliada.*

[SMM96] Strickland, D., Marcus, L. M., Mesibov, G. B. & Hogan, K. (1996). Bried report: Two case studies using virtual reality a learning tool for autistic children. In *Journal of Autism and Developmental Disorders* (1996), 26(6), 651-659.

[TD00] Tortosa, F & De Jorge, E. (2000). Uso de las tecnologías informáticas en un centro específico de niños autistas. *Nuevas Tecnologías, Viejas Esperanzas: las nuevas tecnologías en el ámbito de la discapacidad y las necesidades educativas especiales*, Murcia: Consejería de Educación y Universidades, Spain.

[WAT01] Watkins, A. (2001). Aplicaciones de las Nuevas Tecnologias (NNTT) a las Necesidades Educativas Especiales (NEE). *Middelfart: European Agency for Development in Special Needs Education.* http://www.tecnoneet.org/index.php?f=agencia

[VCH07] Vera, L., Campos, R., Herrera, G. & Romero, C. (2007). Computer graphics applications in the educatin process of people with learning difficulties. In *Computers & Graphics, Elsevier Ltd.* Vol. 31(4), 649-658. ISSN 0097-8493. Doi: 10.1016/ j.cag.2007.03.003.

[VHV05] Vera, L., Herrera, G., Vived, E. (2005).Virtual Reality School for Children with Learning Difficulties. *ACM SIGCHI ACE05*, (June 2005).

In: Multimedia in Education and Special Education
Editors: O. Demir and C. Celik

ISBN 978-1-60741-073-7
© 2009 Nova Science Publishers, Inc.

Chapter 8

DISPROPORTIONALITY IN SPECIAL EDUCATION: SYNTHESIS, ILLUSTRATIONS AND IMPLICATIONS

Amity L. Noltemeyer, Courtney L. Brown,
and Caven S. Mcloughlin[*]
Kent State University, Ohio, USA

ABSTRACT

The overrepresentation of minority students in special education programs has been cause for concern since the original enactment of legislation requiring special education for children with disabilities. Current data suggest that the trend persists.

Given the increasing number of ethnically diverse students in our nation's schools, coupled with the potentially negative outcomes associated with misidentification, it is imperative that educational professionals understand the disproportionality phenomenon as a prerequisite for creating equitable learning environments.

This chapter explores disproportionality in special education. First, it provides an introduction and literature review to acquaint readers with disproportionality and its effects. This includes an overview of definitions, measurement issues, historical and current estimates of disproportionality at the state and national level, factors hypothesized to contribute to disproportionality, and unanswered questions. Next, the methods and results of a study analyzing data from all public school districts in the state of Ohio during the 2006-2007 academic school year are presented to illustrate disproportionality incidence. Ohio has been chosen as the illustration since data are available from every public school district. The state is populous and racially representative of the USA, according to US Census reports, and for many factors it is viewed as a bellwether state reflecting national trends. This study displays the degree to which disproportional identification of African American students continues to exists across disability categories, and displays the association between school district type (e.g., rural, urban, suburban) and disproportionality rates. Finally, the chapter provides discussion of the

---

[*] Address correspondence to Caven Mcloughlin, Ph.D., Professor, School Psychology, 405 White Hall, Kent State University, Kent, OH 44242; telephone: 330-672-2928 or caven@kent.edu

implications and resulting recommendations for addressing disproportionality at the school, district, and state level.

ABBREVIATIONS

For simplicity and clarity, the term MR – and its derivatives Mild Mental Retardation (MMR) and Moderate Mental Retardation (MoMR) – will be used throughout the article since these were the definitions and terms used in most of the research studies. However, legislation in Ohio – the state in which this investigation was conducted – uses the term Cognitive Disability (CD) in place of the federal term MR. In addition, this article uses the term Emotional Disturbance (ED), although previous versions of federal legislation referred to this disability as Severe Behavior Handicap (SBH).

Tabulated data for the 1.6 million subject data-set that describes disproportionality in Ohio's schools (referenced in this chapter) is available from the corresponding author for each disability category and school typology.

Since the issue was first identified forty years ago (Dunn, 1968), the overrepresentation of minority students in special education programs has been cause for concern. Although researchers have expressed interest in the over- and under-representation of multiple ethnic groups across all disabilities, perhaps the most longstanding and alarming trend surrounds the disproportional representation of African American students in Mental Retardation (MR; see Footnote), Emotional Disturbance (ED; see Footnote), and Specific Learning Disabilities (SLD) programs. Despite provisions in the *Individuals with Disabilities Education Improvement Act* (2004) requiring State Educational Agencies (SEA's) and Local Education Agencies (LEA's) to enact policies to prevent such disproportionality, current data suggest the trend persists.

Given the growing number of ethnically diverse students in our nation's schools, coupled with the potentially negative outcomes and wasted resources associated with the misidentification of students for special education, it is imperative that educational professionals understand and address disproportionality. The aims of this chapter, which seeks to focus on disproportionality in special education placements for African American students, are three-fold. First, the chapter will review definitions, measurement methods, estimates, causes, and future directions related to disproportionality. Next, the methods and results of a study analyzing data from all public school districts in the state of Ohio during the 2006-2007 school year will be used to illustrate current disproportionality trends in a bellwether state, with a specific focus on the association between school district type (e.g., rural, urban, suburban) and disproportionality. Finally, the chapter will provide a discussion of the implications and resulting recommendations for addressing disproportionality at the school, district, and state level emergent from the data.

INTRODUCTION TO DISPROPORTIONALITY

Although it has been conceptualized in varying ways, Oswald, Coutinho, Best, and Singh (1999) defined disproportional representation as "...the extent to which membership in a given ethnic group affects the probability of being placed in a specific special education disability category" (p. 198). Dunn (1968) first highlighted this issue when he critiqued the overrepresentation of minority students in Mild Mental Retardation (MMR) programs. Based on observation and experience, Dunn estimated that approximately 60-80% of students identified as MMR came from marginalized backgrounds including poverty and minority status. Using data collected during the same era, Mercer (1973) substantiated Dunn's claims of disproportionality by demonstrating that African American students were represented in MR classes at three times the rate of their representation in the general population.

Following the passage of the Education for All Handicapped Children Act (1975), additional evidence corroborated the disproportionate representation of African American students in some disability categories. For example, using 1978 data collected from the Federal Office of Civil Rights (OCR), Finn (1982) demonstrated that 3.46% of African American students were identified MMR versus 1.07% of White students. Although not in low-incidence disabilities and those with a more observable medical component (e.g., Autism, Orthopedic Impairment, Hearing Impairment), initial evidence suggested African Americans were overrepresented in disabilities involving greater subjectivity in diagnosis (particularly MR and ED).

This finding prompted researchers to action. It presented as such a significant concern that in 1979 that the National Research Council was charged with determining the factors contributing to disproportionality, with a specific focus on MMR (Heller, Holtzman, & Messick, 1982). Despite widespread changes in special education identification procedures, state and federal laws, diversity appreciation, and civil rights over the interim decades, disproportionality persisted at such intensity that the National Research Council initiated additional research on the issue twenty years after their seminal work (Donovan & Cross, 2002). The results of these large-scale studies — along with their smaller-scale counterparts — helped shape current conceptualizations and practice guidelines regarding disproportionality.

Lawmakers, too, responded to disproportionality. For example, the IDEIA (2004) legislation extended the provisions of its predecessors by providing State Education Agencies (SEA) and Local Education Authorities (LEA) the responsibility to define — and enact policies to prevent — disproportional special education identification and placement. However, the IDEIA (2004) added an additional provision aimed at reducing disproportionality. Specifically, LEA's deemed to exhibit significant disproportionality must devote 15% of their Part B funds to early intervention programs aimed at achieving educational equity.

Some researchers (e.g., MacMillan & Reschly, 1998) have questioned why disproportionality in early intervention programs (e.g., Head Start and Title I) has not received the scrutiny afforded to disproportionality in special education programs. The answer to this question appears to relate to the differential outcomes associated with early intervention and special education. First, research and commentary over the years have suggested that special education programming can be ineffective (e.g., Dunn, 1986; *Larry P.*

v. Riles, 1979). Second, identifying individuals with a disability has the potential to be stigmatizing and result in a self-fulfilling prophecy (e.g., Patton 1998). Finally, because special education identification has historically been associated with restrictive placements, there is concern that special education students are at a higher risk for being denied sufficient exposure to typical peers.

MEASUREMENT OF DISPROPORTIONALITY

As a prerequisite for understanding and addressing disproportionality, it is necessary accurately to measure the extent to which it occurs. Researchers and educational agencies have used a variety of methods for achieving this end, each with its own unique strengths and limitations. Three frequently used methods are 'composition index', 'risk index', and the 'odds ratio' (or 'risk ratio').

Composition index measures the percentage of individuals in a particular disability category from a given ethnic group. A composition index is typically calculated by dividing the number of students of a particular ethnic group identified with a specific disability by the total number of students identified with that same disability (Donovan & Cross, 2002).

In contrast, risk index assesses the likelihood that a student in a particular ethnic group will be identified as having a particular disability. The risk index is calculated by dividing the number of students in the ethnic group with a particular disability by the total number of students in that ethnic group in order to determine the percentage of students in the ethnic group who are identified with the disability (Donovan & Cross, 2002).

The odds ratio addresses the primary limitation of each of these methods — namely, the absence of a comparison group — by comparing a particular ethnic group's risk of being identified as having a particular disability to the risk of a peer comparison group. Specifically, the odds ratio is computed by dividing the risk index of one ethnic group by the risk index of another comparison group (Donovan & Cross, 2002). An odds ratio of 1.00 indicates the ethnic group has an equal chance as the comparison group of being identified with the disability (whereas values smaller than 1.00 indicate they have less of a chance and values greater than 1.00 indicates they have more of a chance). For example, if the odds ratio for an African American population in ED is deemed to be 2.0, that means that African Americans are twice as likely to be identified as ED as the comparison population.

The odds ratio has been used not only be researchers, but also by SEA's and LEA's. Burdett (2007) reported the results of survey data collected from 33 SEA's to determine how they defined disproportionality for their LEA's. With regard to special education identification, 18 of the 28 SEA's that had developed procedures for measuring significant disproportionality chose to use an odds ratio (either in isolation or in conjunction with other measurement methods). Of the remaining 10 SEA's, their methods varied, ranging from reviewing LEA policies and procedures to conducting an "analysis of means."

Despite the utility of the odds ratio at the state and national level, unique limitations may occur when analyzing district-level data. For example, wide variations in student enrollments mean that comparing odds ratios from different districts is difficult (Bollmer, Bethel, Garrison-Mogren, & Brauen, 2007). To address these limitations Bollmer et al. proposed modifications to consider when exploring district-level data.

The measurement method used to assess disproportionality ultimately depends on the questions being asked, the audience, and the unique setting. Each method has particular strengths and limitations that must be considered. Some researchers have even called for the use of "multiple gating procedures" which follow the use of one metric or statistic with others (e.g., Hosp & Madyun, 2007). When disproportionality exists across the various metrics or statistics, it can be assumed a significant discrepancy exists. As conductors and consumers of research, it is important to understand that the method utilized may ultimately influence the manner in which the results are perceived and understood.

EXTENT OF DISPROPORTIONALITY

Consistent with early estimates of the overrepresentation of African American students in special education identification (e.g., Dunn, 1968; Finn, 1982; Heller et al., 1982), recent research indicates that this trend persists. Specifically, despite vast educational and societal changes that have occurred over the past thirty years, African Americans continue to be consistently overrepresented in MR and ED identification, and inconsistently overrepresented in SLD identification. This section will provide current estimates of the extent of this phenomenon at the state and federal level.

Oswald, Coutinho, Best, and Singh (1999) were interested in exploring rates and patterns of disproportionality in MMR and ED identification. Using extant data from a representative national sample of 4,455 school districts, the researchers found African American students were 2.4 times more likely to be identified as MMR and 1.3 times more likely to be identified as ED than their non-African American counterparts.

Donovan and Cross (2002) found similar results using data from a 1998 national database. Specifically, African American students were more than twice as likely as White students to be identified as MR, with an odds ratio of 2.24. Although African Americans constituted only 17% of the student population, they represented 33% of the MR population. In addition, with an odds ratio of 1.59, African American students were also at a higher risk for ED identification than any other ethnic group. However, with an odds ratio of 1.08, the researchers did not find significant overrepresentation in SLD among the African American population.

Zhang and Katsiyannis (2002) sought to replicate and extend previous research by exploring patterns of disproportionality across SLD, MR and ED categories and across all reported ethnic descriptions using federal data. The researchers found that compared to other ethnic groups, African Americans had the highest rates of identification across all three disabilities.

In addition to national data, state-level data has also been used to explore disproportionality. For example, using data from 67 Florida school districts, Serwatka, Deering, and Grant (1995) found that African American students were overrepresented in ED programs in 58 of these districts. Defining overrepresentation as the difference between the percentage of African American students in the school district and the percentage of African American students enrolled in ED programs, they found a mean overrepresentation of 10%.

Coulter (1996) was also interested in exploring the disproportional identification of African American students at the state level. For the study, significant disproportionality was defined as ethnic representation in a disability that exceeded 10% of the group's representation in the entire population. Using data from the 66 LEA's in a southern state during the 1993-94 school year, the researcher found that 28 of the LEA's demonstrated significant disproportionate representation of African Americans when considering the entire spectrum of educational disabilities. When examining the judgmental disabilities more specifically, significant disproportionality was identified in 62 of 66 LEA's.

Like Coulter (1996) and Serwatka et al. (1995), Skiba et al. (2004) were interested in exploring disproportionality in identification at the state-level. Using data from Indiana's 304 school districts during the 2003-2004 school year, they found that African American students represented 12% of the state's school-age population but 30.2% of students identified as MMR. With an odds ratio of 3.21, African American students were over three times more likely to be identified with MMR than White students. Disproportionality in identification for African American students was also found, albeit to lesser degrees, in the SLD, ED, MoMR., SMR and Deaf-Blind disabilities.

In addition to exploring disproportionality in identification, Skiba et al. (2004) were also interested in understanding disproportionality in placement. Using the same data set, the researchers found that African Americans were underrepresented in general education settings, proportionally represented in resource room settings, and overrepresented in more restrictive settings (i.e., self-contained class or homebound setting). For example, although African Americans represented 13.25% of students served in special education programs, they represented 30.2% of those served in self-contained classes, with an odds ratio of 2.8.

Skiba, Poloni-Staudinger, Gallini, Simmons, and Feggins-Azziz (2006) were also interested in learning more about the disproportionate placement of African American students in more restrictive environments at the state level. Across five disabilities (MoMR, MMR, SLD, ED, Speech and Language Impairment), these researchers found that African American students were *over*identified in self-contained placements and *under*identified in regular education placements when compared to all students represented in that disability category. For example, African American students were found to be almost three times as likely to be served in a self-contained classroom than other students with disabilities.

Unlike the previously mentioned research, which focused primarily on disproportionality at the identification and placement stages of the special education process, Hosp and Reschly (2003) were interested in exploring disproportionality at the referral stage of the process. Results of their synthesis of individual studies suggested that African American students, with an odds ratio of 1.32, were significantly more likely to be referred than White students. Given that most students who are referred eventually are identified with a disability, these results suggest that African American students may be overrepresented as a result of the frequency with which they are referred.

Together, these studies suggest that African American students continue to be overrepresented in the identification of MR and ED. Related to SLD, there have been conflicting findings, with disproportionality being identified in some studies and not others. In addition to being identified at higher rates than their peers, African American students also appear to be educated in more restrictive placements. Initial studies suggest that, in addition to identification and placement, African American students are also overrepresented in special education referrals.

CAUSES AND CONTRIBUTORS TO DISPROPORTIONALITY

Considering the previously discussed research, which has been conducted in a variety of populations spanning multiple decades, the disproportionate representation of African American students in certain disability categories and placements is no longer in dispute. For this reason, researchers have increasingly shifted from documenting disproportionality to exploring the contributory factors. There have been many such factors posited — ranging from sociocultural differences to bias — with various levels of support garnered for each. This section will highlight some of the empirical support for several hypothesized contributors.

One hypothesis maintains that the stressors associated with poverty may contribute to higher levels of special education identification among African Americans, given increased rates of poverty in this population. The effect of sociodemographic and poverty variables on special education identification has been widely investigated with varying results. For example, using multivariate analyses of district-level data from a Midwestern state's 295 school districts, Skiba, Poloni-Staudinger, Simmons, Feggins-Azziz, & Chung (2005) found that poverty made a weak and inconsistent contribution to special education identification across four disability categories (MMR, MoMR, ED, and SLD). In fact, poverty only predicted disproportionality in MMR identification. Overall, race was shown to be a better predictor of special education identification than poverty.

Oswald et al. (1999), in their previously described study of disproportionality in MMR and SED, also explored the extent to which poverty predicted identification for African American students. Although a clear poverty effect was demonstrated, the direction of the relationship differed for those identified with MMR and SED. Specifically, as poverty increased more African American students were identified as MMR but fewer were identified as SED. The authors concluded that perhaps more affluent communities are more tolerant of African American learning differences than behavioral differences, although this speculation warrants further investigation.

Skiba et al. (2004) also examined the degree to which poverty might explain the disproportional identification of African American students as disabled. In many respects, the results mirrored those of Skiba et al. (2005). For example, Skiba et al. (2004) found that district-level poverty made weak and inconsistent contributions to disproportionality. For ED and MoMR, there was no relationship between poverty and disproportionality, whereas for SLD and Communication Disorders the relationship existed but was opposite the researchers' expectations (i.e., poorer districts had lower levels of disproportionality and wealthier districts had higher levels). Although African Americans were at an overall increased risk of being identified, this risk also increased as district-level poverty increased; this suggest that poverty may serve to exacerbate already existing disproportionality. Interestingly, the most significant predictor of disproportionality was school districts' suspension and expulsion rates, which were associated with higher disproportionality in ED, MoMR, MiMR, and SLD.

This last finding — namely, the relationship between use of exclusionary discipline and disproportionality — suggests that perhaps cultural differences between minority students and their teachers may result in an increased risk for special education referral and identification. For example, White teachers may be more likely to view certain behaviors as deviant even though they may be socially acceptable within African American culture. Serwatka et al.

(1995) sought to explore this issue by examining the relationship between African American disproportionate identification in ED programs and 15 district-level demographic variables. Using correlations between degree of disproportionality and each of the 15 demographic variables, the researchers found that: (a) as the percentage of African American students in the district increased, the degree of disproportionality decreased, and (b) as the percentage of African American teachers in the district increased, the degree of disproportionality decreased. One potential explanation for these results is that as the African American population increases, teachers might become less likely to view culturally different behaviors as deviant. Additionally, African American teachers may be less likely to refer African American students because of an enhanced understanding of such cultural differences.

Using a stratified random sample of 4,151 school districts, Coutinho, Oswald, and Best (2002) also sought to explore the relationship between disproportionality and sociodemographic variables, with a specific focus on SLD. The researchers used nine sociodemographic variables as predictors (e.g., student to teacher ratio, per pupil expenditure, percentage of at-risk children, percentage of non-white children, median income) and found that a statistically significant proportion of the variation in SLD identification could be explained by a combination of these nine predictors. Of particular interest, the researchers found that increased poverty was associated with increased SLD identification among African American, but not White, students. In addition, the researchers found that as the proportion of non-White students increased, SLD identification rates decreased for all ethnic groups.

In addition to differences based on poverty, differences based on region have also been documented. For example, Zhang and Katsiyannis (2002) found significant differences in representation based on region that were not explained by regional poverty differences. Specifically, the percentage of African Americans in MR and ED varied widely based on region of the country. However, the data were aggregated at the state level, and the researchers recommended future research using district-level data to explore the reasons behind these regional variations. For example, the authors recommended exploring such factors as the size of the district, the expenditures of the district, and school district typology (specifically rural, urban and suburban characteristics).

Researchers have also sought to understand better the factors contributing to the disproportionate representation of African American students in restrictive placements. Skiba et al. (2006), in their previously described study, sought to determine whether or not this overrepresentation in restrictive placements was simply an artifact of African American overrepresentation in disability categories that require more restrictive placements. To test this hypothesis, the researchers compared African American students' placements to the placements of other students with the same disability. They found that in four of the five disabilities assessed, African American students were overrepresented in restrictive settings and underrepresented in general education settings even when compared to students with the same disability. In the absence of more intense needs for African American populations, it appears that systemic variables (e.g., cultural differences, implicit bias) might be contributing to this phenomenon.

In addition to implicit bias that might arise from cultural differences, test bias is another factor hypothesized to contribute to the disproportional identification of African American students for special education. Although the judge in the Larry P. v Riles (1979) case opined that intelligence tests used may be biased subsequent research has failed to support this premise in general (e.g., Jenson, 1980) and specifically in terms of the Wechsler test items that he identified as culturally skewed (Koh, Abbatiello & Mcloughlin, 1984). However, after reviewing the literature, Skiba et al. (2008) suggested it is premature to rule out test bias as a contributing factors based on sample limitations in some studies (since most studies were conducted over 20 years ago) and inconsistent evidence in certain areas (e.g., item and examiner bias).

Counter to the test bias argument, some researchers have hypothesized that differences in special education identification may be related to true differences in achievement among ethnic groups. That is, perhaps African American students are more likely to be identified SLD because they are more likely to have achievement deficits or perhaps they are more likely to be placed in restrictive settings because their achievement warrants it. Hosp and Reschly (2002), using data on 230 3rd through 5th grade students from four school districts in Delaware, were interested in exploring the latter argument regarding placement. The researchers concluded that there were no differences in the process of determining special education placement for African American and White students. For both groups of students, the severity of the problem, the presence of behavior problems, and family problems were related to the degree of restrictiveness in setting. This suggests that differences in achievement, rather than bias or cultural differences, may account for differences in placement.

Hosp and Reschly (2004) also sought to investigate the role of achievement — as well as the role of demographic and economic influences — by examining the proportion of variance in special education identification rates explained by academic, demographic, and economic variables using a national data set from the 1997-1998 school year. When considering African American students, the researchers found that: (a) The strongest predictor for MR identification was the set of *economic* variables; (b) the strongest predictor for ED identification was the set of *demographic* variables; and (c) the strongest predictor for SLD identification was the set of *academic* achievement variables. They concluded that perhaps the economic variables were most important for MR identification based on the link between poverty and cognitive abilities, whereas the demographic variables were most important for ED identification because of the importance of a reference group in interpreting the behaviors of others. Finally, the achievement variables were important in SLD identification because a significant factor in the disability definition is underachievement. Overall, these results suggest the causes of disproportionality might be specific to the particular disability under consideration.

This is far from an exhaustive description of the potential factors contributing to disproportionality. Others have proposed inferior instruction, institutional discrimination, or implicit bias in special education decision-making as contributors to the problem, although these forces have been relatively neglected in the empirical literature. Overall, it is clear that the causes of disproportionality are multi-faceted and complex. It is likely that no one cause fully explains disproportionality, and recent research suggests the causative factors may differ by disability condition. Future research will be needed to continue to determine the extent to which each described factor may contribute to disproportionality.

SUMMARY AND FUTURE DIRECTIONS

Over the past thirty years, researchers have uncovered a wealth of information regarding the disproportional identification and placement of minority students in special education programs. Specifically, African American students have consistently been overrepresented in MR and ED identification, with estimates suggesting they are from one to three times more likely to be identified with these disabilities than their peers. In addition, emerging research suggests that African American students may also be overrepresented in SLD identification, albeit with less consistency and smaller magnitude. Although the exact causes of these phenomena are likely complex, researchers have identified several potential contributory factors including sociodemographic, cultural and achievement differences.

Despite this wealth of knowledge on the extent of and contributors to disproportionality, there remain many avenues for continued research. For example, as recommended by Zhang and Katsiyannis (2002), more research is needed to identify specific district-level variables that may contribute to disproportionality. In addition, empirical research on the extent of disproportionality using data since the IDEIA 2004 provisions took effect would help shed light on recent trends. The current investigation will further explore these issues using data from the state of Ohio.

CURRENT INVESTIGATION: DISPROPORTIONALITY IN OHIO

Methods

In March of 2008, two Microsoft Excel™ databases titled "School Typology" and "Enrollment by Student Demographic" were obtained from the Ohio Department of Education (ODE) website representing student data from the 2006-2007 school year. In order to calculate composition indices, risk indices, and odds ratios, the Enrollment by Student Demographic database was used. In order to explore differences in disproportionality based on school typology, both databases were combined into one Excel database. Every school that ODE included in the School Typology database was included in the final dataset. In general, this included all public schools in Ohio and summed to nearly 1,600,000 students. Finally, the data was imported into Minitab 15 Statistical Software (Minitab), a program used for data analysis. The school typologies included: (1) Rural/agricultural—high poverty, low median income, (2) Rural/agricultural— small student population, low poverty, low to median income, (2) Rural/small town—moderate to high median income, (4) Urban—low median income, high poverty, (5) Major urban—very high poverty, (6) Urban/suburban—high median income, and (7) Urban/suburban—very high median income, very low poverty.

Data Analysis

Composition indices, risk indices and odds ratios were each computed on state averages for MR, ED, and SLD identification using the methods described above (Donovan & Cross,

2002) in order to demonstrate how these methods could be used to analyze disproportionality data.

Once the data were imported into Minitab, a Chi Square Test of homogeneity was used to analyze the data. The most significant findings were further examined using Chi Square Residuals. A Chi Square Residual is the calculated difference between the observed value of a response measurement and the value that is fitted under a hypothesized model.

There are circumstances where several proportions in a sample of data are tested simultaneously. A more complex circumstance occurs when several populations have all been classified according to one or more variables. Frequently, there is no working expectation of the equality of proportions for all the variables with all the populations; therefore, there is a need to test the theoretical representative proportions for each variable across all populations. The null hypothesis is that the populations are homogeneous with respect to the classification variables. The test used for testing representative proportions is the Chi-Squared Test of Homogeneity, with hypotheses: H_0: *The populations are homogeneous with respect to the classification variable*, against H_1: *The populations are not homogeneous with respect to the classification variable.*

Results

Statewide, results demonstrated that African American students had a composition index of .317 for ED. This indicates that they represented 31.7% of the students identified as ED, although they represented only 16.4% of the entire student population. African American students were also found to have a risk index of .021 for ED, suggesting 2% of African American students are identified as ED. In contrast, the entire student population had a risk index of .011, suggesting 1% of the entire student population is identified as ED. These figures resulted in an odds ratio of 1.9, suggesting that African American students are at almost double the risk of being identified as ED as the entire student population across the entire state. For MR, the composition index was .314, the risk index was .011 (versus .022 for the entire population), and the odds ratio was 2.0. Finally, for SLD, the composition index was .172 the risk index was .042 (versus .061 for the entire population), and the odds ratio was 1.45

For the variable *school typology*, a Chi Square Test of Homogeneity was conducted to determine the difference between the expected and observed frequency for children diagnosed with an Emotional Disturbance according to each child's reported ethnicity. The omnibus results indicated that a significant differences between the expected frequency and observed frequency existed ($p = 0.001$). Significant residuals were analyzed for important post-hoc differences.

Black-Non-Hispanics were overrepresented in: (a) Typology 1 (rural/agricultural-high poverty, low median income) for CD; (b) typology 4 (urban-low median income, high poverty) for ED; (c) typology 5 (major urban-very high poverty) and typology 6 (urban/suburban-high median income) for CD and ED; (d) and typology 7 (urban/suburban-very high median income, very low poverty) for CD, ED, OHI, and SLD.

Asian or Pacific Islanders were underrepresented in: (a) Typology 1 (rural/agricultural-high poverty, low median income) and typology 7 (urban/suburban-very high median income, very low poverty) in CD, ED, and SLD; and (b) typology 6 (urban/suburban-high median income) in CD and ED.

Hispanics were underrepresented in: (a) Typology 1 (rural/agricultural-high poverty, low median income) and (b) typology 5 (major urban-very high poverty) in CD and ED. Multiracial students were underrepresented in Typology 1 (rural/agricultural-high poverty, low median income), typology 5 (major urban-very high poverty), typology 6 (urban/suburban-high median income) and typology 7 (urban/suburban-very high median income, very low poverty) in CD.

CONCLUSION

It is clear from multiple procedures that African American students continue to be overrepresented in Ohio special education identification. Calculation of composition indices and odds ratios suggest overrepresentation at the state-level across ED, MR, and SLD categories, although to a lesser degree for the latter. Calculation of risk indices suggest disproportionality in ED identification, but not MR or SLD identification. Results of the Chi-Square analysis also indicate that African American students continue to be overrepresented across several disability categories. However, the degree and types of disproportionality appear to differ by school typology. For example, high income urban/suburban districts exhibited significant disproportionality across four disability categories, whereas high income rural/small town districts did not exhibit significant disproportionality across any disability categories. Further research is needed to examine the mechanisms that might account for such differences.

Addressing Disproportionality

It is clear that disproportionality continues to exist at the state and national level. The question remains: What can be done to address it? Based on literature and empirical research, four primary recommendations will be made.

First, monitoring disproportionality at the district level is critical. For example, districts should house a database tracking the numbers of students from each ethnic group: (a) Receiving prereferral intervention, (b) referred for special education, (c) identified as special education, (d) educated in various placements, and (e) receiving exclusionary discipline. Composition indices, risk indices, odds ratios, and other analyses could be computed from this data (see Bollmer et al., 2007 for suggestions analyzing district-level data) and rates of disproportionality compared at each stage of the special education process. Data should also be disaggregated by various district and school level characteristics to identify potential factors contributing to disproportionality. Such a database could also be used to track trends in disproportionality over time.

Second, it is important to consider the use of prereferral intervention to address the needs of all students. In particular, Response-to-Intervention (RTI) has emerged as a systematic framework for maximizing the academic and behavioral outcomes of students from *all* ethnic backgrounds. Grounded in a prevention focus, RTI is typically characterized by a tiered model of support, data-based decision making, problem-solving, evidence-based instruction, treatment fidelity, culturally responsive practices, and professional development (Batsche et al., 2006; Brown-Chidsey & Steege, 2005). RTI has the potential to reduce disproportionality and improve student outcomes by identifying and addressing individual student needs *before* referring students for special education, thereby minimizing inappropriate referrals. Also, due to the reliance on multiple curriculum-based indicators collected over time to determine eligibility within an RTI model, the potential for assessment bias is minimized.

Third, professional development is essential for addressing disproportionality. High quality professional development designed to close performance gaps is needed. These experiences should be content-rich, appropriate to the context, job embedded, builds upon knowledge and skills in collaborating with and teaching diverse individuals, promotes professional learning communities, and builds the capacity of systems (Stollar, Schaeffer, Skelton, Stine, Lateer-Huhn, and Poth, 2008). Such professional development should focus on context-specific disproportionality, culturally responsive instruction, family and community involvement, and understanding cultural differences. Quality professional development should include didactic instruction, modeling, demonstration, simulated practice, application, and consultee-centered consultation (Knotek, 2005).

Finally, it is important to recruit and retain diverse educational professionals within schools (Salend, Garrick Duhaney, & Montgomery, 2002). This is particularly important since preliminary research findings have demonstrated that the degree of disproportionality decreases as the percentage of non-White teachers in a district increases (Serwatka et al, 1995). Efforts for recruiting diverse educators include developing recruitment materials directed to the needs of diverse staff, conducting job fairs, establishing connections with universities, diversifying the committees that recruit and hire staff, and offering incentives to attract diverse staff (Franklin & James, 1990). Efforts aimed at retaining a diverse staff include providing diverse employees with a support network (Salend et al.)

In conclusion, disproportionality is a concern that has persisted for decades. Although much has been learned about the phenomenon, there is more work to be done. By monitoring disproportionality, and looking for its underlying causes, state and local education agencies can begin to build a foundation for addressing the phenomenon. Quality professional development, prereferral intervention programs, and the employment of a diverse staff represent two initial steps toward this end.

REFERENCES

Batsche, G., Elliott, J., Graden, J.L., Grimes, J., Kovaleski, J.F., Prasse, D., Reschly, D.J., Schrag, J., Tilly, D.W. III. (2006). *Response to Intervention: Policy Considerations and Implementation*. National Association of State Directors of Special Education Inc: Alexandria, VA.

Brown-Chidsey, R. & Steege, M.W. (2005). *Response to Intervention: Principles and Strategies for Effective Practice*. New York: Guilford Press

Bollmer, J., Bethel, J., Garrison-Mogren, R., & Brauen, M. (2007). Using the risk ratio to assess racial/ethnic disproportionality at the school-district level. *The Journal of Special Education, 41* (3), 186-198.

Burdett, P. (2007, July). State definitions of significant disproportionality. *In Forum Brief Policy Analysis*. Retrieved May 1, 2008 from http://www.projectforum.org.

Coulter, W.A. (1996, April). Alarming or disarming: The status of ethnic differences within exceptionalities. Paper presented at the Annual Convention of the Council for Exceptional Children.

Coutinho, M.J., Oswald, D.P., & Best, A.M. (2002). The influence of sociodemographics and gender on the disproportionate identification of minority students as having learning disabilities. *Remedial and Special Education, 23*, 49-59.

Donovan, M.S., & Cross, C.T. (Eds.). (2002). *Minority Students in Special and Gifted Education*. Washington, DC: National Academy Press.

Dunn, L. (1968). Special education for the mildly retarded: Is much of it justifiable? *Exceptional Children, 35*, 5-22.

Education for all Handicapped Children Act of 1975 (Pub L. No. 94-142), renamed the Individuals with Disabilities Education Act in 1990, 20 U.S.C., Chapter 33.

Finn, J.D. (1982). Patterns in special education placement as revealed by OCR surveys. In K. Heller, W. Holtzman, & S. Messick (Eds.), *Placing Children in Special Education: A Strategy for Equity*. Washington, DC: National Academy Press.

Franklin, M.E., & James, J.R. (1990). Nontraditional approaches to recruiting and retaining minority future special educators: Two comprehensive models. *Teacher Education and Special Education, 13*, 50-53.

Heller, K., Holtzman, W., & Messick, S. (Eds.). (1982). *Placing Children in Special Education: A Strategy for Equity*. Washington, DC: National Academy Press.

Hosp, J.L., & Madyun, N.N. (2007). Addressing disproportionality with response to intervention. In S.R. Jimerson, M.K. Burns, and A.M. VanDerHeyden (Eds.) *Handbook of Response to Intervention: The Science and Practice of Assessment and Intervention*. New York: Springer.

Hosp, J.L., & Reschly, D.J. (2004). Disproportionate representation of minority students in special education: Academic, demographic, and economic predictors. *Exceptional Children, 70* (2), 185-199.

Hosp, J.L., & Reschly, D.J. (2003). Referral rates for intervention or assessment: A meta-analysis of racial differences. *Journal of Special Education, 37* (2), 67-80.

Hosp, J.L., & Reschly, D.J. (2002). Predictors of restrictiveness of placement for African-American and Caucasian students. *Exceptional Children, 68* (2), 225-238.

Individuals with Disabilities Education Improvement Act. (IDEIA; 2004).

Koh, T. H., Abbatiello, A., & Mcloughlin, C. S. (1984). Cultural bias in WISC subtest items. *School Psychology Review, 13*(1), 89-94.

Knotek, S.E. (1995). Sustaining RTI through consultee-centered consultation. *The California School Psychologist, 10*, 93-104.

Larry P. v. Riles, 343 F. Supp. 1306 (D.C. N.D. Cal., 1972), *aff'd.*, 502F2d 963 (9th Cir., 1974), *further proceedings*, 495 F. Supp. 926 (D.C. N>D. Cal., 1979), *aff'd.*, 502 F.2d 693 (9th Cir. 1984).

MacMillan, D.L., & Reschly, D.J. (1998). Overrepresentation of minority students: The case for greater specificity or reconsideration of the variables examined. *The Journal of Special Education, 32* (1), 15-24.

Mercer, J. (1973). *Labeling the Mentally Retarded*. Berkely: University of California Press.

Minitab 15 Statistical Software. (2006). State College, PA: Minitab Inc.

Oswald, D.P., Coutinho, M.J., Best, A.M., & Singh, N.N. (1999). Ethnic representation in special education: The influence of school-related economic and demographic variables. *Journal of Special Education, 32* (4), 194-206.

Patton, J.M. (1998). The disproportionate representation of African Americans in special education: Looking behind the curtain for understanding and solutions. *The Journal of Special Education, 32* (1), 25-31.

Salend, S.J., Garrick Duhaney, L.M., & Montgomery, W. (2002). A comprehensive approach to identifying and addressing issues of disproportionate representation. *Remedial and Special Education, 23* (5), 289-299.

Serwatka, T.S., Deering, S., & Grant, P. (1995). Representation of African Americans in Emotionally Handicapped Classes. *Journal of Black Studies, 25* (4), 492-506.

Skiba, R.J., Poloni-Staudinger, L., Gallini, S., Simmons, A.B., & Feggins-Azziz, R. (2006). Disparate access: The disproportionality of African American students with disabilities across educational environments. *Exceptional Children, 72* (4), 411-424.

Skiba, R.J., Poloni-Staudinger, L., Simmons, A.B., Feggins-Azziz, L.R., & Chung, C. (2005). Unproven link: Can poverty explain ethnic disproportionality in special education? *The Journal of Special Education, 39* (3), 130-144.

Skiba, R., Simmons, A.B., Ritter, S., Gibb, A.C., Rausch, M.K., Caudrado, J., et al. (2008). Achieving equity in special education: History, status, and current challenges. *Exceptional Children, 74* (3), 264-288.

Skiba, R., Simmons, A., Ritter, S., Rausch, M.K., Feggins, L.R., Gallini, S., et al. (2004, November). *Moving Towards Equity: Addressing Disproportionality in Special Education in Indiana.* Bloomington, IN: Indiana University School of Education, Center for Evaluation and Education Policy.

Stollar, S.A., Schaeffer, K.R., Skelton, S.M., Stine, K.C., Lateer-Huhn, A., & Poth, R.L. (2008). Best practices in professional development: An integrated, three-tier model of academic and behavior supports. In A. Thomas and J. Grimes (Eds.) *Best Practices in School Psychology V* Bethesda, MD: National Association of School Psychologists.

Zhang, D., & Katsiyannis, A. (2002). Minority representation in special education: A persistent challenge. *Remedial and Special Education, 23* (3), 180-187.

In: Multimedia in Education and Special Education
Editors: O. Demir and C. Celik

ISBN 978-1-60741-073-7
© 2009 Nova Science Publishers, Inc.

Chapter 9

WHAT'S IN A NAME? THE INCONSISTENCIES IN SPECIAL EDUCATION DIAGNOSES AND LABELS

Tomoe Kanaya[1,*], *Jaclyn R. MacFarlane*[2] *and Lauren M. Avera*[1]

[1] Claremont McKenna College, CA USA
[2] Muhlenberg College, PA USA

"I read in a book once that a rose by any other name would smell as sweet, but I've never been able to believe it. I don't believe a rose would be as nice if it was called a thistle or a skunk cabbage."

Anne of Green Gables, L.M. Montgomery

ABSTRACT

Although individuals with mental retardation, learning disability, autism and the Gifted are considered to be and treated as separate populations, they share many common characteristics due to the heavy reliance on IQ for diagnosis within the special educational system. By reviewing evidence found in educational, psychological, and legal research over the past century, this chapter demonstrates how a child's special educational diagnosis is based, in part, on his or her race, socio-economic background, year of evaluation, and geographic location rather than his or her educational needs and cognitive ability. The authors also reveal how minor changes in diagnostic policies across the country can have a significant impact on the lives of millions of school children, parents, educators, and school administrators each year. Implications regarding the use of IQ in special education diagnoses as well as variability in diagnostic criteria across the country are discussed. Furthermore, recommendations for future researchers and policy-makers are provided.

Keywords: Diagnosis, IQ, autism, Gifted, Learning Disability, Mental Retardation

---

* Correspondences should be made to Tomoe Kanaya, Department of Psychology, Claremont McKenna College, 850 Columbia Ave, Claremont, CA 91711 or at tkanaya@cmc.edu

INTRODUCTION

Special Education before IDEA

The concept of special education began in France in the late nineteenth century. At this time, the French government commissioned Alfred Binet and Theodore Simon to develop a measure that would determine which children were underperforming due to cognitive deficits. These children were placed into a separate classroom in order to receive a modified curriculum (e.g., special education). After interviewing many children of all ages, Binet and Simon published what would later be referred to as "the first intelligence test" in 1905. There was much interest world-wide for Binet and Simon's scale; it was brought to America by Henry Goddard, who translated and used it on the school children at the Vineland Training Institute for Feeble-minded Girls and Boys in New Jersey (Gould, 1981).

On the other side of the country, Lewis Terman, a professor in the Department of Education at Stanford University, was also using the Binet-Simon scale. Unlike Goddard, who merely translated the scale, Terman standardized it on a large sample of school children in northern California to develop America's first standardized IQ test, the Stanford-Binet, which was published in 1916. Terman, however, was interested in studying individuals at the top end of the intellectual distribution. By repeatedly interviewing children who had obtained an IQ score of 130 points or higher on his scale; he created the longest running, and most comprehensive, longitudinal study on Gifted children to date. Terman's data revealed that, while a few of his subjects became experts in their fields, most went on to live particularly average lives (Minton, 1990; Chapman, 1988).

Many other American psychologists attempted to create their own IQ scales, but none were as successful as David Wechsler, who created the Wechsler Intelligence Scale for Children (WISC). The Stanford-Binet and WISC were quickly embraced by school districts around the country and are still the most widely used IQ tests today. These scales allowed many educators, like Terman, to identify the Gifted. Once identified, Gifted students were often segregated from their peers and provided a more advanced curriculum For example, Leta Hollingworth created the Special Opportunity Class at New York City's Public School 165 in 1922 (National Association for Gifted Children [NAGC], 2008b).

One of the largest breakthroughs in Gifted education came in 1957 when the Soviet Union launched Sputnik. This event caused the United States to reexamine and to increase the quality of education in America. A year later, the National Defense Education Act (NDEA) designated $1 billion to increase the rigor of science, math, and technology curricula in the public schools. While NDEA was meant to push all American children to achieve greatness in academics, the underlying motivation was to support the academic development of geniuses, which would allow the United States to surpass Russia in technology, science, and mathematics (U.S. Department of Education, 2008). Suddenly, all of America was focused on identifying the upper-tail of the IQ distribution in an attempt to foster giftedness across the country.

The Gifted, however, were not the only ones who were set aside and given different educational opportunities due to their cognitive performance. Publications such *as Hereditary Genius* by Sir Francis Galton (cousin of Charles Darwin) in 1869 and *The Kallikak Family: A Study in the Heredity of the Feeble-Minded* by Goddard in 1912, illustrated the genetic nature of intelligence. At the same time, criminality and acts of immorality, including alcoholism and prostitution, were thought to be a result of low intellectual abilities. It is now known that Goddard's data collection methods were far from rigorous, and currently, there is overwhelming evidence that clearly demonstrates the significant role of the environment on deviant behaviors. The preliminary findings of Goddard, Galton and others, however, provided strong support for policy-makers to justify the institutionalization of individuals with cognitive disabilities throughout the nineteenth century. Children who were considered "uneducable" based on their IQ scores were taken out of schools and sent to training facilities like Goddard's Vineland Institute. While some of these facilities did train children on vocational skills and helped them re-integrate into the workforce, most were permanent, life-long institutions that were dedicated to isolating the cognitively disabled from the rest of society. Furthermore, eugenics and forced sterilization laws (which were popular and wide-spread throughout the United States) prohibited the "feeble-minded" from marrying and reproducing (Gould, 1981).

In 1955, the U.S. Supreme Court decision in Brown vs. Board of Education declared that "separate" is inherently "unequal" and made the practice of racially-segregated education illegal. Children with disabilities, however, continued to be turned away from their local, public schools. In 1972, seven children with cognitive and emotional disabilities brought charges against their school district in Mills vs. Board of Education of Washington, D.C. It was revealed that the district refused to enroll or expelled over 12,000 school children with disabilities in the 1971-1972 school year due to financial constraints. Citing that this procedure violated the Fourteenth Amendment of due process, the U.S. District Court ordered the school district to provide "a free and suitable publicly-supported education regardless of the degree of the child's mental, physical or emotional disability or impairment" (Mills vs. Board of Education of Washington D.C., 1972, p. 13).

Four years after Mills vs. Board of Education, the Education for All Handicapped Children Act of 1975 (Public Law 94-142) was implemented across the country; this act required that school districts provide a "free and appropriate education" to all students. Later renamed the Individuals with Disabilities Education Act (IDEA), IDEA eliminated the practice of removing or institutionalizing children with cognitive and physical disabilities. The purpose of IDEA is to support special education services designed to meet children's specific needs, guarantee that the rights of these children and their parents are protected, financially assist states and school districts in providing education for these children, and evaluate the effectiveness of these services and provisions for handicapped children. Now in its third decade, almost 6 million children between the ages of 6-21 receive special education services under IDEA in the 50 states and Washington D.C. (OSEP, 2008).

IDEA IN THEORY

Through IDEA, the Code of Federal Regulations (CFR) provides definitions and diagnostic criteria for the 13 special education categories: Specific Learning Disabilities, Speech or Language Impairments, Mental Retardation, Emotional Disturbance, Multiple Disabilities, Hearing Impairments, Orthopedic Impairments, Other Health Impairments, Visual Impairments, Autism, Deaf-blindness, Traumatic Brain Injury, and Developmental

Delay. While the cognitive disability categories (Mental Retardation, Learning Disability, and Autism) carry the same names as clinical and medical disorders, it is important to recognize that the CFR is created solely for the educational system and may not match clinical criteria. As Table 1 reveals, the special education label placed onto a child based on the diagnostic criteria set forth by the CFR is unique and separate from the criteria set forth by either the Diagnostic and Statistical Manual (DSM-IV; American Psychiatric Association [APA], 2000) used by clinical psychologists or the criteria set forth by International Statistical Classification of Diseases and Related Health Problems (ICD-10; World Health Organization, 2007) used by medical practitioners.

The main difference between the CFR and the clinical/medical criteria is that, for the CFR, any impairment and behaviors must affect educational functioning. School systems are not required to use the DSM-IV or ICD-10 to classify children, and so these diagnostic criteria do not go hand-in-hand. For example, a child who displays all the symptoms of a clinical diagnosis of Autism, but is receiving straight A's in all of his or her classes, will not qualify for any special education services. Likewise, a child who does not have any clinical disorder, but is achieving below his or her intellectual capabilities, would qualify for LD services. The specific differences and similarities between these diagnostic criteria are outlined below.

In the case of Mental Retardation (MR), the CFR provides a somewhat vague definition stating that the student must have poor intellectual functioning and deficits in adaptive behavior to be classified as MR. Unlike the DSM-IV and ICD-10, which are manuals used by psychologists and clinicians, the CFR does not use standardized IQ tests as a basis for qualification of MR. The DSM-IV even specifies that the child must have an IQ of 70 or below and the age of onset must be before the age of 18 to be diagnosed. Likewise, the DSM-IV and ICD-10 distinguish between different degrees of mental retardation (e.g. mild, moderate, severe, profound, etc.).

Currently, the Learning Disabilities (LD)/Severe Learning Disabilities (SLD) category serves the most students out of all of the 13 special education categories. However, prior to changes in IDEA 2004, there was a requirement that students needed to show a "severe discrepancy" between intelligence and academic achievement in order to be classified under SLD. This requirement was eliminated from the criteria because students had to exhibit large deficits and perform poorly for long periods of time in order to qualify for special education services (Cortiella, 2006). When comparing LD in the CFR to LD in the DSM-IV and ICD-10, the main difference between the criteria is that the CFR definition is very broad and encompasses all of the learning disorders specified in the DSM-IV and ICD-10 as well as additional disorders such as dyslexia and developmental aphasia. As is the case with mental retardation, the DSM-IV puts an emphasis on standardized test scores in a particular subject area having to be substantially below what is expected for the child's age, IQ, and education, while the CFR does not include standardized testing in its criteria.

Table 1. Diagnostic criteria for MR, LD and Autism

Category	Special Education: (CFR) [1]	Clinical Psychology (DSM-IV) [2]	Physicians (ICD-10) [3]
Mental Retardation	"Significantly subaverage general intellectual functioning, existing concurrently with deficits in adaptive behavior and manifested during the developmental period, that adversely affects a child's educational performance."	Significant subaverage intellectual functioning is defined as "an IQ of approximately 70 or below on an individually administered IQ test." There must be "concurrent deficits or impairments in present adaptive functioning in at least two of the following areas": communication, self-care, home living, social/interpersonal skills, use of community resources, self-direction, functional academic skills, work, leisure, health, and safety. Age of onset must be before 18 years old. Includes mild mental retardation, moderate mental retardation, severe mental retardation, profound mental retardation, and mental retardation, severity unspecified.	"A condition of arrested or incomplete development of the mind, which is especially characterized by impairment of skills manifested during the developmental period, skills which contribute to the overall level of intelligence, i.e. cognitive, language, motor, and social abilities." Can occur with or without an additional mental or physical condition. Degree of mental retardation is measured through standardized IQ tests. Diagnosis will also depend on a skilled diagnostician's overall assessment of intellectual functioning. Forms of mental retardation include: mild mental retardation, moderate mental retardation, severe mental retardation, profound mental retardation, other mental retardation, and unspecified mental retardation.

Table 1. Continued

Category	Special Education: (CFR) 1	Clinical Psychology (DSM-IV) 2	Physicians (ICD-10) 3
Learning Disability	"A disorder in one or more of the basic psychological processes involved in understanding or in using language, spoken or written, that may manifest itself in the imperfect ability to listen, think, speak, read, write, spell, or to do mathematical calculations, including conditions such as perceptual disabilities, brain injury, minimal brain dysfunction, dyslexia, and developmental aphasia." Does not include learning problems resulting from visual, hearing, or motor disabilities, mental retardation, emotional disturbance, or environmental, cultural, or economic disadvantage.	Learning disorders include reading disorder, mathematics disorder, disorder of written expression, and learning disorder not otherwise specified. Reading and mathematics disorder and disorder of written expression have virtually identical criteria: 1) Achievement, ability, or skill, as measured by standardized testing on the particular subject, "is substantially below that expected given the person's chronological age, measured intelligence, and age-appropriate education." 2) The disorder interferes with "academic achievement or activities of daily living" that requires the particular skill 3) If the child has a sensory deficit, difficulties with the particular subject or skill must exceed difficulties present due to the sensory deficit. Learning Disorder-NOS (not otherwise specified) has no specific criteria but basically encompasses any learning disorder that did not meet the criteria for the three specific learning disorders.	Called specific developmental disorders of scholastic skill and includes specific reading disorder, specific spelling disorder, specific disorder of arithmetical skills, mixed disorder of scholastic skills, other developmental disorders of scholastic skills, and developmental disorder of scholastic skills unspecified. With these disorders, the typical patterns of "skill acquisition are disturbed from the early stages of development." This disturbance is not due to lack of opportunity to learn, a result of mental retardation, or brain trauma or disease.

Autism	"A developmental disability significantly affecting verbal and nonverbal communication and social interaction, generally evident before age three, that adversely affects a child's educational performance. Other characteristics often associated with autism are engagement in repetitive activities and stereotyped movements, resistance to environmental change or change in daily routines, and unusual responses to sensory experiences." A child cannot be classified under autism if their educational performance "adversely affected" mainly due to an emotional disturbance. A child can be diagnosed as having autism after the age of three as long as all of the aforementioned criteria are met.	There must be a total of six or more characteristics from the following 3 sections: 1) impairments in social interaction (manifested by at least two of the four characteristics) 2) impairments in communication (manifested by at least one of the four characteristics) 3) restricted, repetitive, and stereotyped behavior (manifested by at least one of the four characteristics). Onset of autism should be noticed by the age of three in the area(s) of social interaction, language for communication, and/or imaginative play. Rett's Disorder and Childhood Disintegrative Disorder must be ruled out before making an autistic disorder diagnosis.	Called "childhood autism." Defined by: 1) presence of abnormal or impaired development before the age of 3 2) Abnormal functioning in reciprocal social interaction, communication, and restricted, stereotyped, and repetitive behavior. Also common are nonspecific problems that include phobias, sleeping/eating problems, temper tantrums, and self-directed aggression.

[1] Code of Federal Regulations, Title 34, (§) 300.8 (c), revised as of 2007.
[2] American Psychiatric Association. (2000). Diagnostic and statistical manual of mental disorders (4th ed., text rev.). Washington, DC: Author.
[3] World Health Organization. (2007). The ICD-10 classification of mental and behavioral disorders. Geneva: WHO.

Although Autism has been included in the DSM-IV since 1980 (APA, 1980), it was not included as a special education diagnosis until the amending of IDEA in 1990 (National Information Center for Children and Youth with Disabilities, 1996). The CFR, DSM-IV, and ICD-10 definitions all emphasize deficits in social interaction and communication as well as restrictive, repetitive, and stereotypical behavior. The DSM-IV provides subsections and examples of certain impairments, yet most could be interpreted loosely within the context of the CFR and ICD-10 criteria as well. Unlike mental retardation and learning disabilities, the clinical criteria for Autism do not require standardized IQ testing or cut-off scores.

Despite the long-standing history of Gifted programs within the American education system, it is not an official special education category in the CFR or a clinical diagnosis within the DSM-IV. Rather, the educational opportunities of children in Gifted programs have been supported and funded through federal legislation since 1972 (three years *before* IDEA) through the Marland Report. Written by the Commissioner of Education, Sidney Marland, this report states that:

> "Gifted and talented children are those identified by professionally qualified persons who by virtue of outstanding abilities, are capable of high performance. These are children who require differentiated educational programs and/or services beyond those normally provided by the regular school program in order to realize their contribution to self and society" (Marland, 1972, p. 21-22).

It goes on to list six areas in which Gifted children demonstrate achievement or potential ability, from general intellectual ability to creative thinking.

The definition initially set forth by the Marland report underwent slight modifications through the Jacob K. Javits Gifted and Talented Students Program within the Elementary and Secondary School Improvement Amendments of 1988 (Public Law 100-297, 1988), as well as the report entitled "National Excellence: A Case for Developing America's Talent" from the U.S. Department of Education (1994). The latter report defines Gifted children as the following:

> "(c)hildren and youth with outstanding talent perform or show the potential for performing at remarkably high levels of accomplishment when compared with others of their age, experience, or environment. These children and youth exhibit high performance capability in intellectual, creative, and/or artistic areas, possess an unusual leadership capacity, or excel in specific academic fields. They require services or activities not ordinarily provided by the schools. Outstanding talents are present in children and youth from all cultural groups, across all economic strata, and in all areas of human endeavor" (U.S. Department of Education, 1994, p. 26).

Therefore, special education programs for the Gifted, while not in the CFR, are still funded by and protected under federal law.

IDEA IN PRACTICE

Inter-and Intra-state Variability in Diagnostic Criteria

In the previous section, we explained the difference between the educational (CFR) versus the clinical (DSM-IV) and medical (ICD-10) criteria for cognitive disabilities. The purpose of the CFR, however, is to address the educational opportunities and achievements of children with disabilities It is only meant to provide a "bare minimum" criteria that states must adhere to in order to receive federal funding (Turnbull, Wilcox, & Stowe, 2002). Individual states have the flexibility to create their own eligibility criteria as long as it meets or exceeds the federal requirements. And while the IQ cut-off score of 70 points is used consistently across the country for MR diagnoses (DeMatteo, Marczyk & Pich, 2007), other special education categories experience significant inconsistencies in their criteria between states.

Reschly and Hosp (2004) found "enormous" variability in the definition and eligibility criteria used for LD diagnoses between states in the 2001-2002 school year. Their data revealed that "discrepancy between intellectual ability and achievement" was used in 48 of the 50 states, but the operationalized definition of "discrepancy" varied widely. For example, some states require a pre-determined point difference between IQ and achievement scores (e.g., a child's IQ score must be least 15 points higher than his or her achievement score), while other states base a child's diagnosis on his or her predicted achievement score that is calculated from a pre-set regression formula, and some states do not quantify "discrepancy" at all. In addition, the pre-determined point differences and/or regression formulas differed between the states, and as such, the same point discrepancy between IQ and achievement would be considered "severe" enough for LD services in one state, but not in another. Furthermore, states also disagree on the achievement areas (e.g., reading, math, spelling, etc) that can be considered eligible for LD services.

Given LD has the highest prevalence rate of all the special education categories, the variability detailed above have an immediate impact on over 5 million school children each year (OSEP, 2008). However, Hallahan et al. (2007) found that inter-state variability on diagnostic criteria have a relatively little impact on "high incidence" categories such as LD, but have a significant impact on the prevalence rate of "low incidence." Furthermore, they identified that Autism, a diagnosis that accounts for approximately 3% of the special education population each year (OSEP, 2008) will be significantly affected by such variability due to the extensive and specialized services that are required under this category.

In an analysis of the diagnostic criteria for Autism services in all 50 states and Washington, D.C., MacFarlane and Kanaya (in press) found that each state differed in their exact wording and terminology used to explain their criteria for Autism services. While a majority of the states in their sample include Autism Spectrum Disorders (ASDs) within their criteria, there are still many states that do not. Moreover, the states that included ASD in their diagnostic criteria also had higher prevalence rates of children receiving special education services compared to states that relied solely on the CFR. This variability has the most serious implications for students with an ASD, such as Aspergers Disorder, who may qualify for Autism services in one state but not another due to varying state eligibility requirements.

The eligibility criteria for Gifted programs also differ by state. For example, the diagnostic criteria in Alaska is rather vague, and only requires that a child exhibits "outstanding intellect, ability, or creative talent" (Davidson's Institute for Talent Development, 2008) Maine's definition, on the other hand, is more in-depth and specifies the need to show "significant achievement" in "general intellectual ability," which is often operationalized by an IQ score, as well as "specific academic aptitude". Furthermore, most states do not require school districts to recognize Gifted eligibilities from other districts in their own state (NAGC, 2008a). Indeed, less than 15 states have intra-state, standardized policies for the identification of Gifted students across all school districts. In other words, eligibility for Gifted programs is also heavily influenced by a child's geographic location. Moreover, in some cases, 2 children with the same intellectual ability and academic potential will qualify for different educational opportunities simply because they live a street apart from each other.

IDEA and IQ

While none of the diagnostic criteria within the CFR includes IQ, in practice, special education diagnoses rely heavily on IQ scores. This is because school psychologists use the criteria set forth by the DSM-IV or the ICD-10 for MR diagnoses, rather than the vague guidelines outline in the CFR (Reschly, Myers & Hartel, 2002). More specifically, the cut-off score of 70 points or below is the most commonly used measure to determine "significantly subaverage intellectual ability," as it represents the bottom 2% of the IQ distribution (IQ tests are standardized to a mean of 100 points and a standard deviation of 15 points). And while most psychologists and physicians agree that it is also important to measure a child's level of "adaptive functioning," most standardized measures of adaptive behavior, such as the Vineland scale, are highly correlated with IQ (e.g., Bruininks, Woodcock, Weatherman, & Hill, 2000). Therefore, a child's IQ score, and more specifically whether the child is above or below the cut-off of 70 points, is the strongest predictor of an MR diagnosis.

Because of the widely accepted use of the IQ cut-off score of 70 points for MR diagnoses, it is common practice to administer an IQ test to every child who is being evaluated for services. For example, an LD diagnosis will not be considered for a child until it has been determined that he or she is above the MR cutoff (e.g., Kavale & Forness, 1992). In addition, under IDEA, every child in special education must be re-evaluated at least every 3 years to determine if services are still necessary. At this time, an IQ test is usually re-administered As such, children in special education are repeatedly tested on IQ tests throughout their school years. Because of this, any trends or inconsistencies within IQ would generate upheaval in the lives of millions of children each year.

IQ and the Over-representation of Minorities in Special Education Classrooms

There has been much criticism among researchers, practitioners and policy-makers over the disproportionate number of ethnic minority children in special education. The focus on these misdiagnoses have centered predominantly on the overrepresentation of Black males in

MR classrooms (Losen & Orfield, 2002). Indeed, the prevalence rates of MR for Black youth are almost double that for White and Hispanic youth. It is important to recognize, however, that over-representation have been systematically and historically documented across all minority groups, including Hispanic, Native American, Asian American, and children from low socio-economic backgrounds, in all special education categories, including LD (Payette & Clarizio, 1994) and Autism (Yeargin-Allsopp et al., 2003). Furthermore, there is evidence that ethnic minorities and females are under-represented and have a lower retention rate than their white, male counterparts in Gifted programs (Moore, Ford & Milner, 2005).

These trends are partially due to the fact that parents often do not have the financial and/or social resources needed to have their child clinically diagnosed by a pediatrician or clinical psychologist. Therefore, it is not until a child is in school that she or he is able to receive a psychological assessment and services that will enable him or her to overcome a disability. However, the well-documented, 15 point gap seen in IQ scores between African-Americans and Caucasians (an entire standard deviation) is also present in the same populations that overcrowd the special education classrooms. The integral use of IQ tests on special education evaluations is an undeniable, significant contributor to these disproportionate numbers (Neisser et al, 1996).

These racial/ethnic asymmetries have led to litigation that prevent the use of IQ for all MR placement decisions for African Americans in California (Larry P. v. Wilson Riles, 1979, 1986). They have also motivated researchers, practitioners and administrators to emphasize the importance of cultural sensitivity and awareness when referring, testing, and diagnosing disabled children, especially minorities. Ethnic and income-based disparities in special education diagnoses, however, continue to exist across the country, and the heavy reliance of IQ on special education diagnoses must be mitigated if the disparities are to be reduced significantly (Kanaya & Ceci, 2007).

IQ Changes over Time: The Flynn Effect

The heavy use of IQ in special education is also problematic due to the Flynn effect, a phenomenon that refers to the steady rise in IQ scores that has been documented in over 30 countries around the world. Because of this rise, people score almost 10 points higher on an old IQ test that was normed 25 years ago compared to their score on a current IQ test that was normed within that year. In the United States, the Flynn effect is approximately 0.31 points a year on the Stanford Binet and Wechsler Intelligence Scale for Children. In other words, the average IQ of the U.S. population rises from 100 to 106 within a generation. Tests are continually re-normed in a direct effort to compensate for this rise. Re-normed tests reset the mean back to 100, which in turn, 'hide' the previous gains from the old norm. For this reason, a person will score higher on an outdated, old IQ test compared to a brand new IQ test, even when both tests are administered on the same day (Flynn, 1984, 1987).

Due to the Flynn effect and the use of the MR cutoff score, special education diagnoses are based on the year a child is tested and the test norms used, rather than the child's cognitive ability and educational needs. As a test norm ages, and IQ scores rise, fewer and fewer children will obtain an IQ of 70 or below, and therefore, they will no longer qualify for MR services. At the same time, the number of children who score above the cut-off increase, as will the number of children who qualify for LD services. Likewise, more children will obtain the test scores necessary to display "remarkably high achievements" and, therefore, qualify for Gifted programs. These trends, however, would reverse dramatically with the introduction of a newly normed test. Suddenly, MR would increase, while LD and Gifted diagnoses would decrease. Given the criteria for Autism services relies more heavily on social and behavioral symptoms, the Flynn effect should not have a direct or immediate impact on Autism diagnoses (Flynn, 1985).

Indeed, many special education practitioners and researchers have reported that children receiving services lose approximately 5-9 IQ points when re-evaluated on a newly-normed IQ test (e.g., Wechsler, 1991). More alarmingly, Kanaya, Scullin and Ceci (2003), found that this sudden decrease in IQ resulted in a threefold increase in MR diagnoses. Conversely, Gaskill and Brantley (1996) found that more than 40% of the students in their sample no longer met the criteria for SLD when retested on the new WISC-III. This finding was replicated by Truscott and Franks (2001) who found that the number of SLD diagnoses in an entire school district dropped significantly simply due to the introduction of a new IQ norm. In Isreal, where the requirements for the Gifted program are dependent on Terman's original cut-off of 130 IQ points, Cahan and Gejman (1993) found that the introduction of a new norm resulted in a 15 percent decrease in Gifted diagnoses. Therefore, a child's special education diagnosis is based, in part, on the year tested rather than his or her cognitive ability and educational needs.

CONCLUSION

The purpose of this chapter is to illustrate the capricious nature of special education diagnoses for MR, LD, Autism as well as eligibility criteria for Gifted programs. More specifically, the educational opportunities provided to a child are based, in part, on social-cultural factors including ethnicity, socio-economic status, the Flynn effect, and inter-state and intra-state variability in diagnostic policies, rather than his or her actual cognitive ability. These findings have many significant implications for educators, practitioners, school children and policy-makers, which we describe in detail below.

Psychosocial Implications

Educational diagnoses lead to classroom labels that hold significant social implications to the individuals who bear them. Parents will most likely feel delighted and proud of the proclivities exhibited by their "Gifted" child. However, similar to Terman's original sample, Gifted children often report negative psycho-social symptoms due to the social isolation they experience from their peers due to their label (Robinson, Zigler & Gallagher, 2000). The social stigma connected with the MR, LD and Autism labels are also associated with similar, negative social costs (e.g., Baroff, 1999). While it is difficult to determine if escaping the negative consequences of a label outweighs the benefits of receiving special education services, it is clear that a child's social and emotional development is heavily influenced by his or her special education diagnosis.

Financial Implications

Local, state, and federal governments collectively spend billions of dollars on special education and Gifted programs. As such, fluctuations in diagnoses have dramatic, financial implications that go beyond total dollars spent. This variability in special education raises the question of whether the costly services are being properly allocated. For example, in some states, children with an ASD are more likely to be placed in "Other Health Impairment" or "Emotional Disturbance" rather than Autism. The per-pupil expenditures for Autism, however, are over $5,000 higher than expenditures for "other health impairment" and "emotional disturbance" (Special Education Expenditure Project, 2003). This extra cost is required to cover the individualized and intensive services that are highly effective for children with ASD Such services include applied behavioral analysis, which focuses on teaching appropriate and acceptable behaviors, including social skills that increase a child's acceptance with his or her peers as well as academic skills, through small "measureable units" (Dempsey & Foreman, 2001). Although it is possible that ASD children are still receiving these services under a different special education category, doing so can put a great strain on the funding designated for these other disability categories.

Likewise, children whose IQ scores are in the MR range, but who are tested on an outdated, inflated norm will receive an LD diagnosis due to the Flynn effect. This is more likely to occur in low-income school districts that cannot afford to replace their norms in a timely fashion. MR services involve extensive educational interventions such as removal from regular classrooms for all or part of the day to receive instruction from specialists and paid aides (Singer, Butler, Palfrey, & Walker, 1986). However, LD services, which include modifying assignments (i.e., making them shorter and/or easier) are far less invasive, and therefore, less expensive than MR services (Burns, 2003).

The services provided to children in Gifted programs vary greatly between and within states. Some programs have separate classrooms in which intensive educational units are taught to smaller groups of students so that they can explore topics more thoroughly than they would in a regular classroom. Other programs make use of educational field trips. As such, the per-pupil expenditure also varies widely. For example, the Idaho legislature gave over eight million dollars to cover the costs of their Gifted and Talented programs which serve less than approximately 14,600 students (NAGC, 2008a). In comparison, Arizona only spent three million dollars on their Gifted and Talented program that serves 75,121 students that same year. Similarly, Michigan and Colorado had comparable numbers of Gifted students (52,756 and 56,133 respectively) but vast differences in state funding; whereas Michigan gave Gifted and Talented education only $285,000, Colorado gave $7,700,000 (NAGC, 2008a). Therefore, the financial burden placed upon school districts and taxpayers vary between states and over time, regardless of the educational needs and cognitive abilities of the school children who are receiving services.

Legal Implications

Under IDEA, all children have the right to a "free and appropriate education" regardless of his or her disability. However, it does not specify what interventions constitute as "appropriate," and the "appropriateness" of the services provided is the subject of many litigations each year (e.g., Martin, Martin & Terman, 1996). While the problematic nature of IQ is often cited within these litigations (as was the case in Larry P. vs. Riles), the inconsistencies in diagnostic criteria within the Autism category has been the source of over 600 legal cases thus far, making it the "fastest growing and most expensive area of litigation in special education" (Baird, 1999; as cited in Etscheidt, 2003, p.51). Such litigations are costly (financially and emotionally) for parents, school districts, and taxpayers. In addition, these court cases often take years to resolve. Therefore, even if the case has a favorable outcome, the children involved often do not benefit from it, as they have outgrown the services or graduated from the school.

Recommendations

As we have stated, children of the same cognitive abilities and academic potential are receiving different diagnoses and labels due to the lack of consistency found in inter-state and intra-state eligibility criteria as well as the heavy reliance on IQ for special education decisions. While some may say, "what's in a name?" it is evident that these diagnoses and labels carry significant consequences for children, parents, educators, school administrators and taxpayers. Of course, some idiosyncrasies can be expected due to the complex and multidisciplinary nature of special education; however, there are ways in which they could be reduced. We recommend that:

1. Federal guidelines require more consistency between (and within) states' educational guidelines regarding eligibility criteria for special education and Gifted programs;
2. Individual states provide accessible information to parents (particularly those who live in underachieving school districts) regarding the nuances inherent in special education evaluations, as well as to help them deal with the psychological impact of having a child with special needs;
3. Schools address the psycho-social impact of an educational label, including Gifted, as part of the services they provide for their students;
4. School psychologists place less emphasis on IQ scores, and in particular, the MR cut-off score in special education diagnoses

These recommendations will help to ensure that the educational opportunities and experiences are based on a child's needs, rather than race, income, year of evaluation, or geographic location.

ACKNOWLEDGMENT

This research was supported, in part, by a research grant by the Spencer Foundation entitled "What's at stake when we use cut-off scores?" (Grant # 2007-00115) awarded to the first author. This research was also sponsored by an undergraduate, summer research grant entitled "Autism as a special education category" awarded by Muhlenberg College to the second author. Any opinions, findings and conclusions or recommendations expressed in this material are those of the authors and do not necessarily reflect those of the Spencer Foundation or Muhlenberg College.

REFERENCES

American Psychiatric Association. (1980). *Diagnostic and statistical manual of mental disorders* (3rd ed.). Washington, DC: Author.

American Psychiatric Association. (2000). *Diagnostic and statistical manual of mental disorders* (4th ed., text rev.). Washington, DC: Author.

Baroff, G. S. (1999). *General learning disorder: A new designation for mental retardation. Mental Retardation, 37,* 68–70.

Bruininks, R. H., Woodcock, R. W., Weatherman, R. F., & Hill, B. K. (2000). *Scales of independent behavior–revised.* Itasca, IL: Riverside.

Burns, E. (2003). A handbook for supplementary aids and services: A best practice and IDEA guide *"To Enable Children With Disabilities to be Educated With Nondisabled Children to the Maximum Extent Appropriate."* Springfield, IL: Charles C Thomas.

Cahan, S. & Gejman, A. (1993). Consistency of IQ scores among gifted children. *Roeper Review, 15*(3), 140-143.

Chapman, P.D. (1988). *Schools as sorters: Lewis M. Terman, applied psychology, and the intelligence testing movement,* 1890-1930. New York, NY: New York University Press.

Code of Federal Regulations, Title 34, (§) 300.8 (c), revised as of 2007.

Cortiella, C. (2006). *IDEA 2004 close up: Evaluation and eligibility for specific learning disabilities.* Retrieved June 20, 2008 from http://www.schwablearning.org/articles. aspx?r=1063.

Davidson Institute For Talent Development. (2008). *Gifted education policies.* Retrieved June 20, 2008 from http://www.gt-cybersource.org/StatePolicy.aspx?NavID=4_0.

DeMatteo, D., Marczyk, G., & Pich, M. (2007). A national survey of state legislation defining mental retardation: Implications for policy and practice after Atkins. *Behavioral Sciences & the Law, 25*(6), 781-802.

Dempsey, I. & Foreman, P. (2001). A review of educational approaches for individuals with autism. *International Journal of Disability, Development and Education, 48*(1), 103-116.

Etscheidt, S. (2003). An analysis of legal hearings and cases related to individualized education programs for children with autism. *Research and Practice for Persons with Severe Disabilities, 28*(2), 51-69.

Flynn, J.R. (1984). The mean IQ of Americans: Massive gains 1932 to 1978. *Psychological Bulletin, 95,* 29-51.

Flynn, J.R. (1985). Wechsler intelligence tests: Do we really have a criterion of mental retardation? *American Journal of Mental Deficiency, 90,* 236–244.

Flynn, J.R. (1987). Massive IQ gains in 14 nations: What IQ tests really measure. *Psychological Bulletin, 101,* 171-191.

Gaskill, F.W. & Brantely, J.C. (1996). Changes in ability and achievement scores over time: Implications for children classified as learning disabled. Journal of Pscyhoeducational Assessment, 14(3), 220-228.

Gould, S.J. (1981). *The mismeasure of man.* New York, NY: W.W. Norton & Company, Inc.

Hallahan, D.P., Keller, C.E., Martinez, E.A., Byrd, E.S., Gelman, J.A., & Fan, X. (2007). How variable are interstate prevalence rates of learning disabilities and other special education categories? A longitudinal comparison. *Exceptional Children, 73*(2), 136-146.

Kanaya, T. & Ceci, S.J. (2007) Are all IQ scores created equal? The differential costs of IQ cut-off scores for at-risk children. *Child Development Perspectives, 1*, 52-56.

Kanaya, T., Scullin, M.H., & Ceci, S.J. (2003). The Flynn Effect and U.S. policies: The impact of rising IQ scores on American society via mental retardation diagnoses. *American Psychologist, 58*(10), 778-790.

Kavale, K. A., & Forness, S. R. (1992). History, definition and diagnosis. In N. N Singh & I. L. Beale (Eds.). *Learning disabilities: Nature, theory, and treatment.* New York: Springer-Verlag.

Larry P. v. Riles, C-71–2270 FRP. Dist. Ct. Citation (1979, 1986).

Losen, D., & Orfield, G. (2002). *Racial inequality in special education. Cambridge,* MA: Harvard Education Publishing Group.

MacFarlane, J.R. & Kanaya, T. (in press). What does it mean to be Autistic? Inter-state variation in special education criteria for Autism services. *Journal of Child and Family Studies.*

Marland, S. P., Jr. (1972). *Education of the gifted and talented: Report to the Congress of the United States by the U.S. Commissioner of Education and background papers submitted to the U.S. Office of Education,* 2 vols. Washington, DC: U.S. Government Printing Office. (Government Documents Y4.L 11/2: G36).

Martin, E., Martin, R., & Terman, D. (1996). The legislation and litigation history of special education. *The Future of Children: Special Education for Students with Disabilities, 6*(1), 25-39.

Mills v. *Board of Education,* 348 F. Supp. 886 (1972).

Minton, H. (1990). *Lewis M. Terman: Pioneer in psychological testing* (American social experience, No 11). New York, NY: New York University Press.

Moore, J.L., Ford, D.Y., & Milner, H.R.(2005). Recruitment is not enough: Retaining African American students in gifted education. *Gifted Child Quarterly, 49*(1), 51-67.

National Association for Gifted Children. (2008a). *Gifted by state.* Retrieved June 20, 2008 from http://www.nagc.org/index.aspx?id=37.

National Association for Gifted Children. (2008b). *Gifted timeline.* Retrieved June 24, 2008 from http://www.nagc.org/index.aspx?id=607.

National Information Center for Children and Youth with Disabilities. (1996). *The education of children and youth with special needs: What do the laws say?* Retrieved May 23, 2007 from http://www.nichcy.org/pubs/outprint/nd15txt.htm.

Neisser, U., Boodoo, G., Bouchard, T. J., Boykin, A. W., Brody, N., Ceci, S. J., et al. (1996). *Intelligence: Knowns and unknowns.* American Psychologist, 51, 77–101.

Office of Special Education Programs. (2008). State level data files child count 19912006. Washington D.C: *U.S. Department of Education.* Retrieved May 15, 2008 from https://www.ideadata.org/StateLevelFiles.asp.

Payette, K.A. & Clarizio, H.F. (1994). Discrepant team decisions: The effects of race, gender, achievement, and IQ on LD eligibility. *Psychology in the Schools, 31*(1), 40-48.

Public Law 94-142. (1975). *Education for All Handicapped Children Act of 1975.*

Public Law 100-297 (1988*). Elementary and Secondary School Improvement Amendments of 1988.*

Reschly, D.J., & Hosp, J.L. (2004). State SLD identification policies and practices. *Learning Disability Quarterly, 27*, 197-213.

Reschly, D. J., Myers, T. G., & Hartel, C. R. (Eds.). (2002). *Mental retardation: Determining eligibility for social security benefits.* Washington, DC: National Academies Press.

Robinson, N.M., Zigler, E., & Gallagher, J.J. (2000). Two tails of the normal curve: Similarities and differences in the study of mental retardation and giftedness. *American Psychologist, 55*(12), 1413-1424.

Singer, J. D., Butler, J. A., Palfrey, J. S., & Walker, D. K. (1986). Characteristics of special education placements: Findings from probability samples in five metropolitan school districts. *Journal of Special Education, 20*, 319–337.

Special Education Expenditure Project. (2003). *Total expenditures for students with disabilities, 1999-2000: Spending variation by disability.* Washington D.C.: U.S. Department of Education.

Truscott, S. D., & Frank, A. J. (2001). Does the Flynn effect affect IQ scores of students classified as SLD? *Journal of School Psychology, 39*, 319–334.

Turnbull, H.R., Wilcox, B.L., & Stowe, M.J. (2002). A brief overview of special education law with focus on autism. *Journal of Autism and Developmental Disorders, 32*(5), 479-493.

U.S. Department of Education (1994). *National excellence: A case for developing America's youth.* Washington, DC: U.S. Government Printing Office.

U.S. Department of Education (2008). *The federal role of education.* Retrieved on June 25, 2008 at http://www.ed.gov/about/overview/fed/role.html.

Wechsler, D. (1991). *The Wechsler Intelligence Scale for Children-III Manual.* NY, NY: The Psychological Corporation.

World Health Organization. (2007). *The ICD-10 classification of mental and behavioral disorders.* Geneva: WHO

Yeargin-Allsopp, M., Rice, C., Karapurkar, T., Doernberg, N., Boyle, C., & Murphy, C. (2003). Prevalence of autism in a U.S. metropolitan area. *Journal of American Medical Association, 289*(1), 49-55.

In: Multimedia in Education and Special Education
Editors: O. Demir and C. Celik

ISBN 978-1-60741-073-7
© 2009 Nova Science Publishers, Inc.

Chapter 10

REALISTIC MATHEMATICS EDUCATION FOR YOUNG STUDENTS WITH SPECIAL EDUCATIONAL NEEDS

Johannes E. H. Van Luit[1], Jo M. C. Nelissen[2] and Marjolijn C. Peltenburg[2]

[1]Department of Special Needs Education, Utrecht University, The Netherlands
[2]Utrecht University, Freudenthal Institute, The Netherlands

SUMMARY

The common instruction format for students with special educational needs in mathematics education is individually based instruction. We challenge this approach by guided, interactive instruction. The starting point is the student's own informal way of thinking, or in the words of Freudenthal (1991), their 'common sense'. This is the basis for construction, and student interaction in the classroom. The confrontation with each other's ways of thinking can stimulate students' reflection, leading to a higher level of semantization and formalization. We translate this theory into school practice by presenting an instruction format in which students are confronted with rich math problems that are embedded in a context. Working in pairs the students discuss, inquire and construct solutions. Through writing down solutions and conjectures, they have a means to communicate their ideas to their classmates and their teacher. The arising interaction, we think, is an essential element for the emergence of reflective thinking in learning mathematics.

Keywords: Realistic mathematics education, special needs education, guided instruction, learning by interaction

INTRODUCTION

The focus of this study is on the kind of instruction (guided instruction) and mode of interaction (simultaneous interaction) that can be used in mathematics education. Guided instruction has been proved to be effective in a study of students with special mathematical needs (Kroesbergen & Van Luit, 2002), where other research is more pessimistic about the possibilities of this form of instruction for these students (Geary, 2004). In this study we will provide arguments for optimizing mathematics education (curriculum and instruction) for students with special educational needs, in particular learning disabled (LD) and mild mentally retarded (MMR) students.

A general question in education research is that of how an appropriate changeover from traditional to realistic mathematics education (RME) for students with special educational needs can be achieved. The implementation of this type of education is a complicated endeavor and no mean feat at all. The effort should be focused especially on the following issues of discussion and controversy which are connected with the RME theory (Gravemeijer, 1994; Nelissen, 1999; Treffers, 1987).

Students with special educational needs suffer, as is known, from low confidence in their own abilities. For that reason 'drill and practice' is thought to be the best instruction method for these students. This point of view, however, is challenged by Woodward and Montague (2002) who argue in favor of a school practice in which students do have the opportunity to find their own constructions. The next subject of debate is that of whether the use of contexts is distracting for these students, or do contexts contribute to insightful learning? What should be the nature of these contexts? In most cases until now teachers have been inclined to use contexts only rarely. Are students with special educational needs able to learn mathematics in that they are confronted with context problems? It is thought that they are not able to solve problems and many teachers therefore confront these students only with traditional tasks (addition, subtraction, multiplication tasks and so on) in line with the 'step by step' instruction philosophy.

The next question is whether students with special educational needs are able to achieve insights through student discussion in the classroom. Until now it has been thought that they should just individually accomplish their tasks, and that therefore the teacher should focus on drill and practice. In this study we argue that these children are able to interact, learn meaningfully and reflect on their own strategies and those of others. This argumentation is supported by data collected during classroom experiments. In these lessons students are confronted with meaningful context problems. In pairs the students (learn to) discuss and try to find a solution. They use large size scrap paper, also called a poster, to write down and remember their strategy. During classroom discussion the posters are a means to discuss the approaches of the students. This discussion will be the basis for the students to come to reflection (Nelissen & Tomic, 1996). In one of the next sections we will elaborate on this.

'Interaction' is seen as an important concept in this study (Nelissen, 2002). So far the most suitable approach for students with special educational needs was considered to be individually based instruction. The idea is that all students have to cope with their own unique problems and learning trajectory. The consequence of this idea is that there is hardly any meaningful communication between students, and only limited communication between teacher and student, in fact only when the teacher is explaining or correcting work of the students. It was thought, because of language deficiencies, that too much communication would only harm the student's learning. So, in the math lessons, the students miss the encouragement they most need: the encouragement to practice the language that is typical for problem solving, for reflection, for explaining one's own strategies, for comparing different thinking procedures and so on. Moreover they miss the stimulation of the 'thinking processes' that all this is built on.

This individual instructional approach in school practice is often strongly connected with so-called *direct* instruction and with what Woodward, and Montague (2002) typify as 'step by step' instruction. This type of instruction does not fit well with the RME ideas and, moreover, research findings suggest that insights quickly atrophy and fade again (Baxter, Woodward, & Olson, 2001). In contradiction with daily school practice of 'step by step' instruction, and in line with a lot of research, though mostly aimed at 'normal' students (Fosnot & Dolk, 2005; Mercer, 1995; Stone, 1998), we suggest that a suitable instruction form for students with special educational needs can be 'interactive teaching'.

In the next section we elaborate in more detail on the theoretical background. We discuss the alignment of three core concepts of RME: construction, interaction and reflection. Subsequently we discuss several modes of interaction and we clarify how students with special educational needs can take advantage of what is meant in the RME paradigm by meaningful learning, increasing formalization and increasing semantization.

THEORETICAL FOUNDATION

Before we discuss a distinction in several modes of interactive teaching, we present a model which contains an alignment of three core principles of RME. In this model, 'interaction' is placed in a clarifying theoretical context.

Learning Mathematics: A Cyclic and Continuous Learning Process

The first principle is the principle of 'construction'. This principle implies that the learning process should start with the student's own informal way of thinking, or in the words of Freudenthal (1991), with 'common sense'. This way of thinking is elicited in confrontation with meaningful *contexts,* i.e. contexts that derive from the every day life of the students. Construction often leads to interaction, because it makes sense (to stimulate) that the students exchange and discuss the findings that emerged (Kroesbergen & Van Luit, 2002). And so we arrive at a second principle, 'interaction'. In interaction students discuss their ways of thinking, their solutions, the similarities and differences in their approaches. The dialogue with others transforms into dialogue with oneself, and so we arrive at the third principle: 'reflection'. Reflection is interpreted as internalized dialogue and in this statement we recognize the theory of the notable Russian scholar Vygotsky (1978), that all higher functions (speech, thinking, reflection and so on) are originally social functions. In the dialogue the student will anticipate on the expected comments of the discussion partners. This evokes intern dialogue, meaning critical analysis of one's own thinking processes, and that is what we call *reflection* (Nelissen & Tomic, 1996; Slobodcikov & Cukerman, 1990). Moreover, reflection as internalized dialogue emerges, as the Russian psychologists Stepanov, and Semenov (1982) suggest, as a *personal* act as well as an *intellectual* act. Personal means that students attribute sense to their own actions. This is a condition for intellectual reflection, which is aimed at constructing new strategies and modes of thinking.

Reflection is an essential feature of mathematical thinking (Freudenthal, 1991; Nelissen, 1999) and can be considered as a foundation for the development of processes of transfer and generalization as research suggests (Zak, 1976). Figure 1 represents the three principles in connection. In the scheme, learning mathematics is represented as a cyclic and continuous process: construction leads to interaction; interaction or discourse is the basis for reflection and reflection leads to construction on a higher level (Construction 2). And so the process of mathematizing proceeds, because construction again leads to interaction on a higher level (Interaction 2) and so on.

Modes of Interaction

An important question is: do students with special educational needs profit from interactive teaching and learning? Both Stone (1998) and Palinscar (1986) advocate that 'scaffolding' (a term that stems from Bruner, 1967) is feasible for students with learning disabilities. Scaffolding is considered a form of what is called 'interactive teaching'. Whether this succeeds depends on how the dialogue in the classroom is designed and organized. We propose a distinction in three modes of interaction designs: horizontal, vertical and simultaneous. In figure 2 three modes of interaction are represented.

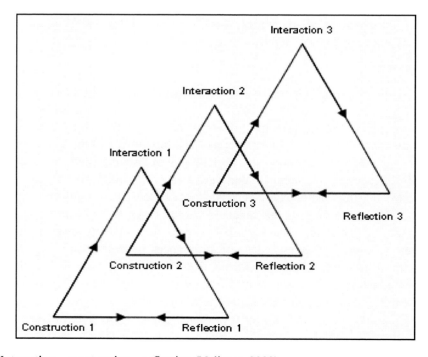

Figure 1. Interaction – construction – reflection (Nelissen, 2002).

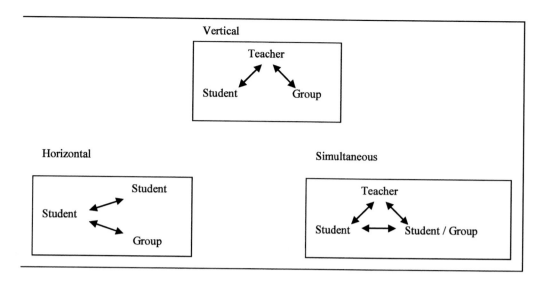

Figure 2. Three modes of interaction (Nelissen, 2002).

'Horizontal interaction' refers to communication and discussion among students. Advantages of horizontal interaction are that students feel free to discuss (Mercer, 1995), that they exchange ideas, that they learn how to put arguments and to improve their speech if needed. A disadvantage however is that students may go under in the group and that the bolder students may dominate the discourse.

We call the interaction between the teacher and a single student, small groups or the whole class 'vertical interaction'. Some special forms of vertical interaction are scaffolding, revoicing and reciprocal teaching (Palinscar, 1986). Scaffolding offers students an opportunity to play a role in their own learning, as Reid (1998, p. 388) stipulates: scaffolding 'redirects our focus to the bi-directional interactive influences'. The student's contribution during the lessons is taken seriously, but that does not imply that the teacher's role is submerged. However, there is sometimes a danger that the teacher will just play a formal role. In such cases interaction shrivels into a mere ritual, a ritual without real *negotiation*. An advantage of vertical interaction is however that the teacher can manage the complicated processes that may emerge during the interaction in the group.

'Simultaneous interaction' reconciles the advantages of horizontal and vertical interaction. For this reason we advocate to use a mix of these two modes of interaction. In the poster lessons all three modes of interaction are incorporated.

Meaningful Learning: Physical Concrete or Common Sense Concrete?

Once (Nelissen, 1999) we asked students - all 10 years old weak students - if they had an idea *why* they were learning math (particularly fractions). Some answers: "Fractions are in our textbooks", "I don't know", "Fractions are very difficult", "For later perhaps?", and so on. How can students like and do math when they don't have any idea why they are learning all these subjects? Several authors (Bottge, 2001; Goldman & Hasselbring, 1997) stress the importance of meaningful learning. Bottge pleads for 'anchored instruction': meaningful problems and contexts. In his research students are asked to manage the problems in cooperation. They should call upon their intuitions or - as we say in RME - informal knowledge. But now the question arises whether it would not be more useful for students with special educational needs to teach them on the basis of concrete and straightforward manipulatives, for after all students would understand what is concrete and tangible such as the well-known Dienes material (MAB-blocks) or the Cuisenaire material, the abacus, cubes and so on. The dilemma seems to be 'concrete or meaningful?'. But what is conceived as concrete?

We propose a distinction in (a) 'material or physical concrete' and (b) 'common sense concrete'. Physical concrete, we believe, mainly ensues from the adult world and is as such not always very meaningful for students. The concept of concrete, however, can also be considered in cohesion with the students' own experience and this we entitle common sense concrete. That is the concrete that stems from a student's own intuitions and experiences, for instance, playing games with dice or sharing candy in a fair way. Such activities contribute to the emergence of number sense, as Woodward, and Montague (2002) assert. Number sense establishes a basis for the use of strategies for addition and subtraction and this illustrates how students achieve progressively more insight in the denotation of math concepts and strategies, and in how these concepts and strategies are semantically related, such as for instance how procedures of addition and multiplication are related. This process of growing understanding of mathematical significance we call 'increasing semantization'.

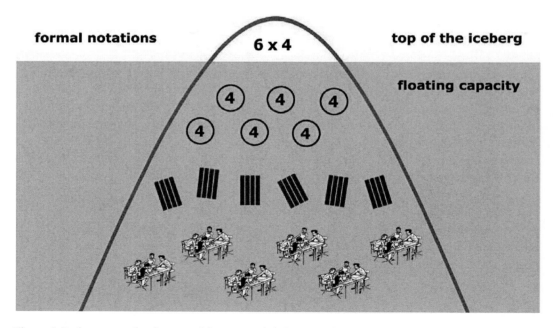

Figure 3. Iceberg metaphor borrowed from Boswinkel & Moerlands (2003).

Increasing semantization goes together with increasing formalization. Formalization alludes to a distinction in levels of mathematizing, as Gravemeijer (1994) points out. Gravemeijer discerns four levels: a situational, a referential, a general and a formal level. The referential level contains the models, descriptions, concepts, procedures and strategies that refer to concrete or paradigmatic situations. By generalization and further exploration, reflection about different strategies becomes more prominent. Then, a formalization of the general level takes place. This means that the general level is the referential level for the formal level.

We find the idea of increasing semantization and increasing formalizations pictured in the metaphor of the iceberg (see figure 3) by Boswinkel, and Moerlands (2003). They use this metaphor in their project 'Speciaal Rekenen' (2001) to make clear the need to invest in activities and insights that are needed to reach a formal level of mathematics, which they call the top of the iceberg. The basic level in the iceberg metaphor can be seen as the situational level of Gravemeijer. Meaning is here the basis for the process of formalization.

The highest level represented in the iceberg metaphor is the formal level. The problem is that the attention of most teachers is focused on this formal level, and so on what is regarded as the final results of the teaching process. These are calculations expressed in formal notations, for example $5+2=7$ and $7x3=21$. The activities leading to this result are more or less neglected and not seen as valuable. These activities are typified as 'floating capacity', for example activities during which students discover the multiplicative structures in packaging. Different models and strategies are discussed in these activities. The problem however is that the 'floating' capacity is not solid enough. Hence learning problems of students with special educational needs do have deeper roots and arise earlier in the learning process and not only at the most formal level. The problems are hidden and not always recognized as such. Moreover, in daily practice it appears that not all students achieve a formal level of addition, multiplication, fractions and so on. If a teacher is confronted with this problem, she should not proceed with 'drill and practice', but be tolerant and leave off the instruction. We should realize that the highest formal level is not attainable for all students with special educational needs (Kroesbergen & Van Luit, 2003).

Just as Boswinkel and Moerlands (2003) Whitson's (1997) represents, as we believe, the way in which semantization and formalization are *interwoven* with each other. The learning process starts with concrete people with whom the student can feel emotionally connected (see Figure 4). Just as in the iceberg metaphor, this is a meaningful start of the learning process. These persons have names. On a higher level one can represent them by fingers and subsequently with numbers et cetera. Students achieve a higher level over and over again but the meaningful basis never disappears. In other words, as Whitson (1997) put it, the signifier or representation always arises from signifiers at a lower level, and are meaningful experiences. At a higher level students come to understand that (for instance) counting and addition are related math activities. This process, which we characterize as increasing semantization, is of great significance when students with special educational needs learn mathematics. After all, for many of these students mathematics does currently not have much meaning, if any at all.

But not only these students, every individual, as research suggests (Girotti, 2004, p.122) is inclined to reason on the basis of meaningful information, *more* than on the basis of formal and fixed rules of reasoning. Girotti (2004, p.111): "inferences may be based on mental models, rather than on rules". Stenning, and Monoghan (2004, p.146) as well as Girotti characterize human reasoning as logic "that is not about mechanisms", but about meaningful interpretation.

Figure 4. Levels of formalization (See Whitson, 1997).

LEARNING MATHEMATICS BY INTERACTION

The core question of this study is: Can the access to mathematics of students with special educational needs be increased by guided, interactive instruction, meaningful learning and learning to solve problems reflectively? These core concepts are reconciled in the idea of interactive problem solving lessons.

What is Meant by Interactive Problem Solving Lessons and how are these Lessons Designed

In the poster lessons the students will be confronted with context problems. In small groups (two or three students) they try to find their own approach and they discuss possible solutions for the problem. This first phase of the students' activities is called the 'construction phase' or better the 'co-construction phase', because in the small groups the students are involved in close cooperation. This is similar to what Fosnot, and Dolk (2001) call a 'math workshop'- when learners are inquiring, investigating and constructing. As a result of the small group activities, the students exchange their thoughts and findings with the members of the other groups. This is the 'interaction phase'. Interaction can result in new insights in the way of thinking of other students as well as in a growing awareness of one's own problem solving activities, which leads to reflection. Fosnot, and Dolk (2001) call this a 'math congress' as a follow up of the math workshop. After investigating and writing down solutions and conjectures, the students communicate their ideas, solutions and thinking to each another. Posters can be helpful in this.

The whole process of interaction, reflection and construction is represented in Figure 1. As one can see, we try to integrate meaningful problem solving and interactive teaching and learning. The lessons are organized in such a way that there is plenty opportunity for both horizontal and vertical interaction, hence for simultaneous interaction. Students are confronted with meaningful problems, and of course it is an important research activity to find out what kind of contexts are inviting and appreciated the most by the students. The lessons supply enough opportunity for interaction to create a basis for the emergence of reflective thinking, which is of great significance for the learning of mathematics.

How the Lessons Actually Take Place

The role of the teacher during the poster lessons is crucial. She should not play a dominant role and the students should feel free to collaborate in their own way. At the same time the teacher has to carefully look at the complicated social processes that emerge during the lesson.

1. The teacher introduces the problem to be solved and she explains the working procedure:
   - look at the problem;
   - discuss the approaches you both favor;
   - try to find a shared approach;
   - write down your ideas and discuss these with your partner (in each pair);
   - a scratch paper or poster can be helpful for yourself and a resource for reflection,
   - the teacher explains what will be her function and role while the students are collaborating; she will not intervene, but she is always available to give information or to support when a pair has a problem.
2. The students work in pairs and try to solve the problem.
3. The students are encouraged to present their work and thinking activities to the whole group. However, special attention has to be paid to shy students. In the try-outs it was observed that for them intervening questions by the teacher was a stimulus for informing the other students about their own work.
4. In a whole class discussion, guided by the teacher, the couples inform each other about their findings and solutions.
5. The teacher looks back, in retrospection, together with all the students, on the merits of the different proposals. The proposals are discussed and the students are requested to review critically their own strategies and solutions.

PRACTICAL IMPORTANCE

Mathematics education for students with special needs was in the past mostly characterized by a practice of step-by-step instruction, and drill and practice. Teachers believe that they should always give these students a helping hand, because of their learning weaknesses. The consequence of this pedagogic is that the students do not get the opportunity to learn to think and reflect on their own. This results in a growing dependency of the students and thus a self-fulfilling prophecy, because the students' low confidence will lead to continuous requests for support which the teachers mostly are inclined to supply.

In two pilot studies (Verbruggen, 2005; Abels, Peltenburg & Verbruggen, 2007) we have seen that students with special educational needs are in fact more capable than is often thought in current school practice and that this competence can be stimulated by realistic mathematics education, especially by interactive teaching. Interactive problem solving lessons, we believe, can be a suitable resource to enhance skill in solving problems and the interactive and reflective skills of students with special educational needs.

RESEARCH IN YOUNG STUDENTS WITH SPECIAL NEEDS

Mathematics learning has been conceptualized as a constructivist process through which students construct mathematical knowledge by linking newly learned knowledge to previously acquired concepts (Van Luit & Naglieri, 1999). The premise of this perspective is that individuals set goals that lead to the construction of new knowledge, which in turn leads to new goals and new knowledge, thus producing a spiral effect in learning. In this view, social and affective development, and the context of learning, are regarded as influential factors in mathematical learning, next to cognitive development (Montague, 1997). Appropriate problem solving behavior in mathematics requires different skills: adequate orientation, planning, and systematic working, controlling and evaluating the solution process and elaborating the most important results (Veenman, Kerseboom & Imthorn, 2000).

In education for students with special educational needs, especially for the learning disabled (LD) and the mild mentally retarded (MMR) students, the number of students with mathematics disabilities seems to increase (Ruijssenaars, Van Luit & Van Lieshout, 2004). These difficulties begin at an early stage in the student's school life. Many students in special education schools are unable to learn the four basic math operations of addition, subtraction, multiplication and division before leaving primary education at the age of about twelve years. Since the seventies, many studies have investigated whether students, either mentally retarded students or learning disabled are better able to learn and/or memorize by teaching them skills like executive processes, performance and learning processes (Van Luit & Naglieri, 1999). It has been shown that education based on the use of open verbalizations by students about the choices they make in the solution procedure has a number of advantages. For example: two students have to solve problems like 'You can put 8 eggs in a box. How many eggs can you put in 7 egg boxes?' The students have to solve 7x8 or 8x7. If they do not know the answer automatically, they can use a backup strategy to solve this problem (Siegler, 1998). One possibility would be 5x8 + 2x8 = 40+16 = 56, while a less efficient strategy could be 1x8 = 8, 2x8 = 16, ..., 7x8 = 56.

In interactive problem solving lessons the students' problem solving and mathematical thinking within and between domains (especially addition, subtraction and multiplication) has to be taken into account. For example, students with mathematics disabilities usually do not combine new information with already known information. Within the domain of multiplication they do not make the connection between an already known task (5x9 = 45), and a new task (6x9 =?). In the lessons the following goals are designed to increase the student's:

- orientation on the problem and making a first plan for a possible solution.
- application of addition, subtraction and multiplication in real and imagined situations (for example by making a picture of the situation).
- understanding of number system and the premises of some problem solving strategies like reversibility (5x9 = 9x5), associations (9x7 = 10x7 - 1x7), and doubling (8x6 = 4x6 + 4x6) in discussion with another student.
- understanding and using control activities to check the chosen solution strategy and the answer together with another student.

A new math domain or a new level within a domain always starts with an orientation phase, and then the task can be solved with the help of materials or drawings, or later on through imagining. After that the connection will be made with the solution for adequate (mental) problem solving. The students then have to learn to check these solutions together. Finally, this cycle ends with the control phase - shortening - elaborating- reflection - generalization. The most common and adequate strategy can be elaborated on a poster (see Figure 5).

Figure 5. students working in pairs on a problem.

Figure 6. Students presenting their strategy and solution to their classmates.

At the end of each lesson some pairs will present their poster to their fellow students. This will result in discussions in which the presenting duo will defend their solution or will choose an idea of one of the other students in the class (see Figure 6).

The poster lessons involve an opportunity for problem solving strategy generation and use. Students are given the opportunity to apply their own solution or strategy to problems. The teacher's task is to lead the discussion in the direction of the use of adequate strategies and to facilitate the (group) reflection of the strategies put forward by the students. Student can use any problem solving strategy they wish, but the teacher assists the students in discussion and reflection about the choices made. For example an initial strategy for 8x7 could be: $7 + 7 + 7 + 7 + 7 + 7 + 7 + 7$. Some students may find this strategy too long and use: $4x7 + 4x7$, or $5x7 + 3x7$, for example. The teacher ensures that each student understands the different strategies and encourages them to use and to reflect on the most efficient strategy. The main goal is to help students to think mathematically about an adequate strategy with the use of simple facts in solving more complex problems.

DISCUSSION

With this study we suggest that interactive problem solving lessons can be employed in teaching mathematics to students with special educational needs who have mathematics difficulties. This idea is based on other research results (Van Luit & Kroesbergen, 2005; 2006). The lessons facilitate, as we have seen in two pilot studies (Verbruggen, 2005; Abels, Peltenburg & Verbruggen, 2007), students learning to think about different ways of problem solving, and learning from presenting their own solutions and discussions about alternatives. We expect that students who have worked with the lessons will become capable of thinking about the best possible problem solving strategy for regular mathematics tasks and their capacity for reasoning and using arguments will be better than before.

We suggest that students with special educational needs may improve in mathematics if they are provided with the underlying principles and given the opportunity to reflect and to generate their own procedures for solving mathematical problems, and that this may result in generalization of knowledge. In an earlier experiment (Van Luit & Kroesbergen, 2006), generalization was possible for most of the LD-students, but not for the MMR-students. Geary (2004), noting the complexity of the difficulties faced by the latter students, remarks that the most likely consequence of these difficulties is the lack of transfer. One important reason for the lack of transfer is that students who show transfer are also proficient in strategy use (Van Luit & Naglieri, 1999).

We will conclude with the expectation that interactive problem solving lessons will have a positive influence on the achievement of students with special educational needs, especially on their adequate problem solving strategies and transfer. Furthermore the arguments mentioned before facilitate regular and remedial teachers with ideas to help students with disabilities improve their math thinking performance.

REFERENCES

Abels, M., Peltenburg, M. C. & Verbruggen, I. (2007). *Probleemoplossen in interactie* [Problem solving in interaction]. Utrecht: Freudenthal Instituut.

Baxter, J., Woodward, J., & Olson, D. (2001). Effects of reform-based mathematics instruction in five third grade classrooms. *Elementary School Journal, 101*, 529-548.

Boswinkel, N., & Moerlands, F. J. (2001). Speciaal Rekenen [RME for students with special needs]. *Tijdschrift voor Nascholing en Onderzoek van het Reken-WiskundeOnderwijs, 19*(3), 3-14.

Boswinkel, N. & Moerlands, F.J. (2003). Het topje van de ijsberg. [The top of the iceberg] In: K. Groenewegen (Eds.), Nationale Rekendagen 2002 - een praktische terugblik, Utrecht: Freudenthal Instituut, 103-114.

Bottge, B. A. (2001). Reconceptualizing mathematics problem solving for low-achieving students. *Remedial and Special Education, 22*, 102-112.

Bruner, J. S. (1967). *Towards a theory of instruction.* Cambridge, UK: Harvard University Press.

Fosnot, C. T., & Dolk, M. (2001). *Young mathematicians at work: Constructing number sense, addition, and subtraction.* Portsmouth, NH: Heinemann.

Fosnot, C. T., Dolk, M., Cameron, A., & Hersch, S. B. (2005). *Turkey investigations.* Portsmouth, NH: Heinemann.

Freudenthal, H. (1991). *Revisiting mathematics education; China lectures.* Dordrecht, The Netherlands: Kluwer.

Geary, D.C. (2004). Mathematics and learning disabilities. *Journal of Learning Disabilities, 37*, 4-15.

Goldman, S. R., & Hasselbring, T. S. (1997). Achieving meaningful mathematics literacy for students with learning disabilities. *Journal of Learning Disabilities, 30*, 198-208

Gravemeijer, K.P.E. (1994). *Developing realistic mathematics education.* Utrecht, The Netherlands: CD-B Press.

Kroesbergen, E. H., & Van Luit, J. E. H. (2002). Teaching multiplication to low math performers: Guided versus structured instruction. *Instructional Science, 30,* 361-378.

Kroesbergen, E. H., & Van Luit, J. E. H. (2003). Mathematics interventions for children with special educational needs: A meta-analysis. *Remedial & Special Education, 24,* 97-114.

Kroesbergen, E.H., & Van Luit, J.E.H. (2005). Constructivist mathematics education for students with mild mental retardation. *European Journal of Special Needs Education, 20, 1,* 107-116.

Mercer, N. (1995). *The guided construction of knowledge: Talk amongst teachers and learners.* Clevedon, UK: Multilingual Matters.

Montague, M. (1997). Cognitive strategy instruction in mathematics for students with learning disabilities. *Journal of Learning Disabilities, 30,* 164-177.

Nelissen, J. M. C. (1999). Thinking skills in realistic mathematics. In J. H. M. Hamers, J. E. H. Van Luit, & B. Csapo (Eds.), *Teaching and learning thinking skills* (pp. 189-213). Lisse, The Netherlands: Swets & Zeitlinger.

Nelissen, J. M. C. (2002) Interactie: Een vakpsychologische analyse [Interaction: A psychological analysis]. In: R. Keijzer & W. Uittenbogaard (Eds.), Interactie in het reken-wiskundeonderwijs (pp. 11-41). Utrecht, The Netherlands: Freudenthal Institute.

Nelissen, J. M. C., & Tomic, W. (1996). Reflection in Russian educational psychology. *Educational Foundations, 10*(1), 35-57.

Palinscar, A. S. (1986). The role of dialogue in providing scaffolding instruction. *Educational Psychologist, 21,* 73-98.

Reid, D. K. (1998). Scaffolding: A broader view. *Journal of Learning Disabilities, 31,* 386-396.

Ruijssenaars, A. J. J. M., Van Luit, J. E. H., & Van Lieshout, E. C. D. M. (2004). Rekenproblemen en dyscalculie. Theorie, onderzoek, diagnostiek en behandeling. [Mathematics disabilities and dyscalculia. Theory, research, assessment and intervention]. Rotterdam, The Netherlands: Lemniscaat.

Siegler, R. S. (1998). *Childrens' thinking.* Upper Saddle River, NY: Prentice Hall.

Slobodcikov, V. J., & Cukerman, G. A. (1990). Genezis refleksivnogo soznaniya v mladshem shkol'nom vozraste [Development of reflective thinking in young school children]. *Voprosy Psichologii, 9,* 25-36.

Stepanov , S. J., & Semenov, I. N. (1982). Problema formirovaniye tipo refleksii v reshenii tvorcheskih zadach [Problems in the development of types of reflection in solving (creative) tasks]. *Voprosy Psicholgii, 1,* 99-104.

Stone, C. A. (1998). The metaphor of scaffolding: Its utility for the field of learning disabilities. *Journal of Learning Disabilities, 31,* 344-364.

Treffers, A. (1987). *Three dimensions. A model of goal and theory description in primary mathematics education. Wiskobas.* Dordrecht, The Netherlands: Reidel.

Van Luit, J. E. H., & Kroesbergen, E. H. (2006). Teaching metacognitive skills to students with mathematical disabilities. In A. Desoete & M. V. J. Veenman (Eds.), *Metacognition in mathematics education* (pp. 177-190). Hauppauge, NY: Nova Science.

Van Luit, J. E. H., & Naglieri, J. A. (1999). Effectiveness of the MASTER program for teaching special children multiplication and division. *Journal of Learning Disabilities, 32,* 98-107.

Veenman, M. V. J., Kerseboom, L., & Imthorn, C. (2000). Text anxiety and metacognitive skillfulness: Availability versus production deficiencies. *Anxiety, Stress, and Coping, 13*, 391-412.

Verbruggen, I. (2005). Interactie in het reken-wiskundeonderwijs [Interaction in mathematics education]. Utrecht: Freudenthal Institute. (Internal report).

Vygotsky, L. S. (1978). *Mind in society.* London: Harvard University Press.

Whitson, J. A. (1997). Cognition as semiotic process: From situated mediation to critical reflective transcendence. In D. Kirshner & J. A. Whitson (Eds.), *Situated cognition* (pp. 97-151). London: Lawrence Erlbaum.

Woodward, J., & Montague, M. (2002). Meeting the challenge of mathematics reform for students with LD. *The Journal of Special Education, 36,* 89-101.

Zak, A. Z. (1976). Psichologichkiye osobennosti teoreticheskogo peshenii zadat [Psychological particularities in theoretical task solving]. *Novye Issledovanye v Psichologii, 2,* 17-20.

In: Multimedia in Education and Special Education
Editors: O. Demir and C. Celik

ISBN 978-1-60741-073-7
© 2009 Nova Science Publishers, Inc.

Chapter 11

USING UNIVERSITY-BASED CONSULTATION TO IMPLEMENT POSITIVE BEHAVIOR SUPPORT INTERVENTIONS IN THE CLASSROOM

Morgan Chitiyo[1] and John. J. Wheeler[2]
[1]Southern Illinois University at Carbondale, Carbondale, Illinois 62901, USA
[2]Tennessee Tech University, Cookeville, Tennessee 38505, USA

ABSTRACT

Consultation has become common among special education teachers since the 1997 and 2004 reauthorizations of the Individuals with Disabilities Education Act (IDEA), which require teachers to use positive behavior support interventions in addressing the behavioral needs of children who exhibit challenging behavior. At present, many school teachers and school systems lack the capacity to effectively utilize these research validated practices and oftentimes they rely on consultation in order to meet these legal requirements. The purpose of this chapter is to describe a university based consultation model for implementing evidence based practices in positive behavior support interventions in classroom settings. A case illustration is presented to demonstrate how such a model can be utilized effectively to maximize positive outcomes.

INTRODUCTION

Consultation models vary across disciplines like mental health, organizational development, and behavioral (Sheridan & Welch, 1996). Although it is defined differently in these professions (West, & Idol, 1987), throughout history consultation has been used as a way to solve one's problems with another person's expertise (Budde & Summers, 1991). According to Zins and Ponti (1990) consultation is:

A method of providing preventatively oriented psychological and educational services in which a consultant and consultee(s) form a collaborative partnership in a system context to engage in a reciprocal and systematic problem solving process to empower consultee systems, thereby enhancing students' well-being and performance (p. 674).

The application of consultation in school settings was popularized in the 1960s with the emergence of the behavioral movement and it flourished in the early 1970s as a credible means of working with children in schools (Friend, 1988). In recent years the use of consultation in school settings has heightened because of the need to educate children with disabilities in the least restrictive environment (Gutkin, 1996). The 1997 as well as the 2004 reauthorizations of the Individuals with Disabilities Education Act (IDEA) require that children with disabilities be educated in a setting that promotes maximum contact with children without disabilities. The result has been that more children with disabilities are now being included in the general education classroom (Scott, Park, Broadway & Landers, 2007). Gutkin (1996) identified two reasons why the need to educate children with disabilities in the least restrictive environment has led to a growing emphasis on consultation services. First, most general education teachers are not prepared to teach students with disabilities with their diverse educational needs (Coombs-Richardson & Mead, 2001) and thus need additional support to maintain these students along with the same-age peers in their classrooms. Second, the law mandates prereferral intervention, which entails a referring general education teacher collaborating with special services personnel to develop intervention for maintaining students in general rather than special education placements. Consultation therefore, is used to help general education teachers who teach children who for a variety of reasons are considered difficult to teach. According to Martens and Ardoin (2002) teachers seek consultative assistance because their usual methods of responding to students' problems have proven unsuccessful.

Furthermore, the IDEA reauthorizations also require teachers to consider using positive behavior support (PBS) for students with disabilities who display challenging behavior (Yell & Katsiyannis, 2000). PBS is a behavioral management approach emphasizing proactive strategies involving designing effective environments to prevent problem behavior and teaching appropriate behaviors that promote positive and acceptable outcomes among students with disabilities (Sugai et al., 2000). Since its utility has been repeatedly demonstrated (Hieneman, Dunlap, & Kincaid, 2005, Lewis et al., 2002, Oswald, Safran, & Johanson, 2005, Artesani & Mallar, 1998, Lassen, Steele & Sailor, 2006, Kennedy et al., 2001) PBS has gained credibility as evidence based practice. Nevertheless, these practices are not widely utilized across school systems today (Malouf & Schiller, 1995) possibly because many school systems lack the capacity to adopt and implement these research-validated practices (Muscott et al. 2004; Sugai et al. 1999).

The purpose of this chapter is to provide an overview of behavioral consultation. We discuss a conceptual framework for university based consultation and present a case illustration to demonstrate how school personnel can utilize university-based consultation to improve the behavioral and academic outcomes of children with disabilities in classroom settings.

CONSULTATION FRAMEWORK

Tharp and Wetzel (1969) suggested a triadic consultation model of using behavioral principles in school settings, which involves three levels: consultant (support professional), consultee (teacher), and client (student). In this model, the consultant helps the teacher to analyze the student's problem, design intervention strategies, implement, and evaluate the efficacy of the intervention in reducing or preventing challenging behavior. Behavioral consultation has adherence to protocol as one of its signature features (Lueselli, 2002). The consultation process has to be delineated up-front with the implementation stages clearly defined. This helps both the consultants and consultees to implement the problem-solving approach more effectively. Lueselli (2002) identified four stages that should be followed in implementing the consultation process that is problem identification, problem analysis, intervention plan intervention and intervention plan evaluation. Along these stages, Wheeler and Hoover (1997) described a model to guide behavioral consultants with the implementation. According to Wheeler & Hoover's model the first phase of the consultation process involves formalizing the consultative agreements. After receiving request for assistance, the consultant should plan to meet the consultee to establish the purpose of the consultation. Next, the consultant and consultee should identify targets, specify roles of team members and identify competencies needed by all team members. Once the targets have been identified, roles agreed on, and competencies identified, the process of assisting with the development of school-based teams (in the case of school-based services) or individual intervention plans (in the case of individual student interventions) begins. The consultation process should culminate in evaluation of the outcomes and intervention activities and the consultant should develop a follow along plan to help while the consultation services are gradually faded.

CONSULTATION MODELS

School-Based Consultation

School based consultation involves school psychologists assuming the role of consultant to assist classroom teachers to analyze student problems, design and implement interventions (Feldman & Kratochwill, 2003). This type of consultation has been used by general education teachers in fulfillment of mandates requiring prereferral intervention for students suspected of having a disability (Gutkin, 1996). In this context if a teacher suspects that a student may be in need of special education, they will first seek help from special education personnel who will assist them to develop and implement interventions before that student can be referred for evaluation. Such prereferal consultation services, which are usually applied in general education settings, have been touted as being effective at reducing the number of children eligible for special education (Gutkin, 1996).

Apart from being used as part of the prereferal process school-based consultation has also been utilized by special educators in order to enhance interventions for students with disabilities. This is usually true when special education teachers lack the "capacity to identify, adopt, and sustain policies, practices and systems that effectively and efficiently meet the needs of [students with disabilities]" (Sugai, et al. 2000, p132).   In such cases special educators seek the help of school psychologists who will guide them through the process of designing and implementing appropriate interventions.   Although school-based consultation has been found to be effective at remediating students' academic and behavioral problems (Feldman & Kratochwill, 2003; Kratochwill, Elliot & Busse, 1995; Medway & Updyke, 1985; Sheridan, Welch, & Orme, 1996; Wilkinson, 2003), research has found it to be less effective than consultation provided through university teams (Doll et al., 2005). This is possibly because university based consultation teams are more research oriented and thus utilize evidence-based procedures which "have been validated in university laboratories and public school classrooms [and thus are likely to yield better outcomes]" (Fuchs & Fuchs, 1996, p387.

University-Based Consultation

University-based consultation usually involves university teams (consultants) providing assistance to school personnel (consultees) on how to solve students' (clients) problems via implementation of evidence-based practices. Extant research on university-based consultation seems to support its effectiveness (Chitiyo & Wheeler, In press; Taylor et al. 1996; Vaughn et al., 1998) and even its superiority over other consultation models (Bahr et al., 1999; Doll et al., 2005). Vaughn and colleagues (1998) described a model used by the East Tennessee State University's Make a Difference (MAD) project to provide consultation to schools vis-à-vis-using functional behavioral assessment to design behavioral interventions for students exhibiting challenging behavior. Through this project the MAD team assists teachers to conduct functional behavior assessments, develop function-based interventions, provide ongoing technical assistance during implementation of the interventions and gradually withdraw their technical assistance once the teachers demonstrate the ability to independently sustain the application of the procedures.

Chitiyo and Wheeler (In press) described a similar model utilized by the Tennessee Technological University's TTU PBIS project which assists teachers and schools in 23 counties of the Upper Cumberland region of Tennessee to implement positive behavior supports in their school systems. The project utilizes a three phase framework where the first phase involves meeting with school teams to establish a relationship and to analyze the problems and type of support the school teams need. The second phase involves assisting school teams through development and implementation of interventions which culminates in the final phase during which the consultant and consultee jointly evaluate outcomes.

CASE ILLUSTRATION

The following case illustration demonstrates how school personnel can utilize university-based consultation to implement research validated practices in their classrooms in order to improve the behavioral and academic outcomes of children who exhibit challenging behavior. In this case two children were referred for consultation to a university-based team. The university team met with the teacher to formalize the relationship and to discuss the teacher's needs vis-à-vis the two students. This was followed by functional behavioral assessments which led to development of intervention plans for the two students. Based on results of the descriptive functional behavioral assessments (FBA) the research team developed the interventions and taught the teacher how to implement them; the team provided ongoing technical support during implementation of the intervention and collected data, through observations, in order to evaluate outcomes. The consultation process ended with evaluation of the process which demonstrated favorable outcomes for both students.

The Students

Frank was a 16 year old boy in grade 10 and Beth was a 17 year old girl in grade 11. Both students exhibited high rates of challenging behavior and were referred for consultation for off-task behavior. Off task behavior for both students involved taking eyes off one's work and looking around for extended periods of time lasting more than a minute. Frank's off task behavior also included talking to other students about any topic not related to his current assignment. While completing their independent assignments, students were required to maintain their attention on the task, to refrain from talking to and touching other students or leave their seats.

Functional Behavioral Assessment

The university team conducted two 30 minute functional assessment interviews for each of the students. The first interviews were conducted with the student's teacher. Each teacher interview was followed by a student interview which also lasted about 30 minutes. The two sets of interviews were conducted using the Functional Assessment Checklist for Teachers and Staff (FACTS) (March et al., 2000). The FACTS was slightly modified to suit the student interview and the two sets of interviews yielded information about Frank and Beth's problem behaviors including a description of the problem behavior, variables that predicted the behavior, as well as variables that maintained the problem behavior. The university team also conducted three ten-minute observations for each student during independent work sessions in the resource classroom using the A-B-C approach (Crone & Horner, 2003) where events were recorded prior to and following instances of off task behavior. Results of the interviews and observations suggested teacher attention as the function of off task behavior for both participants. The team designed an intervention following the FBA.

Intervention

A multiple baseline across subjects design was used in this case because it does not require withdrawal of the intervention in order to demonstrate experimental control and thus is more suited for applied settings. During baseline condition the team members observed the students during independent work sessions. The observers recorded the frequency of off task behavior using partial interval recording. Each observation session lasted 10 minutes and was divided into 60 ten-second intervals (Richards et al, 1999).

Intervention was introduced for Beth after the baseline trend in off task behavior had stabilized. Frank continued on baseline until the trend had stabilized as well at which point the intervention was introduced. The interventions involved putting the behaviors on extinction using extinction by omission. Since it was hypothesized that off task behavior for both students was maintained by teacher attention, it was postulated that by withholding teacher attention contingent on the target behavior there would be reduction in off task behavior for both students. The teacher was therefore, instructed to systematically ignore the students each time they engaged in the target behavior.

Interobserver Agreement

Interobserver agreement (IOA) was calculated for the frequency of the target behavior during both the baseline and interventions on all direct observation sessions for Beth and during 75 percent of direct observation sessions for Frank. Two members of the research team served as observers. The IOA was calculated by dividing the number of agreements by the number of agreements plus disagreements and multiplying that by 100. The IOA for Beth was 99 percent and 98 percent for Frank.

Percentage of Nonoverlapping Data

Percentage of nonoverlapping data (PND) was used to assess the effectiveness of the intervention (Scruggs, Mastopieri & Casto, 1987). PND is a procedure used to evaluate the effectiveness of single case interventions by quantifying the outcomes and it is calculated by "dividing the number of data points in intervention that did not overlap with data points in baseline by the total number of data points in the intervention phase" (Scattone, Tingstrom, & Wilczynski, 2006, p. 217). According to Scruggs, Mastropieri, Cook and Escobar (1986) a PND of at least 90% should be considered very effective, 70% to 90% should be considered effective while 50% to 70% is questionable and anything less than 50% represents an ineffective treatment. The PND for Frank and Beth, separately, was found to be 100% which indicates highly effective interventions.

Outcomes

Figure 1 shows the frequency of problem behavior across baseline and intervention for the two participants. Putting the behavior on extinction resulted in marked reduction in off task behavior in both cases. For Frank there was a reduction from a mean frequency of eight during baseline to zero occurrences after introduction of the intervention. For Beth disruptive behavior occurred during baseline at a mean frequency of 3.25 and dropped to zero occurrences with the introduction of the intervention package.

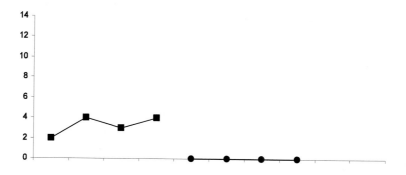

Figure 1. Frequency of problem behavior across sessions

SUMMARY

The case illustration is intended to demonstrate the application of university based consultation to help schoolteachers to implement PBS interventions in their classrooms. In this case the university-based team conducted functional behavioral assessments and designed function-based interventions which the teacher implemented with the assistance of the university team. The team used a three phase framework described by Chitiyo and Wheeler (in press). It is important to note that for this model to be effective the consultant and consultee should collaborate in sharing responsibility during all stages of the consultation process (Buysse & Wesley, 2004) and the collaboration should be based on trust, openness, and cooperation (Zins, & Ponti, 1990).

The intent of a university-based consultation team is to assist public school providers with the formation of school-based teams in the delivery of positive behavior supports within their respective settings. This is accomplished through the delivery of technical assistance and support in the area of training aimed at capacity building in terms of skill development and professional competencies on the part of school personnel. The goal is that external technical assistance as provided by university-based consultation teams will be faded over time as the school-based team refines both their level of professional competency and the system for delivery of PBS services and supports.

The university-based consultation team will provide systematic follow-along of school-based teams over time at regular intervals e.g. 2 week, 4 week, 3-month, 6-month, 1-year intervals. Re-training and or continuing supports should be available should school-based teams find themselves in need of these services. By providing such on-going consultation and technical support the goal of providing evidence-based practices in the area of PBS is attained and the fidelity of these services and supports better ensured through such quality assurance.

CONCLUSION

Consultation appears to be an effective way to bridge the research-to-practice gap that currently exists in special education. There is ballooning evidence pointing to the effectiveness of university based consultation in this regard. In fact, extant research supports the superiority of university based consultation over other models such as school-based consultation. This chapter described how schoolteachers can use university-based consultation to implement evidence-based practices in PBS in their classroom settings. By adopting this approach, school teachers may be able to utilize best and effective practices which will promote positive behavioral and academic outcomes among their students with disabilities. Future research should address generalization issues and examination of moderating variables that may contribute to favorable outcomes associated with university-based consultation compared to other models.

REFERENCES

Artesani, A. J., & Mallar, L. (1998). Positive behavior supports in general education settings: Combining person centered planning and functional analysis. *Intervention in School and Clinic,* 34(1), 33-38.

Budde, J. F., & Summers, J. A. (1991). Consultation and technical assistance. In J. L. Matson & J. M. Mulick (Ed.), *Handbook of mental retardation* (pp. 489-502). New York: Pergamon Press.

Buysse, V., & Wesley, P. W. (2004). A framework for understanding the consultation process. *Young Exceptional Children,* 7(2), 2-9.

Chitiyo, M. & Wheeler, J.J. (In press). Analyzing the treatment efficacy of technical assistance model for providing behavioral consultation to schools. *Preventing School Failure.*

Coombs-Richardson, R. & Mead, J. (2001). Supporting general educators' inclusive practices. Teacher Education and Special Education, 2(4), 383-390.

Crone, D. A., & Horner, R. H. (2003). *Building positive behavior support systems in schools: Functional behavior assessment.* New York: The Guilford Press.

Doll, B., & Haack, K., Kosse, S., & Pray, B. (2005). The dilemma of pragmatics: why schools don't use quality team consultation practices. *Journal of Educational and Psychological Consultation,* 16(3), 127-155.

Feldman, E.S. & Kratochwill, E.R. (2003). Problem solving consultation in schools: past, present, and future directions. *The Behavior Analyst Today,* 4(3), 1-12.

Friend, M. (1988). Putting consultation into context: Historical and contemporary perspectives. *Remedial and Special Education,* 9(6), 7-13.

Fuchs, D., & Fuchs, L. S. (1996). Consultation as a technology and politics of school reform: Reaction to the issue. *Remedial and Special Education,* 17, 386-392.

Gutkin, T.B. (1996). Core elements of consultation service delivery for special service personnel: Rationale, practice, and some directions for the future. *Remedial and Special Education,* 17, 333-40.

Hieneman, M., Dunlap, G., & Kincaid, D. (2005). Positive support strategies for students with behavioral disorders in general education settings. *Psychology in the Schools, 42*(8), 779-794.

Kennedy, C.H., Long, T., Jolivette, K., Cox, J., Tang, J., & Thompson, T. et al. (2001). Facilitating general education participation for students with behavior problems by linking positive behavior supports and person-centered planning. *Journal of Emotional & Behavioral Disorders, 9*(3), 161-172. (11)

Kratochwill, T.R., Elliot, S.N., & Busse, R.T. (1995). Behavior consultation: a five-year evaluation of consultation and client outcomes. *School Psychology Quarterly,* 10, 87-117.

Lassen, S.R., Steele, M.M., & Sailor, W. (2006). The relationship of school-wide positive behavior support to academic achievement in an urban middle school. *Psychology in the Schools, 43*(6), 701-712.

Lewis, T.J., Powers, L.J., Kelk, M.J., & Newcomer, L.L. et al. (2002). Reducing problem behaviors on the playground: An investigation of the application of schoolwide positive behavior supports. *Psychology in the Schools, 39*(2), 181-190.

Lueselli, J.K. (2002). Focus, scope, and practice of behavioral consultation to public schools. In Lueselli, J.K. & Diament, C. (Eds.), *Behavioral psychology in the schools: innovations in evaluation, support and consultation,* (p.5-21). Philadelphia, PA: Haworth Press, Inc.

Malouf, D.B. & Schiller, E.P. (1995). Practice and research in special education. *Exceptional Children,* 61, 414-424.

March, R., Horner, R.H., Lewis-Palmer, T., Brown, D., Crone, D., Todd, A.W. & Carr, E. (2000). *Functional assessment checklist for teachers and staff (FACTS).* Department of Educational and Community Supports, Eugene, OR: University of Oregon.

Martens, B. K., & Ardoin, S. P. (2002). Training school psychologists in behavior support consultation. In J. K. Luiselli and C. Diament (Eds.), *Behavior Psychology in the schools: Innovations in evaluation, support and consultation* (pp. 147-163). New York: Haworth Press Inc.

Medway, F. J., & Updyke, J.F. (1985). Meta-anslysis of consultation outcome studies. *American Journal of Community Psychology,* 13, 489-504.

Muscott, H.S., Mann, E., Benjamin, T.B., Gately, S., Bell, K,E., & Muscott, A.J. (2004). Positive behavior supports in New Hampshire: Preliminary results of a statewide system for implementing schoolwide discipline practices. *Treatment of Children, 27*(4), 453-75.

Oswald, K., Safran, S., & Johanson, G. (2005). Preventing trouble: Making schools safer places using positive behavior supports. *Education and Treatment of Children, 28*(3), 265-278.

Richards, S.B., Taylor, R.L., Ramasamy, R. & Richards, R.Y. (1999). *Single subject research: Applications in educational and clinical settings.* Belmont, CA: Wadsworth Thomson Learning.

Scott, T.M., Park, K.L., Swain-Bradway, J., & Landers, E. (2007). Positive behavior support in the classroom: facilitating behaviorally inclusive learning environments. *International Journal of Behavioral Consultation and Therapy, 3*(2), 223-235.

Scattone, D., Tingstrom, D.H. & Wilczynski, S.M. (2006). Increasing appropriate social interactions of children with autism spectrum disorders using Social Stories. *Focus on Autism and Other Developmental Disabilities,* 21(4), 211-222.

Scruggs, T.E., Mastropieri, M.A., & Casto, G. (1987). The quantitative synthesis of single subject research: Methodology and validation. *Remedial and Special Education*, 8(2), 24-33.

Scruggs, T. E., Mastropieri, M. A., Cook, S., & Escobar, C. (1986). Early intervention for children with conduct disorders: A quantitative synthesis of single-subject research. *Behavioral Disorders*, 11, 260-271.

Sheridan, S. M., Welch, M. (1996). Is consultation effective? *Remedial and Special Education*, 17(6), 341-355.

Sheridan, S. M., Welch, M., & Orme, S. F. (1996). Is consultation effective? A review of outcome research. *Remedial and Special Education*, 17, 341-358.

Sugai, G., Horner, R. H., Dunlap, G., Hieneman, M., Lewis, T. J., Nelson, C. M., Scott, T., Liaupsin, C., Sailor, W., Turnbull, M. P., Turnbull, H. R, III., Wickham, D., Wilcox, B., & Ruef, M. (2000). Applying positive behavior support and functional behavioral assessment in schools. *Journal of Positive behavior Interventions*, 2(3)131-143.

Sugai, G., Horner, R. H., Dunlap, G., Hieneman, M., Lewis, T. J., Nelson, C. M., Scott, T., Liaupsin, C., Sailor, W., Turnbull, M. P., Turnbull, H. R, III., Wickham, D., Ruef, M., & Wilcox, B. (1999). *Applying positive behavioral support and functional behavioral assessment in schools. Technical assistance guide 1, version 1.4.3.* Washington DC: Center on Positive Behavioral Interventions and Support. (ERIC Document Reproduction Service No. ED443244).

Taylor, I., O'Reilly, M. F., & Lancioni, G. E. (1996). An evaluation of an ongoing consultation model to train teachers to treat challenging behavior. *International Journal of Disability, Development, and Education*, 43(3), 203-221.

Tharp, R., & Wetzel, R. (1969). *Behavior modification in the natural environment.* New York: Academic Press.

Vaughn, K. Hales, C., Bush, M., & Fox, J. (1998). East Tennessee State University's "Make a difference" Project: Using a Team-Based consultative model to conduct functional behavioral assessments. *Preventing school failure*, 43(1), 24-30.

West, J. F., & Idol, L. (1987). School consultation (Part 1): An interdisciplinary perspective on theory, models, and research. *Journal of Learning Disabilities*, 20(7), 388-408.

Wheeler, J. J., & Hoover, J. H. (1997). A consultative model for the provision of behavioral supports to children with challenging behaviour: Practical approaches for the development of school-based support teams. *B.C. Journal of Special Education*, 21(1), 4-15.

Wilkinson, L. A. (2003). Using behavioral consultation to reduce challenging behavior in the classroom. *Preventing School Failure*, 47(3), 100-105.

Yell, M. L, & Katsiyannis, A. (2000). Functional behavioral assessment and IDEA'97: Legal and practice considerations. *Preventing School Failure*, 44(4), 158-171.

Zins, J. E., & Ponti, C. R. (1990). Best practices in school-based consultation. In A. Thomas and J. Grimes (Eds.), *Best practices in school psychology -- II* (pp. 673-694). Washington, DC: National Association of School Psychology.

In: Multimedia in Education and Special Education
Editors: O. Demir and C. Celik

ISBN 978-1-60741-073-7
© 2009 Nova Science Publishers, Inc.

Chapter 12

PATIENT EDUCATION IN AN ACUTE CARE SETTING.

FEASABILITY AND MEDIUM-TIME EFFECTS OF A SHORT PARTICIPATORY PATIENT-EDUCATION FOCUSING ON HYPERTENSION IN ELDERLY PATIENTS WITH NON-INSULIN-DEPENDENT DIABETES

H. Burkhardt[*], A. Koffner, R. Gladisch
IV. Medizinische Klinik, Schwerpunkt Geriatrie, University of Heidelberg,
Universitätsmedizin Mannheim, 68135 Mannheim, Germany

ABSTRACT

Patient education is crucial in preventive medicine to achieve and maintain a healthy and appropriate lifestyle and hereby minimize the burden of morbidity due to chronic disease. The framework concept of shared decision making encourage health care professionals to apply a participatory approach in patient education. Feasability and effects of such an approach has already been described in ambulatory settings but little is known about implementation in acute care. Also participatory approaches are often referred as less appropriate in the elderly. To examine the feasability and medium-time effects of a participatory educational session offered in an acute care setting a pilot-study was done in elderly patients with diabetes and hypertension.

Patients were recruited from general internal medicine and geriatric wards. They were eligible if acute illness was controlled or partially recovered. Exclusion criteria were dementia, delirium, instable clinical condition and remaining prognosis below 1 year. Patients were randomized to an intervention group consisting of a short (30 minutes) participatory education session focussing on self-management of hypertension. Reassessment of participants by telephone took place 3 months thereafter.

[*] Corresponding author. H. Burkhardt MD. IV. Medizinische Klinik, Schwerpunkt Geriatrie, University of Heidelberg, Universitätsmedizin Mannheim, 68135 Mannheim, Germany. E-mail: heinrich.burkhardt@umm.de Fax: 49/621/3832182; Phone: 49/621/3835980

44 patients (29 women and 15 men, age 57-88) took part in the study. After three months in the intervention group (N=20) significantly more participants showed reduced blood pressure values, both systolic (120-160mmHg) and diastolic (70-90mmHg), body weight (50-121kg) and HbA1c (5.8-11.3%). However, only 4 patients in the intervention group achieved blood pressure values of 130/80mmHG or below. Also median weight reduction was limited (2kg).

Participatory patient education when applied in an acute care setting is feasible and provides beneficial effects on blood pressure control, weight reduction and metabolic control in elderly but well-functioning patients with diabetes. Therefore this approach may effectively supplement usual ambulatory patient education.

Keywords: Hypertension, HbA1c, diabetes, patient education, participatory decision making

INTRODUCTION

It is widely accepted that reducing mortality and morbidity resulting from vascular disease resembles the main therapeutic goal in treatment of patients with diabetes. In this context the STENO 2 study was a milestone and established the concept of multifactorial treatment in patients with diabetes, focussing on NIDDM [1]. This included besides metabolic control also a strict control of elevated blood pressure with target values below 130/80 mmHg. The ability of successful self-management of different aspects of diabetes predicts metabolic control and hereby also the prognosis of the disease [2]. Therefore the general goal of patient education in diabetes and hypertension is an effective self-management covering correct dosage of medication and insulin, monitoring tasks such as blood-pressure and glucose measurements, and life-style aspects such as nutritional aspects and exercise.

Although the topic of blood pressure control is regularly implemented in standardized education programs for patients with NIDDM, a substantial and unacceptable high portion of patients remains with elevated blood pressure [3,4]. Those patients are also frequently seen in hospital departments for treatment of acute medical problems either related to diabetes or not. Understanding patient education as an ongoing process to reinforce self-management by a continuing counseling [5], patient education should also be offered and implemented in an acute care setting not o leave any patient with an unsatisfactory blood pressure control unrecognized. Patient education in this setting may serve not only as updating of previously given information and advice but also as an education option which may reach patients who had not yet succeeded in optimizing self care behavior and had no opportunity to take part in a structured education program.

Patient education in an acute care setting is a neglected area both in clinical practice and research. Clinicians and scientist often are discouraged to focus on this topic. Several reasons may explain this lack. Structured patient education usually covers several sessions to establish, maintain and reinforce changes in patient´s attitudes and behavior. Therefore in an era of ongoing shortening of days spent in hospital and simultaneously increasing burden of diagnostic procedures, the focus of clinical attention shifts from the close encounter with the patient and personal advice towards standardized and technical procedures [6].

Patient education itself has changed from solely advice of certain behavioral aspects such as the cessation of smoking towards a more holistic approach and aiming at more general concepts such as empowerment. Empowerment as an approach has become popular across several disciplines from medicine to policy. It involves a process and outcomes whereby people, organizations, and communities increase or gain mastery and control over their lives and become active participants in efforts to influence their environment [7]. The role of the educator in this concept is to help and strengthen patients abilities to learn new behavior. This underlines the active role of the patient. Four cognitive key dimensions are essential in this process: meaningfulness, competence, self-determination and impact [8]. Recent developments in education theory underline the importance of shared decision making in this context and encourage educational strategies which utilize a participatory approach [9]. However, there is an ongoing discussion whether this approach is applicable in general or better has to be tailored to the individual needs of certain populations. In this context elderly patients have been found not to prefer a participatory educational approach [10]. But these results are mainly derived from studies in oncological diseases.

In summary, little is known about the effects and especially the long- and medium-time effects of patient education offered in an acute care setting. We therefore performed a pilot study to examine the feasibility and efficacy of a short educational intervention implementing a participatory approach by shared decision making and describing individual short- and medium-time therapy goals.

METHODS

Participants were recruited within a 5-month period from patients admitted to a ward for general internal medicine and geriatrics of a large acute-care hospital. Patients were eligible if both non-insulin-dependent diabetes and arterial hypertension were present, either as primary diagnosis or comorbidity. Exclusion criteria were dementia, delirium, unstable vital parameters, remaining prognosis below 1 year and deteriorating clinical condition. All patients gave informed consent according to the declaration of Helsinki.

Participants were randomized in two groups. The control group received regular advice during inpatient treatment usually provided by the physician during go-rounds and at the end of the inpatient treatment. The intervention group received an additional short and individualized patient education (30 minutes) from one of the investigators (AK). This education session covers advice concerning medication management, self-measurement of blood-pressure and self-care behavior. Patients were regularly advised to maintain or achieve normal body weight, to adhere to regular medication and daily blood pressure measurement. Patients were encouraged to strengthen their self care behavior according to the philosophy of empowerment [5]. Each patient was asked to describe an individual treatment-goal he agrees to achieve within the next three months. The treatment goal was then written by the patient on a flyer also containing general rules for patients with hypertension, hereby serving as reminder of the individual treatment goal. Patients were also asked to keep this flyer at home.

Data concerning functional abilities, social support, residence and diabetes related aspects, such as regularly performed self-management, diabetes duration, previous diabetes education and vascular diseases were assessed applying a semi-structured interview [11]. Data acquisition and patient education took place when the patients clinical condition has stabilized. Data concerning regular medication was taken from the patient-chart. Blood pressure was measured by the nurse on the ward at the day of assessment and education with the patient sitting in an upright position.

Three months after the education session all patients were reevaluated utilizing a telephone-assessment. Also data from the general practitioner caring for the patient were included in the analysis. This data covered the actual body weight, recent values for blood pressure, HbA1c and regular medication.

Descriptive data is given as median value (minimum – maximum). Differences between groups were analyzed applying the Wilcoxon non-parametric test with regard to continuous variables and Fisher's exact test with regard to dichotomous variables. To alleviate the analysis of changes between the two measurement points clinically significant increments were calculated and their frequency analyzed applying Fisher's exact test. Furthermore Kendalls tau B was calculated. Clinically significant changes were defined as follows: any reduction in systolic or diastolic blood pressure values, decrease of the BMI < 2,5%, increase in the frequency of hypoglycemic episodes from less then 1 per week to at least 1 per week, reduction of the HbA1c value of > 0.5%, increased adherence to blood pressure monitoring to regularly performed daily measurements, change in medication concerning aspirin, ACE-inhibitors or AT-antagonists, sulfonylurea, metformin and insulin. Statistical analysis of the data was performed utilizing the SAS-software package.

RESULTS

44 patients (29 women and 15 men) took part in the study. 20 were assigned for the intervention group and 24 resembled the control group. At time of reevaluation 4 patients were lost for follow-up, leaving 23 in the control group and 17 in the intervention group. Table 1 shows baseline data stratified according to the intervention. There were no significant differences between both groups at baseline except the frequency of medication with ACE-inhibitors respective AT-antagonists, which was found to be lower in the control group. There were no major barrier observed to perform this short educational intervention in the setting of an acute care ward. All participants were able to take part in the developing-process of the individual short- and medium time treatment goal. 12 patients (70.6%) chose reduction of body weight as an individual goal for the next three months to be written on the flyer.

Three months after the short intervention, patients in the intervention group reported lower median values for systolic (150mmHg (120-160) versus 160mmHg (130-180)) and diastolic (80mmHg (70-90) versus 90mmHg (70-100)) blood pressure values. Only 4 patients achieved the STENO2 goal: blood pressure 130/80mmHg or below (2 in the control and 2 in the intervention group). Body weight was found to be increased in the control group (median value +2kg (0 to 4)), whereas in the intervention group body weight was reduced (median value –2kg (-6 to +2). This effect was seen in the whole range of BMI (figure 1). Median values for HbA1c were increased in the control group (8.2% (4.1-12.1), whereas in the intervention group HbA1c was decreased after 3 months (6.9% (5.8-11.3). There was no change in the frequency of self-reported hypoglycemia in the intervention group, but in the control group the frequency of self reported hypoglycemia slightly decreased (only 2 patients reported a frequency > 1 episode per week). Regularly self-management of blood glucose monitoring was improved in the intervention group (15 patients (88.2%), whereas this was found to be slightly decreased in the control group (16 patients (69.6%)). Only 14 patients (60.9%) performed daily blood measurements in the control group, whereas in the intervention group the frequency of daily blood pressure management was found to be unchanged compared to the baseline (15 patients (88.2%)). No change were observed concerning the need for regular support in daily activities and the ADL-scores compared to baseline values. At time of reevaluation there was a lower rate of prescription of ACE-inhibitors or AT-antagonists in both groups: 14 (60.9%) in the control group and 10 (58.8%) in the intervention group. Aspirin was more frequently prescribed in the control group (9 (39.1%)) whereas this was unchanged in the intervention group (5 patients (29.4%)). In both groups the frequency of insulin therapy was found to be increased after 3 months (13 (56.5%) in the control group and 11 (64.7%) in the intervention group). In summary there were only minor changes in prescription patterns and a remarkable low rate for both aspirin and ACE-inhibitors respective AT-antagonists. As the number of total observations was rather low, tests for significant differences revealed significant differences only with regard to diastolic blood pressure ($p=0.028$) and tendencies concerning systolic blood pressure ($p=0.053$), HbA1c ($p=0.080$) and the frequency of self-reported blood pressure measurements ($p=0.079$).

Figure 1. Scatterplot depicting BMI (kg/m2) and change in body weight (kg) three months after the educational session. Circles represent the intervention group, triangles represent controls.

Table 1. Baseline characteristics

		Controls	N	Intervention	N	p.
Age (years)		77 (59-88)	23	71 (57-83)	17	0.268
BMI (kg/m2)		28.3 (23.0-47.2)	23	30.9 (19.9-43.8)	17	0.236
Women		13 (56.5%)	23	14 (82.4%)	17	0.103
Comorbidity		6 (3-10)	23	5 (4-7)	17	0.293
Diabetes duration		8 (0.5-41)	23	10 (0.5-40)	16	0.744
Hypertension duration		10 (0.5-41)	23	10 (0.5-40)	17	0.806
HbA1c (%)		7.6 (3.9-11.4)	23	7.9 (5.9-15.5)	17	0.241
Baseline blood pressure systolic		160 (120-80)	23	160 (120-180)	17	0.741
Baseline blood pressure diastolic		85 (60-100)	23	90 (55-100)	17	0.461
Residence	With family	13 (56.5%)	23	10 (58.9%)	17	1.0
	Single	8 (20.0%)	23	6 (35.3%)	17	1.0
	Nursing home	2 (8.7%)	23	1 (5.9%)	17	1.0
Regular support		7 (30.4%)	23	4 (23.5%)	17	0.730
Manual performance	Impaired	6 (26.1%)	23	3 (17.7%)	17	0.707
Visus	Impaired	10 (43.5%)	23	7 (41.2%)	17	1.0
ADL-score		95 (40-100)	23	100 (70-100)	17	0.385
Vascular disease and/or PNP		5 (21.7%)	23	5 (17.7%)	17	1.0
Hypoglykemia ≥ 1 per month		3 (13.6%)	23	3 (17.7%)	17	1.0
Self-management glucose monitoring		17 (73.9%)	23	12 (70.6%)	17	1.0
Self-management blood pressure measurement		17 (73.9%)	23	15 (88.2%)	17	0.428
Insulin therapy		11 (47.8%)	23	9 (52.9%)	17	1.0
Previous diabetes education		10 (43.5%)	23	7 (41.2%)	17	1.0
Meal preparation		12 (52.2%)	23	14 (82.4%)	17	0.092
Medication with ACE-inhibitor or AT-antagonist		18 (73.9%)	23	17 (100%)	17	0.030
Medication with aspirin		7 (30.4%)	23	5 (29.4%)	17	1.0
Medication with diuretics		9 (39.1%)	23	7 (41.2%)	17	1.0
Medication with sulfonylureas		7 (30.4%)	23	2 (11.8%)	17	0.256
Medication with metformin		7 (30.4%)	23	4 (23.5%)	17	0.730

Data is presented as median (min-max) in case of continuous variables and as N (%) in case of categorial variables. Fisher´s exact test (categorial variables) resp. Wilcoxon-two.sample test (continuous variables). ADL: activities of daily living (range 0-100); PNP: polyneuropathy.

Table 2. Effects 3months after inpatient treatment

	Controls	N	Intervention	N	τ	SE	p
BMI reduction > 2.5%	0	23	8 (47.1%)	17	0.582	0.097	<0.001
Systolic blood pressure reduced	4 (17.4%)	23	11 (64.7%)	17	0.483	0.140	0.003
Diastolic blood pressure reduced	7 (30.4%)	23	13 (76.5%)	17	0.455	0.140	0.010
Frequency of hypoglykemia increased	2 (8.7%)	23	1 (5.9%)	17	-0.053	0.152	1.0
HbA1c (%) reduced > 0.5	0	23	9 (52.9%)	17	0.627	0.096	<0.001
Adherence to daily monitoring of blood pressure increased	3 (13.0%)	23	5 (29.4%)	17	0.202	0.157	0.250
Medication with ACE-inhibitor or AT-antagonist stopped	3 (13.0%)	23	7 (41.2%)	17	0.321	0.150	0.066
Medication with aspirin established	2 (8.7%)	23	1 (5.9%)	17	-0.053	0.152	1.0

τ: Kendall's tau β; SE: standard error; p: results from Fisher's exact test.

Table 2 shows results for increments calculated form the data depicting significant changes over time. Both systolic and diastolic blood pressure was more often reduced in the intervention group. Furthermore a decrease of HbA1c-values >0.5% was present only in the intervention group and finally a clinically significant reduction in body weight was also found in the intervention group only.

DISCUSSION

The above described short educational intervention was found feasible to be easily implemented in an acute care setting after patients acute illness is controlled or has substantially recovered.

Although in both groups only a small minority achieved the STENO2 goal blood pressure equal or below 130/80 mm Hg [1], there was a significant decrease in the intervention group compared to the controls. A previous comprehensive review of the literature [12] found educational interventions largely unsuccessful to improve medication adherence and blood pressure control. Overall they found the effect of educational efforts contradictory to previous more optimistic reports [13]. In previous studies a variety of educational approaches were applied, ranging from group education and nurse telephone calls to regularly home visits and counseling, but often the direct influence on blood pressure control was not reported. Also various criteria for medication adherence and therapy compliance were used, which may bias the interpretation and comparison of results. As the primary therapy goal is to prevent vascular complication by normalizing blood pressure values, blood pressure values represent one of the major efficacy criterion of any therapeutic intervention. In this context our results are quite clear and describe a significant medium-time effect of educational efforts, notwithstanding the fact, that the majority of patients in the intervention group did not reach the goal given in the STENO2 protocol [1].

Furthermore we found a significant effect on body weight as participants reduced their body weight only in the intervention group. However, the net effect of this weight reduction was limited. A majority of patients with diabetes are overweight and obesity is a major barrier for successful metabolic control [14,15] and there is a close association between obesity and high blood pressure. Despite an ongoing debate, whether there is a causal relation between both, it is yet accepted, that weight reduction in case of obesity also represents an important therapeutic goal when treating patients with hypertension [16]. This is especially true in patients with diabetes, where weight loss was found to be associated with a substantial reduction of mortality [17]. It has been demonstrated previously that even a modest weight loss can result in significant long-term reductions of blood pressure values [18]. In this trial - The Trial of Hypertension prevention - the medium weight loss achieved in the intervention group was 4.4 kg after 6 months of repeated educational intervention. Today there is also consensus that successful long-time weight reduction requires a multifactorial approach [19]. An intensive educational intervention to change sedentary life-style and optimize dietary patterns may then result in a mean weight reduction up to 10kg or average BMI-reduction of 10% [20]. However, many trials reported a less pronounced weight reduction Tuomilehto et al. [21] e.g. found after 1 year and 7 sessions of nutritional advice a mean weight reduction of 4.2kg. In this context a medium-time BMI reduction of 2.5% although limited appears nevertheless remarkable taken in mind that it may result from a short educational intervention.

Although improvement of metabolic control was no primary aim of the educational intervention provided, there was a clear decrease of HbA1c in the intervention group. This is in good accordance with a prior study [22]. Woodward et al. found an improved glycemic control as an unintended effect of regular attendance to a nurse-led cardiovascular risk reduction clinic, where improvement of metabolic control was not part of the health education protocol. In contrast to our intervention, they applied continuous care and repeated educational interventions hereby possibly reassuring the patients health beliefs and reinforcing beneficial health care behavior. Our study demonstrates, that significant improvement in hypertension control, metabolic control and weight reduction may also be achieved by single educational interventions, if they support the philosophy of empowerment. The simple flyer given as a reminder of the self-chosen goal may provide a greater impact on behavioral changes than repeated advice given in a standardized manner. In conclusion, single educational interventions supplied in an inpatient setting may play a significant role in supplementing educational efforts in outpatient clinics or in the primary care setting. They are not necessarily inferior to standard education programs.

The efficacy of self-management education programs, although accepted for diabetes and other chronic diseases, is still in debate and a recent review found the overall effects only small to moderate [23]. The efficacy however, may be inadequately assessed taken only limited surrogate markers and omitting important aspects eg. quality of life. In our study we focussed on a participatory design of the educational intervention. Heisler et al. [24] demonstrated the role of a participatory approach together with physician communication style as positive predictors of self-management. Our results underline in this context the significance of educational style and approach, which may result in similar effects compared to more time-consuming conventional patient teaching session. Educational style may be more important than frequency or duration of the educational intervention.

Nevertheless this pilot study is limited by a rather low number of observations. Therefore a more detailed analysis of patients primary health beliefs and other patient characteristics, which may serve as predictors for effective educational intervention was not possible. Among those a more detailed analysis may disclose, whether age also is an independent predictor of successful patient education with regard to participatory approaches in the field of diabetes and hypertension. Nevertheless, this pilot was done mainly in elderly patients and found no result pointing to an age-related barrier. This may encourage further studies to analyze these possible predictors of successful patient education especially in the elderly.

In summary we demonstrate significant effects of a single participatory educational intervention. Therefore physicians should find themselves encouraged to apply participatory educational sessions, train their educational style and approach and describing individual treatment goals together with their patients.

REFERENCES

[1] Gaede P, Vedel P, Larsen N, Jensen GV, Parving HH, Pedersen 0. Multifactorial Intervention and cardiovascular disease in patients with type 2 diabetes. *N Engl J Med.* 2003; 348:383-93.

[2] Heisler M, Smith DM, Hayward RA, Klein SL, Kerr EA. How well do patients´assessments of their diabetes self-management correlate with actual glycemic control and receipt of recommended diabetes service. *Diab Care* 2003, 26:738-743.

[3] Andrade SE, Gurwitz JH, Field TS, Kelleher M, Majumdar SR, Reed G, Black R. Hypertension management: the care gap between clinical guidelines and clinical practice. *Am J Manag Care.* 2004;10:481-6.

[4] Resnick HE, Fester GL, Bardsley J, Ratner RE. Achievement of American Diabetes Association clinical practice recommendations among U.S. adults with diabetes, 1999-2002: the National Health and Nutrition Examination Survey. *Diabetes Care.* 2006; 29:531-7.

[5] Funnell MM, Anderson RM, Arnold MS, Barr PA, Donnelly M, Johnson PD, Taylor-Moon D, White NH. Empowerment: an idea whose time has come in diabetes education. *Diabetes Educ.* 1991; 17:37-41.

[6] Kapocsi E. High-tech medicine and the physician-patient relationship. *Ehtics Medicine* 2003, 19:69-74.

[7] Rappaport J. Terms of empowerment / exemplars of prevention: towards a theory for communicatiy psychology. *Am J Comm Psychol* 1987, 15:121-128.

[8] Lee M, Koh J. Is empowerment really a new concept? *Int J Hum Res Management* 2001, 12:684-695.

[9] Montori VM, Gafni A, Charles C. A shared treatment decision-making approach between patients with chronic conditions and their clinicians: the case of diabetes. *Health Expect.* 2006; 9:25-36.

[10] Beaver K, Luker K, Owens R, Leinster S, Degner L, Sloan J. Treatment decisions making in women newly diagnosed with breast cancer. *Cancer Nurs* 1996, 19:8-19.

[11] Burkhardt H, Gehrlein M, Eisenhofer S, Elfert-Hartl B, Gladisch R. Individualizing education for patients with diabetes attending an acute care unit. *Med Klin (Munich).* 2003; 98:601-8.

[12] Schroeder K, Fahey T, Ebrahim S. How can we improve adherence to blood pressure-lowering medication in ambulatory care? Systematic review of randomized controlled trials. *Arch Intern Med.* 2004; 164:722-32.

[13] Dubar-Jacob J, Dwyer K, Dunning EJ. Compliance with antihypertensive regimen: a review of the research in the 1980s. *Ann Behav Med* 1991, 13:31-39.

[14] Centers for Disease Control and Prevention (CDC). Prevalence of overweight and obesity among adults with diagnosed diabetes--United States, 1988-1994 and 1999-2002. *MMWR Morb Mortal Wkly Rep.* 2004; 53:1066-8.

[15] UKPDS Group. UK Prospective Diabetes Study 7: response of fasting plasma glucose to diet therapy in newly presenting type II diabetic patients, UKPDS Group. *Metabolism.* 1990; 39:905-12.

[16] Pickering TG. Obesity and hypertension: what should we do? *Ann Intern Med.* 2001; 134:72-4.

[17] Williamson DF, Thompson TJ, Thun M, Flanders D, Pamuk E, Byers T. Intentional weight loss and mortality among overweight individuals with diabetes. *Diabetes Care.* 2000; 23:1499-504.

[18] Stevens VJ, Obarzanek E, Cook NR, Lee IM, Appel LJ, Smith West D, Milas NC, Mattfeldt-Beman M, Beiden L, Bragg C, Millstone M, Raczynski J, Brewer A, Singh B, Cohen J; Trials for the Hypertension Prevention Research Group. Long-term weight loss and changes in blood pressure: results of the Trials of Hypertension Prevention, phase II. *Ann Intern Med.* 2001; 134:1-11.

[19] Franz MJ, Bantle JP, Beebe CA, Brunzell JD, Chiasson JL, Garg A, Holzmeister LA, Hoogwerf B, Mayer-Davis E, Mooradian AD, Purnell JQ, Wheeler M; American Diabetes Association. Nutrition principles and recommendations in diabetes. *Diabetes Care.* 2004; Suppl 1:S36-46.

[20] Anderson JW, Konz EC, Frederich RC, Wood CL. Long-term weight-loss maintenance: a meta-analysis of US studies. *Am J Clin Nutr.* 2001; 74:579-84.

[21] Tuomilehto J, Lindstrom J, Eriksson JG, Valle TT, Hamalainen H, Ilanne-Parikka P, Keinanen-Kiukaanniemi S, Laakso M, Louheranta A, Rastas M, Salminen V, Uusitupa M; Finnish Diabetes Prevention Study Group. Prevention of type 2 diabetes mellitus by changes in lifestyle among subjects with impaired glucose tolerance. *N Engl J Med.* 2001; 344:1343-50.

[22] Woodward A, Wallymahmed M, Wilding J, Gill G. Improved glycaemic control— an unintended benefit of a nurse-led cardiovascular risk reduction clinic. *Diabet Med* 2005; 22:1272-4.

[23] Warsi A, Wang PS, LaValley MP, Avorn J, Solomon DH. Self-management education programs in chronic disease: a systematic review and methodological critique of the literature. *Arch Intern Med.* 2004; 164:1641-9.

[24] Heisler M, Bouknight RR, Hayward RA, Smith DM, Kerr EA. The relative importance of physician communication, participatory decision making, and patient understanding in diabetes self-management. *J Gen Intern Med.* 2002; 17:243-52.

In: Multimedia in Education and Special Education
Editors: O. Demir and C. Celik.

ISBN 978-1-60741-073-7
© 2009 Nova Science Publishers, Inc.

Chapter 13

EMBRACING DATA: POTENTIAL USES FOR DATA LOGGING IN ONLINE LEARNING ENVIRONMENTS

Erik W. Black
Assistant Professor, College of Medicine, The University of Florida, USA
Kara Dawson
Associate Professor, College of Education, The University of Florida, USA

ABSTRACT

Business and government have embraced data logging applications to provide for a more comprehensive web-based user experience. The vast majority of web-based educational applications have yet to incorporate even the most rudimentary forms of data-logging. The incorporation of data-logging and tracking applications can aid in the enhancement of a individual's learning experience by aiding in the creation and maintenance of community, logistical planning and instructional individualization. Educational researchers and application developers can apply lessons learned in the commercial and government marketplace when using data collection tools to advance an online learners educational experience.

INTRODUCTION

According to Guthrie (2007, p.1):

"there are few 21st century operations as outmoded as educational data systems….Wal-Mart managers routinely know more regarding the location…of a toy bear manufactured in China, from the original point of purchase manufacturing specifications to the vendor's ocean shipping arrangement, to local store delivery and shelving and time of final placement into a customer's shopping basket than school district administrators know regarding the day-to-day status and school progress of their enrolled students."

Guthrie's comments, while aimed at brick and mortar K-12 institutions, certainly hold true for online learning providers both at the K-12 or collegiate level (Black, Ferdig & DiPietro, 2008). Fortunately, there is indication that the online learning community has begun to embrace the potential that educational data systems can offer. In particular, online administrators and researchers are beginning to consider the use of learning management system (LMS) data logs to gain a more comprehensive understanding of the online learning experience (Black, Dawson & Priem, 2008; Romero, Ventura & Garcia, 2007; Zhang, Almeroth, Knight, Bulger & Mayer, 2007). The analysis of data logs derived from online learning environments has the potential to transport online educational data systems into the category of dynamic informational interchange applications synonymous with current 21st century web-based services (Pahl, 2004; Zaiane, 2001).

Whether derived from a learning management system, router or web-based analytic application, data logs can be used in a myriad of different manners to advance the online learning experience (Romero, Ventura & Garcia, 2007). This commentary discusses and outlines the potential for the utilization of LMS derived quantitative data logs in contemporary online education. Issues addressed include utilizing data logs to build, evaluate and maintain online communities, and enlisting log data for instructional individualization, finally, the commentary will address regulation and ethical issues surrounding the use of data logs.

AN OVERVIEW OF ONLINE EDUCATION
AND DATA-LOGGING IN THE U.S.

The online education in the United States has seen unprecedented growth in both the availability of and participation both degree granting, certificate and professional continuing education programs. At present, there are over 3.2 million online students at the college and university levels (Allen & Seaman, 2007) and over 96% of the very largest higher education institutions in the U.S. have online course offerings (Allen & Seaman, 2006). Over 700,000 students also participate in K- 12 online education (Smith, Clark, & Blomeyer, 2005). Faced with double digit annualized growth, budget and technological limitations, online education administrators have their hands full just trying to meet students' basic needs (Ferdig & Cavanaugh, in press). Further, many LMS vendors do not provide their customers with ready access to logging information (Black, in press). These limitations have hindered the development of methods and tools for tracking and evaluating users' experiences within online learning communities, creating a situation in which field of education lags far behind industry and government in the use of logged, or automatically collected, data to support decision making (Black, Dawson & Priem, 2008; Black, Ferdig, & DiPietro, 2008). Learning management systems, many of which automatically keep logs of student activity, present an exciting means of narrowing this gap (Black, Dawson & Priem, 2008).

The process of analyzing data logs derived from an LMS is similar to the methods used to analyze data generated by other web-based technologies including web-servers, firewalls and routers. This process, presented in a simplified format, involves four basic steps and typically employs the use of a database and the aid of a statistical software package (Romero, Ventura & Garcia, 2007).

4 Step LMS Log Analysis Process
1. Data Collection – native data logs are collected from the learning management system
2. Data Preprocessing – logs are cleaned and formatted for analysis
3. Data Analysis – analysis is conducted according to inquiry
4. Interpretation and Evaluation – output of the analysis is interpreted and implications are derived by the user

The continued incorporation and adoption of data analytic techniques prevents the opportunity to revolutionize the online learning world. The vast majority of online educators fail to utilize data analysis as a component of course feedback, instead, operating on intuition and student feedback alone. By ignoring the opportunity to analyze click streams and add this analysis to other forms of course feedback, educators are perpetuating the fallacies synonymous with the historical incorporation of computers in education (Foshay & Bergeron, 2000; Jonassen, Davidson, Collins, Campbell, & Haag, 1995).

DATA LOGS AND ONLINE COMMUNITY

Research by Black, Dawson and Priem (2008) highlights a simple, yet innovative data-logging application. This exploratory study utilized Rovai's Classroom Community Index (Rovai, 2002), regressing survey results against a student's raw data log totals for the duration of a course. Results indicate that data logs were predictive of a student's perception of community. The simplistic nature of this study allows for the development of future investigation and refinement of a predictive model. For instance, Black et als study did not differentiate between the type of data log generated by a student. It would be plausible to assign differentiated value to logs, understanding that a forum post generates is more contributive to the course environment then a syllabus view. Research by Dawson (2008) focusing solely upon forum post quantity and their relation to community indicates that a qualitative classification of the forum post may be necessary in order to create an association with community. This notion is supported by Lowes, Lin and Wang (2007) who found that posts that do not provide new content, question or challenge thoughts and ideas, are of inconsequential, if not negative, value to creating a constructive learning environment.

DATA LOGS FOR LOGISTICAL PLANNING

Building a reliable, cost effective infrastructure while adhering to the constraints of a budget requires considerable skill (Lorenzo & Moore, 2002). A comprehensive mining of LMS data conducted by Heathcote and Dawson (2005) provided Queensland University with a wealth of data regarding utilization and capacity planning. Data analysis allowed distance learning administrators to effectively plan down-time for server and software updates around periods of low-utilization, it also allowed for investigations into server and bandwidth load utilization. These investigations allowed Queensland to proactively manage their infrastructure needs. Given the rapid growth typified by online education in the U.S. and abroad, capacity planning is a critical component of ensuring a quality learning experience.

DATA LOGS FOR INSTRUCTIONAL INDIVIDUALIZATION

Consumer focused websites have been tailoring content based upon input from cookies and browser and server based tracking software since the initial deployment of Netscape Navigator (Whalen, 2002). Cookies are an essential component of our user experience as web denizens. Without the assistance of these bits of code, websites we frequently visit would have no record of your previous visits, thus precipitating a generic and uninspiring experience. Whalen's analogy, relating cookies to dry cleaning, aptly describes their importance:

> "You drop something off [at the dry cleaner], and get a ticket. When you return with the ticket, you get your clothes back. If you don't have the ticket, then the laundry man doesn't know which clothes are yours. In fact, he won't be able to tell whether you are there to pick up clothes, or a brand new customer. As such, the ticket is critical to maintaining state between you and the laundry man."(p.1)

At the present time, LMSs create the same generic learning experience for each individual within a course, regardless of this individual's learning style, needs, wants or desires. By tracking user patterns, the LMS may determine that a user typically reads forum postings prior to engaging in other activities within a course environment. Shouldn't the LMS accommodate this by placing the latest forum posts in a easily accessible location? All learners are not the same; to ignore the opportunity to customize the learning environment specifically to an individual removes a central affordance of the Internet. To this effect, Van Dyk and Conradie (2007) utilized the Felder Index of Learning Styles and simple data mining procedures to correlate WebCT tool use with specific student learning styles. Results provided statistically significant evidence that individuals with differing learning styles utilized intra-LMS tools to different degrees.

DATA LOGS AND ETHICS

The present state of privacy protection in the United States is a complex interactive web of federal and state constitutions, statutes, and regulations (Sipior, Ward & Rongione, 2004). The vast majority of the focus regarding online data collection ethics is aimed at corporate entities who seek to utilize consumer information for marketing, sales and promotional means. Little concern has been given to online learning providers, some of which are for-profit entities. Questions remain as to whether the student learning experience will be altered due to the knowledge that activities in a learning environment are being monitored. Research by Berendt, Günther and Spiekermann (2005) provides evidence that an individual's privacy concerns tend to be forgotten when they are engaged in a compelling online interaction. It goes without saying that students should be made aware that they will be monitored while online, they should understand the extent of the monitoring and analysis techniques that will be employed. In effect, this is no different then taking attendance in a classroom setting, or monitoring whether students are participating in activities.

CONCLUSION

Business and government have eagerly applied the rich data from web systems to guide strategic and day-to-day decision making (Montgomery, Li, Srinivasan & Liechty, 2004); as previously outlined, e-learning has been slow to follow this good example (Pahl, 2004; Zaiane, 2001). Recent developments within the online learning research community lend credence to the notion that LMSs will soon experience some dramatic changes in the way they facilitate the exchange between student, teacher and course content.

The creation and deployment of an automated tool to augment the simple embedded analysis applications found in some LMSs (eg: Moodle) is a likely step for future research. Such a tool, designed to perform simplistic counting functions could serve as a beta-test for more complex and costly undertaking. Unlike complicated data mining techniques, counting total log entries would be easy to automate for use in real time, representing a very practical step toward a system to comprehensively broaden an online instructor's perception of his or her students (Black, Dawson & Priem, 2008).

Future research should seek to discern whether there is consistency between data log totals inter-course-instance, the relationship between course content and course evaluation and data log production, and whether data logs have predictive relationships with other affective variables correlated with student success.

REFERENCES

Berendt, B., Günther, O. & Spiekermann, S. (2005). Privacy in e-commerce: Stated preferences vs. actually behavior. *Communications of the ACM,* 48(4), 101-106.

Black, E.W. (in press). *An evaluation of familial involvements' influence on student achievement in K-12 virtual schools.* University of Florida.

Black, E.W., Dawson, K. & Priem, J. (2008). Data for free: Using LMS activity logs to measure community in an online course. *The Internet and Higher Education,* 11, 65-70.

Ferdig, R.E. & Cavanaugh, C. (Eds.) (in final submission). Effective practice in virtual schools. *To be published by the North American Council for Online Learning* (NACOL; Vienna, VA) in 2008.

Foshay, R., & Bergeron, C. (2000).Web-based education: A reality check. *TechTrends,* 44, 16−19.

Guthrie, J.W. (2007). Data systems linking resources to actions and outcomes: One of the nation's most pressing education challenges. *Peabody Journal of Education,* 82(4), 667-689.

Heathcote, Elizabeth and Dawson, Shane (2005) Data Mining for Evaluation, Benchmarking and Reflective Practice in a LMS. In Proceedings E-Learn 2005: *World conference on E-learning in corporate, government, healthcare & higher education,* Vancouver, Canada.

Jonassen, D., Davidson, M., Collins, M., Campbell, J., & Haag, B. B. (1995). Constructivism and computer-mediated communication in distance education. *The American Journal of Distance Education,* 9, 7−26.

Lorenzo, G., & Moore, J. (2002). *The Sloan Consortium report to the nation: Five pillars of quality online education.* Retrieved 11/10/2008 from http://defiant.corban.edu/ jjohnson/Pages/Teaching/pillarreport.pdf

Lowes, S., Lin, P., &Wang, Y. (2007). Studying the effectiveness of the discussion forum in online professional development courses. *Journal of Interactive Online Learning,* 6(3), 181−210.

Pahl, C. (2004). Data Mining Technology for the Evaluation of Learning Content Interaction. *International Journal on E-Learning,* 3, 47-55.

Romero, C., Ventura, S. & Garcia, E. (2007). Data mining in course management systems: Moodle case study and tutorial. *Computers and Education,* 51(1), 368-384.

Rovai, A. P. (2002). Sense of community, perceived cognitive learning, and persistence in asynchronous learning networks. *Internet and Higher Education,* 5 (4), 319-332.

Sipior, J.C., Ward, B.T. and Rongione, N.M. (2004). Ethics of collecting and using consumer internet data. *Information Systems Management,* 21(1), 58-66.

Zhang, H., Almeroth, K., Knight, A., Bulger, M. & Mayer, R. (2007). Moodog: Tracking students' online learning activities. In C. Montgomerie & J. Seale (Eds.), Proceedings of World Conference on Educational Multimedia, Hypermedia and Telecommunications 2007 (pp. 4415-4422). *Chesapeake,* VA: AACE.

Whalen, D. (2002). The unofficial cookie FAQ, v2.6. *Cookie Central.* Accessed 11/5/2008: http://www.cookiecentral.com/faq/

Van Dyk, L & Conradie, P 2007. Creating business intelligence from course management systems, *Campus-Wide Information Systems,* 24(2), 120-133.

Zaiane, O. R. (2001). Web usage mining for a better web-based learning environment. *Proceedings of Conference on Advanced Technology for Education,* 60–64.

INDEX

B

C

S